Mastering Catastrophic Risk

"'Be Unsurprised by surprise.' This final piece of advice in *Mastering Catastrophic Risk* captures what this book offers. The authors provide a guide to senior executives on how to prepare for the one low probability event that will surprisingly affect their firm. This book will help executives survive and thrive their next predictable surprise. Failing to read this book will expose your firm to unnecessary risk!"

—Max H. Bazerman, Straus Professor,
Harvard Business School, and author of *The Power of Noticing*

"A smart and timely read on coping with the increasing frequency of catastrophes. From underlying psychological biases to wise preparations and savvy responses, the authors offer rich examples to explain the hows and whys of avoiding or at least, lessening the toll of unexpected disasters. An essential book for wise leaders."

—Kathleen M. Eisenhardt, S.W. Ascherman M.D. Professor
at Stanford University and co-author of *Simple Rules:
How to Thrive in a Complex World.*

"This excellent book draws on the many lessons learnt from catastrophic failures and avoided mistakes to show why and how risk management must be improved. Risk management is everyone in business's business and I know of no better starting point than this book."

—Ian Goldin, Professor of Globalization and Development,
Oxford University; co-author of *The Butterfly Defect:
How Globalization Creates Systemic Risks, and What to Do about It*

"As one who has spent a career in discovering biases in risk perception and decision making, it is exciting to see them portrayed in such an informative way through interviews with executives and risk managers from major firms. In this way, this valuable book gives essential lessons for avoiding these biases and the catastrophic consequences they may cause."

—Paul Slovic, President of Decision Research and Professor
of Psychology at the University of Oregon

Mastering Catastrophic Risk

How Companies Are Coping

with Disruption

HOWARD KUNREUTHER

MICHAEL USEEM

OXFORD
UNIVERSITY PRESS

OXFORD
UNIVERSITY PRESS

Oxford University Press is a department of the University of Oxford. It furthers the University's objective of excellence in research, scholarship, and education by publishing worldwide. Oxford is a registered trade mark of Oxford University Press in the UK and certain other countries.

Published in the United States of America by Oxford University Press
198 Madison Avenue, New York, NY 10016, United States of America.

Library of Congress Cataloging-in-Publication Data
Names: Kunreuther, Howard, author. | Useem, Michael, author.
Title: Mastering catastrophic risk : how companies are coping with disruption / Howard Kunreuther, Michael Useem.
Description: New York, NY : Oxford University Press, [2018] |
Includes bibliographical references and index.
Identifiers: LCCN 2017031957 | ISBN 9780190499402 (hardcover : alk. paper) | ISBN 9780190499426 (epub)
Subjects: LCSH: Risk management, author. | Crisis management.
Classification: LCC HD61 .K86 2018 | DDC 658.15/5—dc23
LC record available at https://lccn.loc.gov/2017031957

9 8 7 6 5 4 3 2 1

Printed by Edwards Brothers Malloy, United States of America

Dedicated to the life and memory of

Jay S. Fishman, 1952–2016

Chair and Chief Executive Officer, The Travelers Companies Inc.

Our advisor and friend whose vision made this study possible.

CONTENTS

Mastering Catastrophic Risk

Prologue

On a Sunny Day

Make the best decision that you can with the information that's
available to you at the time. Above all, do the right thing.
—LEE SCOTT, *CEO, WALMART*

This could have been just another weekday morning. Millions of people
were already at work or getting there after dropping their children at school.
The weather was beautiful with clear skies and warm temperatures, a great
morning in New York City. But that morning would soon become catastrophic for thousands, a terrifying moment for America and the world,
marking a new era of extreme disruption.

Employees of Morgan Stanley, one of America's premier banks, had
begun their workday on Tuesday, September 11, 2001, in the South Tower
of the World Trade Center. It looked to be another routine start, but at 8:46
a.m., American Airlines flight 11 slammed into the North Tower. Morgan
Stanley's director of security, Richard Rescorla, asked the Port Authority,
the towers' landlord, for immediate guidance.

The landlord recommended against evacuating the South Tower, but
Rescorla requested that his chief executive, Philip J. Purcell, approve the
instant evacuation of all employees, then spread across twenty floors. Such
a request was not to be taken lightly. It could cost millions of dollars in
lost business and executive reputations if it proved unnecessary or even
endangering. Given that Rescorla had limited information on what had just

happened, he was taking a significant risk himself in asking his chief executive for the immediate and full evacuation.

Rescorla's calculus was informed though by his own experience with a prior disaster in the same building: he had lived through the 1993 al-Qaeda truck bombing of the World Trade Center. That attack did not bring down the towers, but it had killed six people. Fearing how many might have perished if that assault had succeeded in collapsing a building, Rescorla had instituted quarterly evacuation drills, making sure that new employees were trained and veteran workers did not become complacent. Now, eight years later, he ordered a well-practiced evacuation, though this time it was not a drill.

Rescorla and his staff succeeded in moving most of Morgan Stanley's 3,700 staff members down the South Tower's stairwells before the second aircraft slammed into that tower at 9:03 a.m. Virtually all of the employees managed to exit the building before its collapse at 9:59 a.m. Just six staff members of Morgan Stanley were still inside when the tower finally imploded, among them Rescorla himself and three deputies who had returned to the offices to make sure no others remained inside.

To anyone who worked for Morgan Stanley in the South Tower that day, the bank's risk managers became martyred heroes. Morgan Stanley's chief operating officer Robert Scott later offered an instructive observation on Richard Rescorla's preparation for and nearly complete evacuation of the Trade Center on 9/11: "If you wait for a crisis to begin to lead," he said, "it's too late."

Seven years later, and in a very different context, the leadership of insurance and asset-management giant AIG proved woefully ill-prepared to avert its own collapse after Lehman had failed. Though warned by regulators, AIG's top management had not fully appreciated that the company's credit worthiness—a measure of the financial strength of a firm—might be threatened. But a major rating agency found that AIG, via its London subsidiary, held large amounts of the same toxic subprime mortgages that had pushed Lehman over the edge on September 15, 2008. Alarmed, the rater downgraded AIG's credit rating from AAA to A–.

To those outside the insurance industry, the downgrade might seem like just another of those arcane Wall Street resets, but to AIG executives the reduction meant that they had to instantly find tens of billions of dollars to post as collateral to back up the insurance policies that the London subsidiary had written against the possibility of mortgage defaults. Company executives had set aside no such funds, never imagining they would ever be needed. But now they were needed, and as collateral calls from customers exploded, they drained the company of $32 billion by the end of the month and $61 billion by the end of the year, leading to the greatest annual loss in business history. The US federal government eventually injected nearly $180 billion to save AIG from complete ruin, the largest corporate bailout ever.

Such disruptions can serve as a powerful source of instruction, as Walmart, the world's largest retailer, came to appreciate in 2005. When Hurricane Katrina—then the most costly natural disaster in American history—hit the US Gulf Coast in August, Walmart applied its technical understanding of complex global supply chains and its careful tracking of the storm itself to assist the region's recovery when other institutions faltered: "Make the best decision that you can with the information that's available to you at the time," chief executive officer Lee Scott had urged his employees, and "above all, do the right thing." On that premise, swift decisions followed, including Walmart's dispatch of 2,500 trucks to deliver food, blankets, and clothing to thousands of hurricane-affected families for weeks after Katrina's landfall. In some affected areas, Walmart delivered assistance ahead of that of even the US Federal Emergency Management Agency.

In the years that followed, Walmart built on its Katrina experience to strengthen its risk management worldwide for all kinds of disruptions, not just natural disasters. It invested in an emergency operations center and a central coordination and response hub, and when the US Center for Disease Control confirmed in 2014 that an Ebola-infected traveler from Liberia had landed in the United States, the emergency center sprang into action, monitoring millions of Walmart employees and customers for signs that those who had been exposed to Ebola might be working or just shopping in one of its 11,000 stores worldwide. Following Hurricanes Harvey, Irma, and Maria in 2017, Walmart committed $30 million toward hurricane relief efforts.[1]

Larry Fink also learned about risk management through adversity. He had been enjoying great success at investment bank First Boston until his team lost $100 million in a single quarter of 1986 as a result of a risky bet that interest rates would increase, when instead they decreased. A quarter of a century later, he still vividly recalls how painful—and instructive—the loss was. "We built this giant machine," he recalled, referring to a computer system for trading decisions, "and it was making a lot of money—until it didn't." And that, he concluded, was because "we didn't know why we were making so much money," and "we didn't have the risk tools to understand the downside of our trading decisions." The resulting precept: "You should analyze your portfolio just as much when you are making money [as when you are losing it], because you could be taking on too much risk.'"[2]

Several years later, Larry Fink created what would become BlackRock. In three decades under his leadership, the firm has emerged as the world's largest asset holder, with $6 trillion of assets under management by the end of 2017. Instructed by Fink's early career experience, BlackRock built its business model on a host of risk management principles. It created, for instance, Aladdin, an operating system that incorporates risk analytics along with traditional portfolio management and trading tools. More than 25,000 investment professionals now utilize Aladdin, and it is applied by organizations managing a total of $15 trillion in assets, including the United States. When the 2008–2009 financial crisis struck with its enormous risks for all, the federal government turned to BlackRock for help in managing its bailout programs.

Overconfidence about the benefits of risks and an underinvestment in their mitigation is, however, still evident in other firms. Wells Fargo Bank faced a public scandal in 2016 that damaged the firm's reputation and undercut its sales and market capitalization. Incentivized by a draconian pay-for-performance system that required consistently meeting aggressive sales goals without strongly disallowing their unethical execution, thousands of its retail bankers increased their paychecks by creating fake bank and credit card accounts—some two million in all—in the names of customers but without their knowledge. And then, as these practices became known within the bank, management forced out some five thousand frontline employees over several years, but continued the incentive system until it became publicly known.

According to later congressional testimony by Wells Fargo CEO John Stumpf, the flawed incentive system was not a hidden middle-management misstep; it was known—but not curtailed—by top management and the governing board. Executives and directors began discussing the faulty incentive compensation in 2013, but it was not until 2016 that the board finally intervened, forcing out the chief executive and calling for an overhaul of the system. Warren Buffett, chief executive of Berkshire Hathaway, Wells Fargo's largest single investor with nearly 10 percent of its stock, bluntly criticized the inaction by company executives and directors: "It was a bad incentive system," he complained. "The main problem is that they didn't act when they learned about it." In the end, it cost Wells Fargo billions of dollars in litigation expenses, settlement costs, and foregone revenue. To improve its risk management, the bank forced top executives out, tightened internal controls, brought in a new board chair, a former Federal Reserve Board governor, and appointed a new chair to the board's risk committee, a former president of Bank of New York Mellon.[3]

Executives and directors need not suffer their own crisis to ready their enterprise for the next disruption. By learning from others' experiences and through scenario planning exercises, their ability to manage adverse risks more deliberatively can be strengthened without having to individually undergo a calamity. *Mastering Catastrophic Risk* is intended to facilitate that mastery. And given the increasing pace and scale of disruptive events, there is no time like the present to do this. Lessons learned from the experience and wisdom of others calls for more disciplined thinking in advance of the unimaginable, for recognizing the shortcomings in human and organizational behavior in dealing with low-probability but high-consequence events, and for preparing for the long run even when short-term pressures prevail.

We take you into those defining moments when catastrophic risks— whether physical, financial, or reputational—threaten a firm's performance or even its existence. These adverse events sometimes emerge from within the company itself: the sudden death of a CEO, as experienced by McDonald's, Sara Lee Corporation, and SAP SE; executive fraud that proved fatal for Enron and WorldCom; or massive recalls of faulty products that whipsawed General Motors, Merck, and Toyota.

Often the disruptions are industry-wide: toxic subprime mortgages proved fatal to dozens of financial institutions in 2008–2009; the unanticipated fall of oil prices in 2016 severely affected energy companies and the communities where they operated. Sometimes the hazards are a product of global interdependencies: the shutdown of auto-parts makers near the Fukushima nuclear reactors in 2011 forced car factories around the world to close, and the WannaCry cyberattack affected firms in more than 150 countries in 2017. Other disruptions are the result of a technological revolution—think how digital platforms have changed the way we consume information and learn today, and how value is created or destroyed by the few corporations that own these platforms.

This book is about the challenges faced by firms threatened by or actually experiencing extreme events—and what we can learn from their successes and and the adverse events that they weathered. There are many examples of firms that have vastly improved their strategies in recent years, with enterprise risk management emerging as a critical area for board attention, executive planning, and front-line accountability. When companies focus on what McKinsey & Company has termed their "big bets"—those major decisions that all firms have to make—many have become far savvier about the hazards that can derail or even blow them up. Others, less prepared, are still pondering where to start and how to manage disruptions.[4]

This book offers a four-phase journey, starting with an exploration of the new risk environment in which corporations now operate (Part I). We then develop a framework on how enterprise decisions are made for managing low-probability, high-consequence events by highlighting how companies can recognize their systematic biases and behave more deliberatively by assessing and managing their risks (Part II). We next examine several accounts of companies in the United States and Germany that have dealt with catastrophes (Part III). We also report study findings on how companies' management of catastrophic risk affects their stakeholders—internal and external (Part IV). We conclude with a practical checklist for managing potentially disruptive events before they occur to mitigate their impacts and facilitate recovery.

While risk-taking has always been part of business, our story is about the fundamental transformation in how companies are preparing for large-scale disruptions. This shift promises to have major societal impacts, affecting all of us as consumers, employees, investors, and citizens.

From interviews we have undertaken with directors, executives, and managers of more than a hundred companies in the Standard & Poor's 500 Index—America's 500 largest publicly traded firms, known as the S&P 500—we have gained a broad appreciation for how many are now mastering catastrophic risk management. They have candidly shared their experiences in coping with and learning from disruptions, decisions that in hindsight they would have done differently, and how they are now better prepared to deal with adverse events in the United States and abroad. We also draw on recent research from the social sciences to better understand the behavioral biases and decision rules that have sometimes inadvertently led firms to experience severe disruptions.

With guidance from an advisory council of senior business and government officials, we asked company leaders how they have prepared for and responded to severe setbacks, both externally generated and self-inflicted. Gaining a deeper understanding as to what works and what falls short, we hope that other business leaders can take actions now to avoid later lamenting, "I wish we had taken steps to prepare for this disaster that we felt could never happen to us!"[5]

The firms whose leaders we interviewed vary by industry, size, and sector. Their annual revenues ranged from $1 billion to more than $400 billion (average revenue: $29 billion). Their workforces varied from a few thousand to hundreds of thousands (average number of employees: 70,000). A quarter of the firms are in financial services, a quarter in retail, and smaller fractions in information technology, healthcare, and manufacturing, a sectoral distribution comparable to the S&P 500 as a whole. Virtually all of the firms operate in a range of countries that have exposed them to an array of disruptions worldwide.[6]

We have also drawn on a host of other sources, including company disclosures, risk surveys, public data, and government reports. Looking outside the United States, we have examined how several large corporations in Germany—Europe's largest economy—have coped with catastrophic risks. Taken together, we have sought to distill the best deliberative thinking and risk practices for business firms anywhere.

Many of the findings reported here should be applicable not only to the risk management strategies of business firms, but also to public and nonprofit organizations. The tangible leadership experience of those at the helm of some of the world's largest enterprises can offer invaluable guidance for all who seek to build a more resilient organization of their own in an era of rising disruption—and who want to be better prepared to face what might one day prove to be their own "big one."

PART I

A More Risky Era

Risk on the Agenda

Take calculated risks. That is quite different from being rash.
—US GENERAL GEORGE PATTON

Taking calculated risks and avoiding others is an intrinsic part of any firm's agenda. A vital decision facing all company managers is choosing what risks to take and which ones to avoid—and then how to hedge against the potential consequences of risks that are taken. Recognizing that careful analysis takes time and money, how methodical should the firm be in becoming more resilient when facing potential disruptions and adverse events?

It is evident that protective measures have become more essential as risks have attracted far more public attention and concern in recent years. Media references to *risk* rose worldwide from 1990 to 2016 by a factor of twenty-five—and in the United States double that. *Risk* has entered the lexicon of virtually every company manager. Headlines with the word "crisis" and the name of one of the top hundred companies ranked by *Forbes* appeared 80 percent more often in the 2010s than in the previous decade. The now widely used acronym ERM—enterprise risk management—has become one of the essentials for almost everybody in business.[1]

The growing importance of the concern is evident in influential business gatherings. The World Economic Forum, with which the two of us have been collaborating for over a decade, provides a barometer. In the 1990s, the Forum devoted only a few of the sessions in its annual meeting in Davos, Switzerland, to risk issues. Of its nearly 250 sessions at the 1997 annual gathering, for instance, just a dozen were explicitly focused on the topic. By the mid-2000s, however, a third of its sessions touched on risk, and by the 2010s nearly half. Recent discussion has centered on how to manage these risks more effectively to foster a culture of resilience.[2]

Understanding, reducing, and managing risk are no longer the province of just technical specialists, but involve the entire enterprise. Catastrophic risk has even entered boardroom deliberations as directors have come to appreciate that cyberattacks and cyclones can depress their firm's performance and their own reputations as much or more than a floundering strategy. Yet there is also an obvious upside: well-managed, calculated risk-taking is one of the drivers of value creation and profitability in any competitive market.

DISRUPTION

Calamity, catastrophe, or crisis; adverse event; a low-likelihood but high-impact shock. A host of words and phrases capture the central focus of this book. We apply them interchangeably but consistently with reference to moments or events that could dislocate the normal business functions or operations of a firm, or cause major financial or reputational damage to it. We use the terms *risk* and *disruption* to characterize company threats and their impacts.

The sources of company disruptions are many. They range from natural calamities such as hurricanes and earthquakes, to human-caused disasters such as terrorist attacks, oil spills, and chemical accidents. Some events are a complex mixture of natural and unnatural calamities, such as Japan's 9.0-magnitude earthquake in 2011 and the resulting tsunami that overwhelmed three nuclear reactors at Fukushima. Economy-wide shocks such as the 2008–2009 financial crisis in the United States caused enterprise disruptions worldwide. So, too, have technological breakthroughs such as digital marketing, selling, and streaming. They have upended established business models across a swath of traditional retailers and media networks. Public regulations and government restrictions, from emission rules to immigration bans, have also threatened some of the best operating enterprises.

Company disruptions can sometimes come from inside the firm's own walls, whether from executive malfeasance, worker sabotage, or fraudulent reporting. Or the unexpected departure of an indispensable executive, an explosion on an oil rig, or the release of a fatally flawed product. Costly litigations, cover-ups, and failed mergers can add their own troublesome waves.

Some events are sudden in onset—think of high-magnitude earthquakes—while others—such as changes in climate patterns—unfold over months, years, or even decades. Some are firm-specific or unique to an industry or a country; others can upend enterprises across markets and oceans. Disruptions can also have ramifications well beyond the firm's formal boundaries, triggering the attention of other parties, including officials, investors, creditors, consumers, reporters, and tweeters.

Whatever the engines of disruption, all deserve explicit attention from company leaders. In the pages that follow we address four complementary questions:

First, *why* is preparing for disruption an essential element of company management today, and what are the major drivers leading firms to take action?

Second, *what* are directors, executives, and managers doing about potentially catastrophic risks—and how can they learn from their past successes and failures as well as those of others?

Third, *when* do interested parties—government officials, company owners, and product consumers—become involved after a firm has been disrupted by an adverse event?

Fourth, and most importantly, *how* can firms improve their mastery of adverse events by being better prepared for them and better managing them when they occur?

For answers, we have turned to the many company leaders whom we interviewed for this book, asking them how they anticipated and then responded to their own company disruptions. We learned that executives and managers are now appraising their risks in a more deliberate fashion, engaging more directly with their directors in risk oversight, and making risk management an integral part of business strategy.

Company officials also reported that despite the heightened readiness for what they had already seen or experienced, fresh challenges abounded, each very different from any that had come before. Consider the loss of Pan American flight 103 in 1988 over Lockerbie, Scotland, that killed 270 people. A bomb had been loaded onto an earlier aircraft in Malta where securities measures were weak, transferred to a feeder airplane in Frankfurt, and then placed on the Pan Am flight in London. It exploded, as intended, at an altitude of 28,000 feet. Following the crash, airports changed their security protocols around the world to prevent bombs from being stored in checked baggage as if that would now be the primary form of attack that terrorists might use again. On September 11 some thirteen years later, security officials at Boston's airport waved several terrorists through a checkpoint when no bombs were detected in their bags.

Yet it is also from the diverse and ever changing array of adverse events of these kinds that company managers have come to better appreciate the common shortcomings that had clouded or misdirected their efforts in the past. They learned that their own biases and heuristics had sometimes hampered their preparedness for and response to hazards of any kind.

At first blush, the time and resources devoted to enterprise risk management might be seen as limiting company growth. Yet the opposite appears to be the case. The value of enterprise risk management for company performance was evident, for example, when Standard and Poor's appraised the robustness of enterprise risk management among insurers. It found that those insurers that strengthened their risk management capabilities had much lower volatility in their return on equity, a good thing, compared to other insurers that did not give risk management a high priority. It also reported that insurers with strong ERM measures in 2008 outperformed the S&P 500 index by nearly 20 percent, while those with weak risk management underperformed by 40 percent.[3]

Beyond financial returns, the value of enterprise risk management can be captured via a simple analog with the dual purpose of automobile brakes. They are designed, of course, to slow a vehicle, but they also allow the operator to accelerate since they provide a reassuring means for decelerating when needed. Other risk-reducing measures such as audio warnings against dozing off and crossing lanes offer the same, allowing drivers to more confidently and quickly reach their destinations.

Such risk-mitigation devices might have even saved the life of one of the greatest risk-takers of all time, General George S. Patton. Having aggressively commanded the US Third Army during World War II as it swept through France and Germany after the Allied invasion of Normandy in 1944 and fought back during the Battle of the Bulge in 1944–1945, Patton was severely injured in a minor auto accident not long after the war ended when his car collided with an army vehicle. Paralyzed but conscious, he complained that "this is a hell of a way to die." The accident might well have been prevented by the many risk-mitigation measures that exist on new cars today.

DRIVERS OF DISRUPTION: DISRUPT

Changes in how corporations approach disruptions can be traced to six forces or drivers (D): interdependencies (I); short-term focus (S); regulatory compliance (R); urban concentration (U); greater probability of shocks (P); and pressure for transparency (T). Taken together, these drivers of disruption can be conveniently captured with the acronym DISRUPT, depicted in Figure 1.1.

Driver 1: Interdependencies (I)

The globalization of human migration and economic activity has forced businesses to become more dependent on people, services, and suppliers across the world for research, production, and marketing. The process of global integration and cross-border flows have had very positive economic impacts, but at the same time they have also introduced systemic risks. Severe disruptions in one region can now have more significant repercussions on a

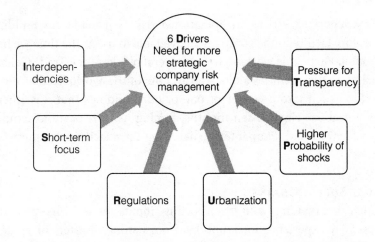

Figure 1.1 DISRUPT: Six Drivers of More Strategic Company Risk Management

firm's far-flung operations elsewhere. Ian Goldin and Mike Mariathasan have documented how the failure of global governance has greatly aggravated these so-called butterfly effects, where small changes in one place can lead to much larger changes elsewhere in the world.[4]

Global connectivity raises questions about the motivation of any organization to invest in protection when its security depends in part on how others behave. If a firm thinks that other enterprises with which it is linked are *not* investing in risk-mitigation measures, its own incentive to invest can be reduced as well. These disincentives are even more pronounced with the prospect that a failure by a competitor or supplier could cause havoc in the entire market. On the other hand, if a firm perceives that other partners and players are investing in risk reduction, it will find it more appealing to do so as well. This decision is thus likely to be subject to both virtuous upward cycles when competitors follow suit—and vicious downward spirals when they do little to protect themselves. Other forms of interdependency are many, and we briefly note several of prominence.[5]

GEOGRAPHIC PROXIMITY

A firm's operations may be adversely affected if one of its facilities is damaged or destroyed after the collapse or explosion of a neighboring structure, as was the case for many firms located near the World Trade Center in September 2001. The chief risk officer of a financial institution caught up in the mayhem explained:

> We categorized 9/11 as an operational risk as it made our building and core facility in the company unavailable to us. At the time we had about 8,000 people working within several blocks of the Trade Center, including two facilities a block away. One of the World Trade Center buildings fell into a corner of one of our buildings that was [then] out for about eight to ten months, forcing us to relocate to temporary facilities and set up intermediate long-term facilities for these ten months.

GLOBAL SUPPLY CHAINS

Companies providing and transporting inputs to a firm's production process may experience interruptions from natural disasters or epidemics that never touch a firm's facilities, but can nonetheless paralyze its operations.

Consider a massive flood that submerged much of Bangkok in 2011. Thailand's capital region manufactured a third of the world's hard-disk drives and served as regional hub for Japanese auto making. The unprecedented inundation damaged or destroyed the facilities of more than 14,000 businesses. Apple CEO Timothy Cook reported that Bangkok's flood had significantly slowed the supply of Mac computer components. Western Digital Corp., the world's largest maker of hard-disk drives, warned that it would post a quarterly loss and that production would not return to normal for months. Toyota suspended its assembly lines for lack of parts, and Ford, which made its Fiesta in Thailand, halted production. Only then did some multinational companies come to fully appreciate that their sole-source suppliers had located factories in flood-prone areas. In the disaster's wake, they expanded from single-source to multiple suppliers for essential inputs.[6]

PROTECTION OF SHARED NETWORK RESOURCES
Most workplaces maintain complex networks of information technologies. A virus entering computer files, cloud storage, and operating systems through the laptop of just a single employee who failed to update the firm's antivirus software may infect applications or erase files across the firm. Those who carry their laptops home and then connect to the Internet without appropriate protection can jeopardize the digital information of the entire company.[7]

CRITICAL INFRASTRUCTURE
Public agencies and private providers sometimes underinvest in maintaining critical components of their infrastructure, such as the local electric grid. It may be as simple as a software error or an underdesigned device, but it can mushroom into a far-reaching disaster.

The 2003 electricity blackout in the northeastern United States that deprived over 50 million people of power stemmed from a small software glitch in the control-room alarm of an Ohio utility, the FirstEnergy Corporation. With no siren sounding, its operators remained unaware of an urgent need to redistribute power after overloaded transmission lines hit unpruned foliage. What would have been a manageable local blackout cascaded into a massive shutdown of the nation's grid. Similarly, the power generators at the Fukushima plant in Japan that were overwhelmed by the 2011 tsunami resulted in a vast disruption of companies in Tokyo and eastern Japan.[8]

CROSS-SECTOR SHOCKS

Large-scale risks in one sector or one country can impact many industries and many nations. The 2008–2009 financial crisis sparked by the failure of a handful of American banks soon sandbagged thousands of nonfinancial companies around the world, as liquidity vanished and sales plummeted in one market after another. An executive of a consumer-products corporation noted, for example, that as other firms began to sharply contract, their downscaling depressed his own firm's operations. Components no longer needed by the firm continued to arrive and inventories piled up, requiring more working capital and damaging relations with long-standing but now struggling suppliers and buyers.

INTERNAL SHOCKS

Interdependencies within a corporation can prove damaging or even fatal when the actions of a single division can seriously disrupt or even bring down the entire firm. Union Carbide operated many chemical plants worldwide, but a massive disaster in just one of its facilities spelled the demise of the entire firm. A gas leak at its operation in Bhopal, India, in December 1984 killed more than three thousand residents, leading to a $470 million legal settlement. Badly weakened, the company sold off some of its most prominent brands, including Glad Bags and Eveready Batteries; fended off a number of takeover attempts; and was finally bought by Dow Chemical Company in 1999.[9]

In 2003, Arthur Andersen, then one of the Big 5 public accounting firms, voluntarily surrendered its license to practice as a result of the criminal actions of its Houston office that had been auditing Enron Corporation. Arthur Andersen employees in offices from Dubai and Frankfurt to Paris and Seattle lost their jobs, even though most of them had nothing to do with Enron nor ever met their Houston colleagues.

Barings Bank, a British institution founded in 1762, was destroyed in 1995 by the actions of a single rogue trader, Nick Leeson, doing his mischief halfway around the world from the home office. Similarly, the illicit actions of a single employee almost brought down one of the largest banks in Europe in 2008. Jérôme Kerviel, a trader at France's Société Générale, secretly exposed the bank to nearly $75 billion worth of risk, more than the market value of the entire bank, leading to a loss of more than $7 billion once the dust had settled. The near-collapse of American International Group (AIG) in 2008 was caused by its 377-person London Unit, AIG Financial Products, that had been given autonomy by the parent and had suffered enormous losses from credit default swaps that it issued and traded. In 2012 a single trader, Bruno Iksil, known as the London Whale, lost more than $6 billion for JPMorgan Chase before the company caught up with his malfeasance.[10]

GLOBAL MOVEMENT

Fast transport and global trade have also increased interdependencies among firms. People and products are moving from country to country more quickly and more cheaply than ever before.

Many travelers might not realize that airfares in the United States have dramatically decreased over the last forty years: it was 50 percent cheaper to fly within the United States in 2011 than in 1978, and the number of passengers tripled. Less than a fifth of Americans in 1965 had ever flown on an airplane, but by 2000 half of the country was taking at least one round-trip flight per year. While this has brought significant personal and economic benefits, it has also facilitated the spread of health risks more rapidly and more globally, as evidenced by the quick dispersion of severe acute respiratory syndrome (SARS) in 2002, the H1N1 virus in 2009, and the Zika virus in 2016. An infectious disease in any part of the world today could very well infect residents in any other place. The Los Angeles airport is the fifth busiest airport in the world with nearly 700 daily flights to 85 domestic cities and more than 900 weekly flights to over 60 cities abroad. It does not take much imagination to foresee that a virus carried by passengers coming from Asia or Africa can be spread quickly in America and then across Europe.[11]

Driver 2: Short-Term Focus (S)

Shortening cycle times in many areas of business have contributed to a right-this-minute mindset at some, leading managers to downplay risk-reducing measures, since benefits would not be realized immediately. That shortsightedness has been exacerbated by investor pressures on publicly-traded firms to consistently improve quarterly performance.

Executive myopia can also lead a firm to engage in excessive risk-taking by assuming that today's market conditions will be not change much in the future. The financial crisis of 2008–2009 had a particularly adverse impact on energy firms, for example, since many had purchased oil under the faulty premise that crude oil prices would remain high in the months to come. But the cost of oil plummeted from over $149 per barrel in July 2008 to just $30 less than five months later.

Driver 3: Regulatory Compliance (R)

The growing interest of firms in risk management has also been stimulated by new government regulations and compliance requirements. In 1938, the Code of Federal Regulations (CFR) totaled 18,000 pages. By 1970 it had nearly tripled to 50,000 pages, and it further soared to 138,000 pages by 2000 and 175,000 pages by 2015. Another measure: the number of pages in the *Federal Register*, a daily US journal that reports agency policies, proposed rules, and public notices. The *Federal Register* began with less than 3,000 pages in 1936, grew to 20,000 pages by 1970, and expanded to more than 80,000 in 2015. Add fifty state regulations and international rules for multinational firms, and the result is a thicket of public directives with potential attendant risks from many of them.

As will be noted later in these pages, we have found that government policies and actions are the most frequently cited hazards when companies disclose major risks in their annual reports. This was true before the financial crisis and became even more so since. The directors, executives, and managers we interviewed reported much the same concern, and they are echoed by the public. A Gallup poll in 2016 reported that 47 percent of the public believed that government regulates business too much and only 22 percent too little.[12]

Ironically, company policies intended to prevent the recurrence of past crises are sometimes perceived as creating costly new risks. The key US legislation to emerge from the 2008–2009 financial crisis is the Dodd–Frank Wall Street Reform and Consumer Protection Act of 2010. Its nearly 9,000 pages of rules represents the most comprehensive financial reform measures taken since the Great Depression, and compliance with them has forced financial institutions to dedicate full-time staffs to implementing its requirements.

It should be noted that while many government regulations are perceived by business leaders as increasing some company risks, they can at the same time reduce others. Well-enforced standards such as building codes to withstand natural disasters and land-use restrictions in flood-prone areas, for example, diminish facility damage and personnel injuries from natural disasters. Financial regulations reduce the likelihood of executive fraud and enterprise insolvency, environmental regulations slow global warming, and flight regulations improve air safety.

Driver 4: Urban Concentration (U)

As firms and markets grow, company operations become more intertwined with more populous regions. Urbanization has given companies ready access to large pools of customers, but it has also brought a greater concentration of risks. In 1990, only 30 percent of the world's population resided in urban areas, but by 2000, half of a far larger number—6 billion—did so. The United Nations projects that by 2050, 60 percent of the world's population will live in metropolitan regions, twice the percentage in 1990. In 1975 there were only three "megacities" with 10 million inhabitants or more—Mexico City, New York City, and Tokyo—but by 2025, twenty-seven megacities are anticipated.[13]

The growing concentrations of people and firms in urban areas and the emergence of megacities imply greater company risks ahead. Disruptions—whether terrorist attacks, disease pandemics, or power failures—are likely to affect more people and more firms. This may be especially the case for the growing concentrations of residents and enterprises in coastal communities when it comes to natural disasters. From 1970 to 2010, populations in shoreline counties of the United States, for example, rose by 39 percent, and in coastal watershed areas by 45 percent. By 2010, 123 million people resided along a coastline, attracted by the appealing amenities, but now increasingly vulnerable to floods, hurricanes, and a rising sea level.[14]

The scale of this increased vulnerability can be appreciated by estimating the total direct economic cost of catastrophes in the past century adjusted for inflation, population, and affluence. A study of mainland US hurricane damage for the period 1900–2005, for instance, found that a hurricane that devastated Miami in 1926 would have been almost twice as costly as Hurricane Katrina, then the most expensive disaster in US history, had the 1926 hit occurred in 2005.[15]

Driver 5: Greater Probability of Shocks (P)

Disasters are by definition low-probability events. Yet when viewed over longer periods, those small likelihoods add up. It is sobering, for instance, to learn that the annual probability is one in six that at least $10 billion of insured property will be destroyed by hurricanes somewhere in Florida. If we extend the time horizon from one year to ten, keeping the population of

Florida constant, the likelihood of at least one hurricane causing damage of more than $10 billion is greater than five in six. Given the continuing population concentration and economic development of shorelines in Florida and the increased intensity of hurricanes in recent years, the chance of a hurricane-inflicted disaster exceeding $10 billion in losses during the next decade will exceed 90 percent in future years.[16]

Similar logic can be applied to catastrophic losses by companies. If each division in a ten-division firm has a one-in-six chance of causing a severe loss to the entire firm—recall how just one of AIG's divisions felled the parent—over a five-year period the prospect of the parent suffering a severe setback during the next half decade is greater than five in six.

Some losses from single events can be massive. In 2011, for instance, global damages exceeded $400 billion, and the lion's share came from the earthquake and tsunami in Japan ($240 billion in 2016 dollars). The Kobe earthquake in Japan in 1995 ran up a tab of $100 billion ($155 billion inflation adjusted). Hurricane Sandy in 2012 cost the United States over $80 billion. In 2017 Hurricane Harvey devastated the Houston region with losses of more than $100 billion; it was followed by Hurricane Irma, whose damages to Florida were estimated at more than $60 billion. Losses from Hurricane Maria in Puerto Rico, just weeks after, were estimated at more than $70 billion as this book goes to press. Such costs are likely to increase in the future with warming temperatures, rising sea levels, and more intense hurricanes.[17]

In the aggregate, economic setbacks from natural disasters worldwide increased from $530 billion during the decade of 1981–1990 to more $1.2 trillion during the decade of 2001–2010. From 2011 to 2015, natural disasters caused an average annual loss of $188 billion (inflation corrected), up from $46 billion in the early 1980s, as seen in Figure 1.2.

Shocks are not limited to natural disasters. The average annual number of media headlines referencing reputational risk among 100 large companies rose from 130 in the 1990s to 570 in the 2000s and 1,030 by the 2010s. Financial penalties of at least $20 million paid by corporations for regulatory infractions grew from $11 billion in 2010 to $59 billion in 2015. American automakers recalled 20 million vehicles in 2010—but 53 million in 2016. The US Food and Drug Administration sent 1,700 warnings to noncompliant organizations in 2011—but 15,000 in 2016.[18]

Cyberattacks are on the rise as well. The Bank of America estimated 80 to 90 million cybersecurity breaches in 2014 in the United States alone, with some four hundred new attacks every *minute,* and 70 percent of them

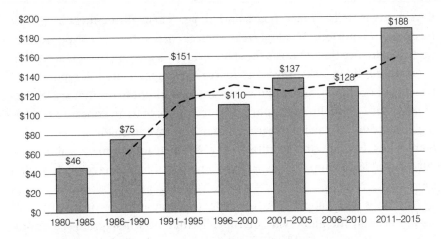

Figure 1.2 Annual Global Cost of Natural Disasters, 1980–2015, in $ Billions
SOURCE: Authors with data from Munich Re GeoResearch; 2016 prices corrected for inflation. The dashed line represents trend over ten-year periods.

remaining undetected. A data breach at Equifax, a consumer-credit reporting agency, in 2017 was estimated to have affected the personal records of approximately 143 million Americans, though the actual number may never be known. Taking into account both the direct damage and postattack recovery expenses, insurers have estimated that cyberattacks are likely to cost firms worldwide as much as $400 to $500 billion annually.[19]

The financial impact of data breaches—when sensitive, protected, or confidential data are copied, transmitted, viewed, stolen, or used by those unauthorized to do so—are also increasing. More than 700 million records had been breached worldwide in 2015, and a study of 350 companies in 11 countries by IBM and a partner found that the per-record cost of a data breach had steadily risen, reaching $154 in 2015.[20]

Driver 6: Pressure for Transparency (T)

Publicly traded firms have been required by the US Securities and Exchange Commission since 2005 to annually disclose their key risks to the equity market. As we report later, those company disclosures have on average doubled in length during the period 2007 to 2014.

Additional pressures for greater risk transparency among companies have been building with the rise of social media. *The Economist* captured that development wells: "Many boards no longer fear that openness is bad for business," it reported. "In some areas, such as corporate social responsibility, there is evidence that it boosts the share price by signaling that management is tackling hidden risks. Investors increasingly appreciate the reputational benefits of openness, and employees want to work for firms that are leaders in disclosure—and, just as importantly, ever more of them appear to see it as their civic duty to leak information if their employer is shady and secretive." Starbucks CEO Howard Schultz crisply summed up the main point: "The currency of leadership is transparency," and social media have made it even more relevant today.[21]

Anything that happens on the planet can now be recorded live and shared around the globe via YouTube, Twitter, and Instagram. Facebook had over 2 billion monthly active users at the end of 2017 and Instagram had 800 million. With the emergence of widely affordable, sometimes even free technology, anyone can become an investigative journalist, whether a critical employee, supplier, customer, neighbor, or shareholder. Small shortcomings become quickly magnified into larger threats. As an executive at a large multinational software company told us: "A cause for concern for me right now is social media. That's something that really is on the forefront. Anybody could say anything they want and you can try to retract as you may, but once it's out there it is reputational risk at the end of the day."

MANAGEMENT PRINCIPLES

Rising disruption risk is changing how directors, executives, and managers view their company agendas and lead their enterprises as a result. The direction is not necessarily toward greater risk aversion, or even greater risk-taking, but rather toward a greater grip on it.

Other studies have found that personally-experienced disasters tend to send executives toward more risk seeking if the setbacks have been modest—but the opposite when the risks have become extreme. A study of the childhood experiences of 1,508 chief executives of S&P 1500 firms from 1992 to 2012, for example, examined whether they had been exposed in their formative years—from ages five to fifteen—to an earthquake, hurricane, wildfire, or other natural disaster that had caused local fatalities. Years later, those CEOs who had experienced events that caused a small number of fatalities were *more* likely to accept operating risks including greater debt for financing, pay higher interest rates, accept a lower rating for company debt, and assent to greater volatility in their stock prices—compared with CEOs who had experienced *no* fatal disasters in their childhoods.[22]

By contrast, those chief executives who had faced *major* disasters in their early years, with large losses of life, tended to build up greater cash reserves, made fewer acquisitions, and allowed for less share volatility than those who had no exposure to fatal disasters. A study of CEOs who had grown up during the Great Depression—another extreme disruption—found much the same: children of the Depression were more likely to avoid borrowing and depend less on external financing.[23]

Our interviews suggest that company directors, executives, and managers are embracing a greater readiness to face up to their risks. While firms still vary in their risk tolerance and those differences are likely to be exacerbated by the rising hazards, many business leaders have become more adept at managing the disruptions that increasingly abound. Yet, as we will see, the level of readiness varies widely among firms.

RISK ON THE AGENDA

1. Attention to disruption among large companies has risen significantly in recent years.
2. The confluence of six drivers of change has thrust enterprise risk management onto company agendas. The Drivers are: Interdependencies, Short-term focus, Regulations, Urbanization, greater Probability of shocks, and pressures for greater Transparency, captured by the acronym DISRUPT.
3. Directors, executives, and managers are more likely to be held responsible—and to take responsibility—for ensuring that their firm is ready to face disruptions and to recover from them.
4. If your organization has not yet experienced a serious disruption or crisis, it is probably not a question of whether it will occur, but when.

Impact of Severe Events

We always thought crises happened outside of New York, and 9/11 changed our minds.

—EXECUTIVE, *Financial Services Company*

When it comes to changing management mindsets about catastrophic risk in a DISRUPT environment, nothing is as consequential as when a firm suffers its own adverse event. Directors focus, executives act, and managers mobilize. Such setbacks are often unique to a firm, one-off interruptions that can devastate the enterprise but leave others unscathed. Yet others leave a swath of destruction. When we asked directors, executives, and managers across industry sectors, "What are one or two of the most adverse events that you have faced as a firm?" many of those we interviewed over the period 2011–2016 singled out at least one of four widely felt events: the terrorist attacks of 2001, Hurricane Katrina in 2005, the financial crisis of 2008–2009, and the Japanese earthquake of 2011. Taken together, these events caused massive disruptions, leading many organizations to strengthen their risk management capabilities.

THE TERRORIST ATTACKS OF 2001

The terrorist attacks of September 11, 2001, wreaked havoc on many American companies. Al-Qaeda's assault on New York City and Washington, DC, killed nearly three thousand and devastated the business center of lower Manhattan. With catastrophic property and infrastructure losses, few major companies escaped at least some tangible cost, and the attacks ushered in a new era of insecurity and risk for many.

Company officials we interviewed recounted that the 9/11 attacks proved to be a seminal event regardless of the direct effect on their business operations—in some cases relatively minor. No longer could their organization avoid thinking about the unthinkable, nor could they comfortably accept that "it could never happen here."

One company executive reported that prior to the terrorist attacks, she and her colleagues had never conceived of a disruptive incident of this magnitude: "We had not done sufficient contingency planning prior to 9/11 because we had not imagined this level of risk could happen." But in its wake, she said, "we developed a new set of business continuity measures," and now "every department determines the kind of contingencies it could face and makes sure that it has a duplicate, such as alternate physical space, available to us. In addition, we needed to find a way of ensuring means to get in touch with our people by knowing their cell phone numbers. And we needed to make sure that we have proper insurance against catastrophic risk so it doesn't affect the basic survival of the company."

Continuity planning, communication rules, and evacuation protocols came to be seen as part of the new normal. A risk manager for a financial services firm captured the sea change: "We always thought crises happened outside of New York, and 9/11 changed our minds about that. So we now spend a lot more time planning our strategic postures. What kind of businesses do we need to reinforce, and which kind of businesses expose us to danger?"

HURRICANE KATRINA IN 2005

Hurricane Katrina devastated the US Gulf Coast in late August 2005. The category 3 storm caused severe damage along the coastline from Florida to Texas, and the levee failure in New Orleans left 80 percent of that city submerged for weeks. Property losses exceeded $100 billion.

Since relatively few American companies had a major footprint in New Orleans at the time of Katrina, it might be assumed that the hurricane's impact on many firms would be modest. But Katrina knocked out Gulf ports through which some 5 percent of the country's trade flowed, and Wall Street got the message. Sensing that the supply chains and global exports of many companies would be compromised, investors reduced their holdings, causing stock prices for major corporations to plummet in the immediate aftermath of the hurricane.[1]

Many of the companies with a direct presence in the Gulf region had already readied for a major hurricane, but few had imagined the worst-case scenario that Katrina had wrought. The risk manager of a consumer-products company with many stores in the area disclosed his firm's inadequate preparation:

> So in the case of Katrina we made a bad decision. We rented about thirty-five generators and tried to position them as close as possible to where the storm was going to hit so that we could get these generators distributed to the stores that were without power, get them up and running so we could sell stuff again. Unfortunately, the decision was made to store the generators in downtown New Orleans. They all went underwater and those that survived got looted immediately thereafter.

It proved a powerful learning experience, reported the risk manager: "Since Katrina, we have coordinated the different business interests within the organization, from store operations to distribution centers to the trucking folks, as well as how we position our response teams, including the generators."

A large chemical company had prepared for a modest outage, but it had never anticipated an event of Katrina's magnitude. To restart a facility, company managers sought the assistance of federal agencies and even private competitors to mobilize employees from the company. Its director of environment, health, safety, and quality explained what had not been planned but was now needed: "We enacted two things to get going in the process: putting teams on the ground and starting to work with all of the national responders from FEMA to the local teams in New Orleans. We also built a small city with a camp to house workers, brought in people from all over the company, and put in place a business and operating team that managed the supply chain issues."

The director of risk management of another large firm reported that Hurricane Katrina furnished a wake-up call for updating and enlarging its business continuity planning. The company had lost a number of stores because it did not have a well-defined protocol for protecting against a major disturbance, but now it does:

The storm is coming in. Let's be careful. Let's try to do what people do with coastal properties and board things up. And let's try to determine where the storm is heading. [Before Katrina], the risk-management department was very young and undeveloped. We only had six people with nobody specializing in property or in catastrophic response. Today we have about eighteen people with a lot of specialties. We have really changed the program as a result of the experiences we've had.

Similarly, a consumer products chain created its own power backup facilities, as its risk manager reported:

We invested in a fleet of generators after the 2004 and 2005 hurricanes so that they can be anywhere we might need them within twenty-four hours. The stores that are in the most storm-prone areas that would have the highest financial impact are all prewired so that when the generator pulls up, they plug it in and we go to work. In 2008 when Hurricanes Ike, Dolly, and Gustav hit we had all twenty of those generators hooked up and servicing our stores so we were able to keep business going.

The company even had assembled a fleet of trucks to fuel and repair the generators after a storm. Many other firms reported that in the post-Katrina era, they had come to view great storms as a fact of life for which backup supplies and equipment were essential. As the CEO of a chemical company concluded: "We will proactively stage equipment within proximity but not in the strike zone, so that we can get generators, water, and other supplies and equipment quickly. We work with local authorities to be able to get our trucks through any kind of police barricades or roadblocks set up in the perimeter around the natural-disaster zone."

FINANCIAL CRISIS OF 2008–2009

The financial crisis of 2008–2009 is considered by many economists to have occasioned the worst source of disruption for business firms since the Great Depression of the 1930s. The crisis began in 2007 with a meltdown in the subprime mortgage market and then ballooned into a full-blown financial calamity after the collapse of Lehman Brothers on September 15, 2008, and Merrill Lynch and AIG in the days that followed.

Most firms were taken by surprise by the severity of the crisis. Many directors, executives, and managers reported that the meltdown felt like a nightmare that had become all too real. But it also proved instructive, exposing the inadequacy of current risk-management practices, especially the ability to track, quantify, and assess the hazards a company faced. Having experienced a worst-case scenario, they were no longer inclined to dismiss the unthinkable, placing a new premium on foreseeing extremes.

Some warned that a lack of transparency about their firm's condition as the crisis intensified had led both employees and external observers to doubt their firms' ability to survive. The risk manager of an insurance company, speaking for many, recalled that the financial crisis had "called into question the financial strength of the company and whether we'd continue to be able to service our policies." Employees were as shell-shocked as the policyholders. "We began getting a lot of phone calls and questions, so our internal workforce was thinking, 'Gosh, what's happening?'"

The chief risk officer of an investment bank reported that its shareholders began to doubt its credit worthiness even though the bank had substantial capital and liquidity and remained profitable. Large investors turned against the firm when they could not quickly secure reassuring details on how the firm planned to navigate through the downturn. A withdrawal of capital from struggling firms had ripple effects with the risk of failure tainting the industry. "There was such a lack of information," recalled the risk officer, "that firms were thrown essentially into a single bucket in terms of analysts' assessments of their credit quality and overall financial strength."

The disruptions of the financial markets spread into sectors that had been seemingly immune from the vagaries of financial hazards. The business leaders whom we interviewed in consumer durables, for instance, recalled that the demand for their products plummeted far more than they had ever forecast or even imagined. One risk manager reported the shock felt by all when demand for his company's goods declined abruptly after three decades of steadily rising sales. It was "a real wake-up call," he said. "Did we have the processes in place to mitigate the risk and understand what we needed to do to address that significant downturn?" Hardly of his own making, he now had to manage the collateral damage.

A manufacturer of home appliances had similarly experienced an abrupt downturn, its sales plunging in ways never anticipated, leaving the company with excessive stockpiles that nobody wanted, recalled its chief risk officer. "It was a surprise to everybody that it took as long as it did to wind down the amount of inventory in transit to us," he reported.

The financial crisis also seriously impacted energy companies when the price of crude oil plummeted. Executives found their firms overextended with projects they could no longer afford, even to the point of potential insolvency. The chief financial officer of a major oil company reported his model upended: "The 2008 fall-off in crude prices, which happened very rapidly over a five-month period from July to December 2008, posed a big cash-flow challenge to us."[2]

Though companies in most sectors were adversely hit by the crisis, the severity varied from enterprise to enterprise, partly a product of their preparedness. If they foresaw the possibility, had clear lines of communication, and eschewed excessive risk, they escaped the worst. A risk manager of an energy company contrasted his firm's experience with others in the industry:

When I look at my peers, there are very clear examples of companies that totally misjudged the financial crisis. They leveraged up right before the meltdown happened, put lots of projects in place when oil was hitting $150. In reality, it was a very short-term spike. Our company is very conservative and we do our planning around a lower projected price, and we don't leverage excessively and carry more cash than we have debt.

JAPAN EARTHQUAKE AND TSUNAMI OF 2011

On Friday, March 11, 2011, the largest earthquake in Japanese history shook much of the country at 2:46 p.m. Tokyo time. At 9.0 magnitude on the Richter scale, the Tōhoku earthquake was the fourth largest earthquake to occur anywhere on Earth within the past century. During the six-minute Tōhoku event, two hundred miles of Japanese coastline dropped two feet, Japan moved eight feet closer to North America, the Earth shifted its axis by ten inches, and the globe's rotation slowed by 1.8 microseconds. Building damage was extensive, despite Japan's tough earthquake-resistant building codes. But far more devastating—what indeed would prove catastrophic— was the earthquake's aftereffect some fifteen to twenty minutes later.[3]

Just forty-five miles off the peninsula of Tōhoku, a ten-foot upward thrust of the sea floor created an enormous outflow of water in all directions. The resulting tsunami rose thirty feet above normal sea level in many coastal regions, sweeping inland for as much as six miles along Japan's northeast shoreline, destroying almost everything in its path. The Japanese government estimated that more than 15,000 people perished in the earthquake and tsunami.

The Tōhoku earthquake and tsunami of 2011—and subsequent nuclear meltdown of the plant at Fukushima—led many American companies and others to recognize the underlying vulnerability of their supply chains, as manufacturing in Japan ground to a halt. Global companies relying on the region for components found themselves suddenly and unexpectedly facing shortfalls in essential inputs, curtailing production a continent away.[4]

Car makers in Detroit, for instance, relied on automotive microcontroller chips from Renesas Electronics Corporation, a company extensively damaged by the earthquake. With no alternative suppliers, auto production lines were temporarily closed. And those companies with operations in Japan were even more directly affected, though many had prepared for the possibility of a major earthquake given the country's long history of seismic activity. As the chief risk officer for one American producer recalled: "We have two large plants in Japan: one on the east coast and, one on the west coast. The east coast plant was damaged, and it took our capacity offline for months. And that had a significant impact on our earnings and ability to supply parts so we lost significant market share during that period. It has taken us 18 to 24 months to regain the share that we lost."[5]

When the earthquake and tsunami first struck, foreign companies in Japan drew on protocols already well established. The treasurer of a manufacturer, for example, reported that his company focused on three preset priorities: "First, validating the status of our employees and ensuring that we knew where they were, the condition of their families and their homes. Second, the safety and security of our facilities. And then the resultant business impact," as inputs from Japanese suppliers had become scarce, leading to a disruption in the firm's production processes and seriously affecting the firm's operations.

Other companies with similarly preset plans for communication and continuity avoided the worst. One firm, for example, instituted a risk management team during the crisis to study the multiple possibilities as events unfolded and to develop flexible plans in response to the varied scenarios:

There was a team here in the United States that was charged with thinking about the unthinkable. If we have to shut the plant down and completely relocate our facilities, what does that do to our whole business picture in Japan? The big factor for us was the radiation issue. We didn't know how bad that was going to get and if at some point we would be forced out of the plant never to return. But it also wasn't something we had ever thought about, quite honestly. It's one of those black swan things that most companies can't even imagine.

Many firms noted the challenge of securing reliable information during the crisis, making it difficult to decide whether to withdraw operations and employees from impacted areas. This was particularly daunting given the great distance between company headquarters and the site of the reactor meltdown, and in light of unreliable media reports and a dearth of first-hand information. An executive of a financial services company highlighted this problem: "Is it safe for us to keep our 1,500 people in place, or did we need to exercise a business-continuity scenario? Or do we need to get our people out and try to run our franchise remotely? So it's a fundamental question that you need to deal with in a catastrophic scenario. Can your business survive in place or do you need to relocate it and try to sew the pieces together in another fashion?" The firm had anticipated the possibility of an earthquake in the region by reaching out to experts and government officials, and it was thus more primed for the event.

About a year before the quake, anticipating that seismic activity was a significant risk factor for our franchise in Japan—we undertook a pretty significant effort regarding earthquake awareness and preparation for our Tokyo operations. That involved making sure our building is designed to the maximum specifications for handling earthquakes, making sure that our staff understood what best practices for earthquakes were, and making sure we had resiliency in our data centers and our communications capabilities given a worst-case scenario we constructed. When the earthquake and tsunami hit and we had the crisis at the Fukushima reactor, we had built pretty good relationships with some very eminent nuclear reactor safety specialists and businesses who were able to give us really accurate information on what the conditions were at the Fukushima plant and the real risk to our staff in Tokyo from radiation. Other firms in the sector were reaching out to us for guidance and advice.

MANAGEMENT PRINCIPLES

Four massive disruptions in recent years have focused company directors, executives, and managers on risk readiness. They are symptomatic of our new era of heightened disruption that has fundamentally altered the way business leaders see and prepare for disasters.

IMPACT OF SEVERE EVENTS

1. Catastrophes such as the terrorist attack of 2001, Hurricane Katrina in 2005, the financial crisis of 2008–2009, and the Japanese earthquake of 2011 led many firms to ratchet up their hazard appraisals and build more robust risk-management agendas.
2. Firms developed a number of scenario-specific plans that they could deploy during a massively disruptive event.
3. Company leaders are now more prepared to think about the unthinkable, and to improve transparency, communication, and readiness to weather the worst.

PART II

Enterprise Decisions for Managing Disruptions

The discipline of economics has until recently paid relatively little attention to decision-making in business organizations. The standard model of choice assumed that managers behaved in ways that led firms to maximize their returns by collecting relevant information and undertaking careful calculations to choose optimal short- and long-term strategies. Firms whose managers behaved imperfectly would be driven out of business by their competitors. As economists were fine-tuning this rational model of firm behavior, a body of research—stimulated by the pioneering work of Herbert A. Simon, beginning with his book on *Administrative Behavior* written in 1947 based on his doctoral dissertation—emerged in other social science disciplines on how managerial choices were actually made. Simon stressed that managers were satisficing rather than optimizing, by stopping short of compiling and analyzing the data required for systematic decision making. Much to the surprise of economists, some of whom were not even cognizant of his work, Simon received the Nobel Prize in Economics in 1978 for his research into the decision-making process in organizations.

More recently, Daniel Kahneman and Amos Tversky developed additional insights into the systematic biases and judgment shortfalls evident even among the most disciplined decision-makers, including those at the top of large corporations. The story of their collaboration was the focus of bestselling author Michael Lewis' *The Undoing Project,* and Kahneman received the 2002 Nobel Prize in Economics "for having integrated insights from psychological research into economic science, especially concerning human judgment and decision-making under uncertainty." And in 2017, Richard Thaler received the Nobel Prize for his pioneering research on behavioral economics.

Part II develops a framework for understanding how directors, executives, and managers reach decisions in preparing for and responding to adverse events where suboptimal biases and heuristics can be especially detrimental. Chapter 3, "From Intuitive to Deliberative Thinking," focuses on how managers in firms behave when confronted with low-probability, high-consequence events that have the potential to cause considerable disruption to the enterprise. Chapter 4, "The Risk-Analysis Cycle," describes how recent adverse events have led many company leaders to be more deliberative in specifying the firm's risk appetite and risk tolerance, and more determined to develop systematic risk-management methods. Chapter 5, "Risk-Management Praxis," details management practices that have emerged from this more disciplined focus on catastrophic risk.

From Intuitive to Deliberative Thinking

The fishermen know that the sea is dangerous and the storm terrible, but they have never found these dangers sufficient reason for remaining ashore.

—Vincent van Gogh

The silver lining in the rising tide of corporate disruptions is an increasing company readiness to face them. Risk management has become an important part of the decision agenda at the highest levels of the firm, including—and this is especially new—the governing board. Directors, executives, and managers have, as a result, come to better recognize their need to be more aware of decision-making shortcomings, both their own and others', that can misdirect their actions in preparing for and responding to adversity.

We start with a brief account of what decades of research have come to identify as deficiencies in decision-making that can lead managers to be ill-prepared for disruptions. It is now well-established that systematic biases and simplified decision rules can predictably impede risk readiness and response, and once such shortcomings in decision-making come to the fore, company leaders can better move to overcome them. As we will see, many directors and executives have embraced a more deliberative style of decision-making by learning from their past experiences and those of others.

HOW MANAGERS MAKE DECISIONS

Professor Herbert A. Simon recognized more than a half century ago that company managers do not make decisions with perfect information in hand. He coined the terms *bounded rationality* and *satisficing* to highlight the limited time and imperfect data typically available to decision-makers. Working with James G. March, Simon built on those concepts to develop a more general theory of organizational decision-making, and then March, working in turn with Richard M. Cyert, extended that model to recognize that company managers are often content to choose a plausible alternative rather than to seek out the single best option.[1]

By undertaking empirical studies of many firms, this trio and their colleagues also foresaw that conflicting goals among divisions within an organization could lead to suboptimal outcomes for the whole firm. For example, a production department might want to limit inventory to reduce storage costs, while a marketing department might prefer more inventory on hand to avoid stock-outs. Unless reined in by top management, division managers predictably focus only on their own goals rather than the firm's overarching objectives.

Enterprise disruptions of the kind characterized in the prior chapters have led company executives and divisional managers to work to subordinate their short-term agendas to the firm's long-term objectives by transcending the managerial shortcomings that Simon, March, and Cyert warned about. However, they still face challenges given a set of systematic biases and simplified decision rules that characterize decision making under uncertainty. For example, decision makers are likely to avoid thinking about the consequences of a potentially serious accident if they feel its likelihood is so low that it is below their threshold level of concern.

To illustrate this point, Cyert and March spent time with a plant manager who hoped to improve the firm's safety record by renovating aging equipment; however, he became proactive only after a crane had fatally pinned an employee against the wall. The manager used the tragedy as a wake-up call to set up a special committee to overcome the resistance within the ranks to effect change. This points to the importance of appreciating the nature and shortcomings of managerial decision-making in dealing with low-probability but high-consequence events, to which we now turn.[2]

MANAGERIAL DECISIONS FOR LOW-LIKELIHOOD DISRUPTIONS

A large body of cognitive psychology and behavioral research has drawn a useful distinction between intuitive and deliberative thinking that is critical for our purposes. It identifies management mindsets that can enhance or get in the way of catastrophic risk management. In our interviews, we heard this distinction repeatedly playing out among company directors, executives, and managers as they characterized their own evolving thinking about their disruptive threats and their readiness to respond.

Daniel Kahneman summarized the differences between these two mental models in his book *Thinking, Fast and Slow*. Intuitive thinking is guided by emotional reactions and simple rules of thumb that have been acquired from personal experience and do not require extensive time or resources when reaching a decision. Deliberative thinking, by contrast, gives greater attention to reasoned analysis and complex protocols before choosing among alternative courses of action.[3]

Intuitive thinking works well when managers have good data on the possible outcomes of their different options based on past experience and when complexity is low. But relying on this mode of thinking is less than ideal for devising steps to reduce the impact of disruptive events and responding to them when such events have never been experienced before. There is a tendency to misperceive the risk by underestimating it prior to a disaster and overestimating it afterward. Here, the more analytic and systematic methods associated with deliberative thinking can better direct a manager's attention to the multifaceted sequences and consequences that characterize low-probability but high-outcome adversities.[4]

A deliberative approach would have key decision-makers work to gain a fuller understanding of the specific risk-related problems that the firm faces and then undertake a comprehensive search for the best alternatives to deal with the situation. For each alternative, expert information would be collected to conceptualize the anticipated outcomes, both positive and negative. The decision-makers then examine the expected downsides and benefits of the alternative courses of action, and opt for the path that optimizes the firm's short- and long-term performance.

Though the two modes of thinking are distinct, they are often combined by those responsible for leading a company through a crisis. Morgan

Stanley's decision to evacuate the World Trade Center on 9/11 stemmed, for example, from the use of both intuitive and deliberative thinking by its security manager, Richard Rescorla. After the North Tower had been hit by the terrorists' aircraft, he had no time to perform a systematic analysis of the tradeoffs between staying or leaving the South Tower. He thus relied on his gut reaction to recommend and then execute a wholesale corporate evacuation. Yet at the same time, Rescorla drew on his own deliberative thinking that had come out of the terrorist incident at the World Trade Center in 1993 that had led him to organize annual evacuation exercises. The two modes of thinking together proved essential for the bank's successful evacuation of nearly its entire workforce when it was needed.

SYSTEMATIC BIASES AND SIMPLIFIED DECISION RULES

While invaluable in many settings, intuitive thinking also suffers from a number of well-known biases and overly simplified decision rules that can be particularly inappropriate when deciding on how to prepare for future adversities and reduce their impact if they come to pass. It is thus essential, in our view, for company leaders to recognize the shortcomings of their intuitive thinking and to take steps to overcome them by moving toward a more deliberative mode.

To illustrate, suppose your firm has decided to locate a plant in a coastal area of Florida. As facility manager, you have been asked to determine what investments should be made to reduce the chances of significant damage to the plant from extreme weather events. The firm has never suffered water-related losses from hurricanes in its other locations, and you have never experienced such an event yourself. How might the lack of company and managerial experience affect your decisions if you chose to rely solely on intuitive thinking? With no personal know-how to draw upon, it is possible that you might be tempted to lowball a risk-mitigation investment in order to ensure funding for other needs as the plant is opened.

To avoid placing short-term concerns ahead of long-term goals, decision makers in an organization need to wisely appreciate these and other common decision traps, how to avoid them, resist them, and even how to take advantage of them when facing catastrophe risks. Here are some of the most frequently encountered pitfalls when intuitive thinking prevails over deliberative thinking.[5]

Availability and Hindsight Bias

Company managers tend to forecast the likelihood of an uncertain event by the ease with which instances of its occurrence can be brought to mind. One's recent personal experience can thus lead to an underestimation of adverse events, and then conversely to their overestimation following an actual occurrence. In the case of a plant that you are overseeing in Florida, your intuitive skullcap would suggest underinvesting in hurricane preparedness since you have never been through one—and then overinvesting after actually experiencing damage from a hurricane.

This behavior is a product of what researchers have termed an *availability bias*. Prior to experiencing a severe setback, we underestimate its likelihood because we have limited data for estimating the risk. But after suffering a disaster's disruption, we overestimate the likelihood of it reoccurring since the event and its consequences are very salient, easily retrievable, and hence "available."[6]

By way of example, companies whose operations are potentially affected by pandemics predictably estimate their likelihood from their own experience and from media coverage of recent outbreaks and their consequences. But we also know that a new pandemic rarely resembles the last one. The Ebola virus outbreak in 2014 in West Africa was followed by the Zika virus outbreak in 2016 in Central and South America. Readying for the latter by preparing for the former would be a fool's errand since a company's defense against Ebola would share little with that against Zika.

To illustrate this point, a senior vice president for global security and safety at a retail company recalled his company's misdirected follow-ups to the early outbreaks of one form of avian influenza, H5N1, that had erupted in several regions during the 2000s and 2010s. He recalled that "when the H1N1 flu outbreak occurred, it became apparent that our H5N1 plan was really not applicable. So we had to reevaluate the plan. A lesson coming out of this experience was that your planning has to have generic elements so that you can modify and tailor it to specific events." Generic elements referred to the importance of undertaking a careful risk assessment in advance of a disruption and developing a risk-management strategy that can apply to a wide range of scenarios rather than focusing on the event that just occurred. After identifying what caused the crisis, managers often believe that they should have seen the disaster coming when, in fact, this may not have been possible—an example of the *hindsight bias*.[7]

The senior vice president of corporate continuity and recovery management for a financial services company warned of this bias when referencing a disabling power outage his firm had suffered: "But of course hindsight is 20/20 and there's no way for us to have known in advance."

There is a silver lining to the hindsight bias in that company leaders are likely to then pay attention to preventive strategies that they should have considered beforehand. This behavior is reinforced by the availability bias: the tendency to focus attention on how to avoid an adverse event such as the one that just occurred, rather than focusing on its low likelihood of recurrence.

Underestimation of Risk

Another intuitive pitfall is the tendency for company leaders to underestimate the likelihood and impact of risks that could disrupt their enterprise. Directors, executives, and managers are often hired, promoted, and rewarded for their can-do attitude and readiness to surmount barriers. It comes as little surprise that they often tend to define risks as challenges to be overcome, cutting them down to manageable size—or perhaps ignoring them altogether if they believe the chances of a future occurrence are below their threshold of concern. Hazards are thus often intuitively seen as more manageable or of less concern than deliberative analysis would suggest.

Novo Nordisk, a Danish pharmaceutical company, employs forty thousand people globally and sells its diabetic-care medications and hormone therapies in 180 countries. Its stock price far outperformed the market in recent years. When a number of employees voiced concerns about the quality of its production system for insulin—one of its bestselling medications—their warnings were ignored by company managers who were riveted on the firm's strong results. But when the US Food and Drug Administration uncovered the quality problems, it forced the company to discard six months of insulin production and asked American drugmaker Eli Lilly to take over most of Novo Nordisk's customer base in the United States.[8]

This underestimation of risk was also evident among those we interviewed as they reflected on the catastrophic events summarized in chapter 2. The chief executive officer of a chemical company, for instance, recalled the miscalculating mindset that had prevailed at the outset of the 2008–2009 financial crisis:

> We saw some signs as early as June that there was a real storm coming economically. We got together all of our leaders in July and we had them work through three different scenarios on what they would do if volumes fell 5 percent, 10 percent, 20 percent, and we had those plans in place. . . . Now, when it hit, it turned out to be a lot worse than the 20 percent that we talked about for some of our businesses.

Having learned that their intuitive thinking needed to be calibrated by undertaking a more systematic analysis in the spirit of deliberative thinking, many company managers vowed to press their colleagues to be wary of underestimated risks. The director of risk management at a medical technology company spoke for many in warning about what might be around the corner: "I am looking at ways just to continually keep people thinking about events outside the organization that are at least plausible and that we should take a look at."

Overconfidence

A third pitfall is the tendency for decision-makers to focus on readily available data that can also lead to overconfidence. More specifically, firms may ignore potential disruptions when information on their likelihood or impact is hard to obtain or simply unavailable. Moreover, success itself can breed overconfidence as company leaders reckon that they have more control over events than is warranted, a shortcoming that we often witness in company acquisitions of other enterprises where failure rates can exceed 50 percent.[9]

By way of example from our interviews, several risk managers noted that an overreliance on quantitative models and predictive algorithms had skewed management thinking toward excessive optimism about the risks it faced. One large bank for instance, learned the hard way that its risk models based on available data were not capturing the full range of the hazards it faced. Its risk manager warned that "retrospective models do not always accurately predict the future." She had as a result pressed her firm to incorporate stress testing and scenario analysis into its models.

Minimum Risk Thresholds

Even if company managers do not underestimate the likelihood of an adverse event occurring, they may tend to ignore the disruptive consequences of the risk if they view its likelihood to be below their threshold of concern. Since all risks cannot be concurrently considered, priorities must be assigned. Given these pragmatic constraints, some hazards must be left on the back burner, at least for the moment; some may later be a focus of attention, but only after an adverse event occurs. This certainly makes intuitive sense, but less so deliberatively, as there is a need to not only consider the likelihood of a disaster occurring but also its consequences.

The tendency to use a simplified decision rule—*minimum risk thresholds*—diverts attention from the impacts of low-probability disruptions. This was evident among insurers before the terrorist attacks of 9/11; they had not priced terrorism coverage in the years running up to the attack despite the World Trade Center bombing in 1993, the destruction of a federal building in Oklahoma City in 1995, and al-Qaeda's attack on the US destroyer *Cole* in Yemen that had killed seventeen sailors in 2000.[10]

That said, specifying the appropriate cut-off for consideration is itself a hazardous business. A manager with an energy company reflected on the challenges of identifying the right risk threshold for his company's attention:

> We've done a rough job, I'll say, of trying to define certain thresholds at which risks are elevated for review. So for example, a $100-million-loss event is one that typically is elevated to regional leadership. Anything that could, we believe, plausibly result in a fatality has to be explicitly elevated to the overall leadership team.

Other potential risks might also be elevated above the threshold if more deliberative analysis is undertaken by focusing on worst-case scenarios and then estimating their likelihoods.

Myopia

Decision-makers tend to be shortsighted when reaching decisions on whether to invest in protection against catastrophic risks. There is a predictable reluctance to incur high upfront costs for loss mitigation measures unless near-term payoffs are evident. Rarely do the expected benefits over the next several years from investing in such measures justify incurring the cost of taking action now given the infrequency of extreme events. This short-term view was introduced as one of the drivers of DISRUPT.

British Petroleum had suffered a string of accidents from 2005 to 2010, for instance, culminating in its massive oil spill in the Gulf of Mexico in 2010. An independent panel that had reviewed an earlier BP refinery explosion that resulted in the loss of fifteen lives concluded that short-term managerial incentives had been a key contributor to the company's underinvestment in process safety:

> The metrics and milestones contained in [BP's] performance contracts have historically focused on short-term performance in areas such as profitability, production, environmental, and injury rates, all of which are measured annually. [Yet] many decisions relating to process safety involve costs and benefits that are both long-term in nature and sometimes difficult to measure.[11]

By way of a parallel, when the Tokyo Electric Power Company decided to construct its Fukushima nuclear reactor power plants in the 1960s, it had estimated that the greatest tsunami would never top four meters. The actual surge after the 2011 earthquake came in at more than forty meters. Had the company looked well back in the history of the region, it might have anticipated the devastation of its plants by the 2011 tsunami. The manager of an industrial company we interviewed drew a lesson for his own company from this avoidable forecasting error that had stemmed from the power company's myopia:[12]

> Was it a black swan event? No. The Japanese only chose to go back to 1890, despite the fact that there's geological evidence indicating that there had been much higher surges than the tsunami that occurred. So we try to use what others have done poorly and translate their

behavior to what we're doing and recognize that we may be as short-sighted as they are.

More deliberative thinking can thus help transcend our limited lines of sight and point to the long-term benefits of near-term measures.

Status Quo Bias

Finally, everything else being equal, managers often find it easier to preserve the status quo than incur the expense of changing operations in anticipation of risk. The potential costs of switching are often weighted more heavily than potential gains. The commitment of additional funds, when abandonment of a current plan is viewed as a performance failure, is dubbed the sunk-cost fallacy.[13]

It is often easier to preserve the status quo than to search for alternatives, for several reasons. It simplifies the process by postponing difficult decisions. The potential downsides of switching may well be given greater weight than projected gains. And those with a vested interest in the status quo may have the power to resist or even block any change.[14]

After the Japan earthquake and tsunami in 2011 and the meltdown of the Fukushima reactors, managers with an American publishing firm began thinking about what could happen if a nuclear power plant near its headquarters was subject to an earthquake. The director of crisis planning perceived the probability of an earthquake at that location to be less than one in ten thousand, but still felt it was a disaster that one should place on the firm's radar screen: "After any catastrophe the firm needs to take a look and ask itself, am I okay with the status quo? What do I need to look at differently?"

LEARNING FROM ADVERSE EVENTS

As we learned in the last chapter, company executives and managers may have toyed with scenarios for potential catastrophic losses, but if the firm had not suffered a severe loss or witnessed one nearby in recent years, company leaders may have concluded that doomsday scenarios remain below their threshold of concern. Adverse events, however, whether personally experienced or witnessed among others, can help trigger immediate soul searching on how to avoid them in the future, driven by the availability bias.[15]

By way of example, Union Carbide's lethal gas leak in Bhopal, India, in 1984 led another chemical firm to reduce inventory of a product that could potentially cause a catastrophic accident. That firm's executives had long wanted to take the precaution, and the Bhopal disaster provided them with the rationale.[16]

Similarly, only after a financial institution suffered huge losses during the 2008–2009 financial crisis did its executives focus on a host of other low-probability but extreme-impact events. In the words of the firm's director of risk management:

> The modeling we use to anticipate these black swans and the resulting capital that we have to set aside for these anticipated risks are taken far more seriously than they were before. There was a sense that things happen in places like Nigeria, but they don't happen in places like New York City. Now we realize they happen everywhere.

Following the 2010 massive oil spill in the Gulf of Mexico, a large energy company decided to completely exit deep-water drilling. The director of risk management explained:

> Although that oil spill didn't impact us directly, it probably has had the single largest impact on the industry I've seen in ten years. We quickly came to the conclusion that we really wouldn't survive an event of that magnitude. It is our view that there is always the potential for something to happen like that. So we spent a lot of time asking, "Is that the type of a business we'd like to be in?"

FROM INTUITIVE TO DELIBERATIVE THINKING

1. Management decisions in preparing for and reacting to low-probability but high-consequence events often reflect behavioral biases and simplified decision rules that characterize intuitive thinking, including an availability bias, hindsight bias, underestimation of risk, overconfidence, minimum risk thresholds, myopia and a status quo bias.

2. Deliberative thinking, by contrast, gives greater attention to systematic analysis and complex protocols, both essential for company readiness for disruptions.

3. Though company costs from disruptions are high, a silver lining has been a shift of company managers from intuitive thinking to more deliberative thinking, creating greater awareness of the biases and heuristics that can skew decisions under risk and uncertainty by learning from adverse events.

The Risk-Analysis Cycle

You know you've got a nice sail, you can gets lots of wind and can get blown all over the place, but unless you have a rudder to direct you, you never know where you're going to wind up until it's too late.

—Chief Risk Officer, *Commercial Bank*

Company directors, executives, and managers are coming to appreciate that a personally experienced adverse event in their organization is one of the best learning moments for anticipating future setbacks. With the benefit of hindsight, company leaders can better appreciate what they should have done in preparing for the past disruption, and thereby become more deliberative in preparing for the next one. They can more systematically identify, assess, and prioritize risks. They can also more purposefully set the company's appetite and tolerance for those risks.

While every firm differs in the details, Figure 4.1 depicts a *risk-analysis cycle* that has emerged from the experience of many enterprises. Building on tangible understanding, executives and managers identify and assess the potential risks faced by the firm, determine the firm's appetite and tolerance for such hazards, and develop the firm's risk-management strategy. They then bring that strategy to life.

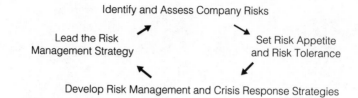

Figure 4.1 The Risk Analysis Cycle

IDENTIFY AND ASSESS COMPANY RISKS

The risk-analysis cycle begins with executives and managers at all levels identifying the disruptive events their operations may face. For that, they often turn to outside experts for estimating event likelihoods and outcomes, though they also draw on their own dedicated staffs. The expert and in-house appraisals are then aggregated to identify company risk as a whole. The vice president of risk management and insurance for a food company summarized the first step of the process: "The comptroller division, finance division, [and] operations division are each asked to identify the risks that they see as important so that we don't miss these."

Most firms have formalized their risk assessment process with dedicated reviews. Among firms where we interviewed, more than nine in ten do so at least annually, and nearly half do so semiannually or even continuously. The chair of the risk-management committee for another firm explained: "Our committee has a representative from each of our major business units as well as representatives from internal audit. We meet quarterly and construct a list of the top risks we currently face as well as emerging risks. We then analyze their potential impacts, probability, speed of onset, and the effectiveness of any mitigation measure," all with an eye to the firm's overall risk profile.

Firms apply a variety of methods for assessing the risks. Two-thirds of directors, executives, and managers with whom we had contact reported that their firm used quantitative methodologies such as scenario analysis and stress tests. Scenario analysis entails constructing a set of possible future events and outcomes rather than painting an exact picture of the future. Stress tests examine prospective outcomes to determine how the firm will fare if they actually occurred. The chief risk officer of an insurance firm, for instance, reported that his firm "fully tests the spectrum of scenarios" in identifying and quantifying key risks. A bank executive applied stress tests to identify whether there is a scenario where it would have insufficient capital. An executive with another financial services company affirmed that her enterprise built detailed scenarios around a spectrum of extreme events, while a manager with a manufacturer reported that his firm wanted "to make sure that it has stressed their system to be able to take care of decisions to reduce the risk if either its frequency and/or severity were classified as high."

With experience over time, companies have also made their methods more sophisticated, comprehensive, quantitative, and forward looking. The chief risk officer of a bank reported that many modeling techniques that the industry had previously utilized had failed to anticipate the extreme events that had actually hit the industry. "We were all very confident in our risk models," she said, "that were backward looking." By contrast, "today we have added stress testing and scenario testing into our models to determine what could happen if this type of calamity occurs or if that type of an economic scenario happens to take place."

Some companies classify their risks by quantifying frequency and severity. An executive with an industrial firm, for instance, noted that it sought to identify "some of the tails or extreme risks" to make sure that it has stressed its system to reduce the risk "if either its frequency and/or severity were classified as high." After imposing appropriate controls, emerging from the appraisal, the firm moved most of its risks to the low-frequency/low-severity category.

Still, many firms continue their reliance on more qualitative approaches in the belief that quantitative databases are often incomplete and sometimes inaccurate. The danger, warned a number of managers, is that their executives and directors could be drawn to what was measurable more than what was vital. In the words of a bank risk manager, "there is an element of judgment regarding the likelihood of particular events occurring that make them difficult to quantify." Even so, he affirmed that his bank must realistically factor them into its planning process.

Whatever the upsides and downsides of quantitative and qualitative methods, virtually all of the companies where we interviewed had moved toward more comprehensive and systematic analysis, the essence of deliberative thinking. In the words of an executive of an insurance firm: "It's very easy to allow yourself psychologically to believe that certain events can be remote, but there's got to be that balance between probability and severity. Sometimes I find probabilities very difficult to quantify. Severities are much easier to quantify." The executive reported that he still sought to identify the likelihoods of all events, however extreme they might be, even if many were difficult to estimate with precision.

Once risks are assessed, both quantitatively and qualitatively, they are passed up—and down—the company ladder. The identified threats, some-times in the hundreds, are aggregated through reporting systems and brain-storming sessions, and priorities among them are then set. Less threatening hazards are left to the responsibility of their originating units, while the most important ones are brought to the attention of the chief executive or even the directors.

The director of corporate risk for a healthcare company, for instance, classified and then ranked his firm's risks in twenty-one categories. He then took only the top-ranked risks up to executives who report directly to the chief executive and the governing board. Defining the top risks: "They are the ones that are likely to make the most significant difference in the per-formance of the organization. They are often ones requiring more effort and investment to manage, so they need to be discussed at a strategic level by the top management and the board."

SET RISK APPETITE AND RISK TOLERANCE

A firm's *risk appetite* is the amount and kind of risk it is willing to take to achieve its objectives, and its ascendance in corporate planning has come with an obvious corollary: Is the company ready to bear the downsides if its risk-taking turns into negative reality? *Risk tolerance* is the company's willingness to accept a loss from an adverse event knowing the likelihood that it could cause significant disruption to the firm.[1]

Specifying the firm's risk appetite and risk tolerance often entails test-ing the company's resilience at the extremes by applying scenario analyses and stress testing to see how far the company could go but still survive if pushed to the brink. While the degree of financial distress is usually the first benchmark for answering those questions, it is not the only ranking criterion at many companies. The impact of risk on a firm's brand and credibility is frequently also important as it is generally recognized that a damaged reputation can severely impair a firm's earnings. As one company's chief risk officer warned: "The firm's appetite for risk is typically measured in losses, but often it can be measured in damage to the firm's reputation that can have long-term adverse consequences to the firm's revenues and earnings."

Companies rarely used the concept of risk appetite before 2000. It gained general currency, however, in the regulatory wake of the 2008–2009 financial crisis when investment banks and other financial service companies were required to meet legislative requirements under the Dodd–Frank Act of 2010.

While risk assessment is a largely bottom-up process, the determination of risk appetite and risk tolerance normally comes with top-down specifications that are then carried into the firm's risk-management and crisis-response strategies, the next step in the risk-analysis cycle of Figure 4.1. Without a centralized definition, the divisional inputs to a company-wide view of risk are likely to range all over the map. In the metaphor of a bank's chief risk officer, going without a firm-wide specification of risk appetite and tolerance is akin to "sailing in the Atlantic Ocean without a rudder. You know you've got a nice sail, you can gets lots of wind and can get blown all over the place, but unless you have a rudder to direct you, you never know where you're going to wind up until it's too late."

The specification of risk appetite and risk tolerance is normally a tiered process in which specific risks are initially identified at lower levels of the firm and then aggregated by upper management. This process works well when the specific risks are accurately appraised by operating managers and reported up the chain of command. As a business-unit risk manager for a chemical company explained: "We delegate authority in these matters to our most senior business heads, who all sit on the corporate executive committee. For those of us in my role, our obligation is to support those business heads with the right information to help them enable that decision making process."

Explicit specification of the firm's appetite and tolerance provides managers throughout the enterprise with a compass needle, though it can prove difficult for a given business unit to make the pointer operational. Still, a clear-minded and widely communicated statement is an essential first step, reported at many of the firms, as one risk officer explained: "In determining

our risk appetite, we are aiming for a return of 20 percent on this investment but based on our risk tolerance we are not willing to have a likelihood
greater than 5 percent that the investment will lead to a loss of more than
50 percent of our existing capital." As noted by another chief risk officer:
"I have a report on my desk as we speak that's going to be distributed this
afternoon which codifies and quantifies every risk we have in the firm,
whether it be catastrophic or small. And it outlines our risk positions to the
whole organization to make sure that everybody understands what they are
and that they're within our risk appetite."

Oft-repeated and widely dispersed messages of the firm's risk appetite
and risk tolerance gradually transform executive signaling into company
culture. As the chief risk manager for a bank told us: "Risk appetite is the
critical driver of culture. You can have the craziest organizational structure,
but if you have the right culture, you'll be okay. [And] a well-defined risk
appetite that is measured, monitored, and reported back to the board of
directors is a critical component of that culture."

Companies have found numerous ways to communicate their risk
appetite and tolerance up and down the hierarchy. Executive statements,
performance indicators, and regular appraisals are among those used in
many firms to focus divisions on these risk-related measures. As described
by the chief risk manager for a conglomerate firm: "We've created a risk-
appetite statement in words and in metrics, so that we can measure our
performance against these words, and that is something that we have
instituted and approved at the board level. We do monitoring across our
portfolios of business to ensure that the risks that they are taking and the
outcomes that they are achieving are within the risk appetite approved by
the board."

BALANCING APPETITE AND TOLERANCE FOR RISK

Company hunger for risk and a willingness to live with risk inherently
coexist in uneasy tension, since a greater risk appetite implies a higher
tolerance for risk. Finding the right balance between the two has become
a management challenge that requires deliberative thinking. It helps
explain the rise of the role of the chief risk officer in many firms. At the
turn of the century, few companies had designated the position of a chief

risk officer, but today it has become a standard fixture on many organizational charts.

The chief risk officer's principal responsibility is to synthesize inputs from company divisions and operating units, and to evaluate their data against the backdrop of the firm's avowed risk appetite and risk tolerance. From headquarters, might the company's liquidity be threatened by its current levels of appetite and risk? From the operating units and divisions, could any of their vulnerabilities put the entire firm at risk? The chief risk officer of a food processing corporation made those considerations explicit in rendering her advice on company actions: "How much risk does the senior management want to retain? Will they feel uncomfortable if their earnings per share significantly decrease because we had an earthquake in Chile, or will they respond by saying, 'This is a one-time event?'"

The challenge in balancing risk appetite and risk tolerance comes to a head when firms are taking sharp-edged decisions to expand, change, or contract a given business. It is then that the chief risk officer is often asked to weigh in on competing priorities and serve as an arbiter for the tradeoffs between appetite and tolerance. The chief risk officer of a medical technology company, for example, affirmed that the tradeoff question would arise whenever the company was considering entry into a new geographic region, new product line, or new business. "You need to balance the inherent risks in each activity," he warned, and as a result, "we may only want to move into some of them." Similarly, the chief risk officer of a financial firm reported that she was working to ensure growth while limiting the risk of a severe loss: "Risk management is a mixture of creating economically viable options for growth, but it's also a mechanism to improve controls so that catastrophes do not happen."

The tradeoffs are less fluid, however, in the case of criteria for which there is little or no tolerance for any risk. Health and safety, bribery and corruption, and integrity and responsibility are among the most common no-tolerance zones even if short-term gains from compromising them might be perceived. Several executives and managers in consumer healthcare companies, for instance, were unwilling to consider any tradeoff if a product or device might jeopardize the health or safety of its patients or customers. In practice, however, it can prove hard to police all the no-tolerance zones within an enterprise.

DEVELOP RISK-MANAGEMENT
AND CRISIS-RESPONSE STRATEGIES

Once a company's risk appetite and risk tolerance have been specified, managers at all levels can then build their risk-management and crisis-response strategies, the third stage of the risk-analysis cycle. These are the blueprints for improving a firm's protection against extreme events and enhancing its resilience when one of the risks becomes reality. A survey of 1,843 companies worldwide in the fourth quarter of 2016 revealed that the larger the firm, the more likely it was to have a formal risk-management department. More than 90 percent of companies with at least $1 billion in annual revenue now report this dedicated function. Company directors, executives, and managers are consequently devoting greater attention to risk-management plans across a range of low-probability but high-consequence events. Here, too, we see deliberative thinking making its way into operating divisions, the executive suite, and more recently, the boardroom.[2]

Firms often cited specific events, most notably the terrorist attacks of 9/11, the financial crisis of 2008–2009, the Deepwater Horizon drilling-rig explosion in 2010, and the 2011 Japanese trifecta—earthquake, tsunami, and nuclear meltdown—as sparking their own more deliberative calculations. Company learning was event-driven, with the era's great disasters serving to catalyze a focus on risk appetite, tolerance, and management in ways that lesser disasters had not.

A particularly striking development has been the increased engagement of company directors in guiding the firm's risk-management strategy. At virtually all of the firms where we interviewed, the board has become increasingly involved in specifying levels for both risk appetite and risk tolerance, often by drawing on reports from divisions and functions across the organization. As described by the chief risk officer of a financial services firm, "Our board is very engaged. Every quarter we spend about an hour and a half with them going through a detailed discussion of the enterprise risk profile of the company. Our board adopted a statement of risk appetite, which articulates our business strategies and how much risk we're willing to take in pursuit of those strategies."[3]

The board's concern with these issues places a premium on deliberative thinking among the chief risk officer and other executives so that they can effectively inform the directors on the tradeoffs between risk appetite and risk tolerance. The chief risk officer of an insurance company, for example, stressed that her directors understand "what these risks are so that there is no argument after the fact as to whether or not we will have had a loss. If somebody, especially our chairman, sees that these risks could be bigger than they are or thinks that possibly they're bigger than they should be, then it's time to do something about them."

Though directors have been pulled into the formulation of risk-management strategies, executives generally resisted board guidance regarding appropriate crisis-response strategies. Directors were generally seen as incapable of reaching the kinds of informed and rapid decisions required of a company during a crisis. As the senior vice president at a man-ufacturing firm cautioned: "The board is very interested in doing this, but they're not management. Their job is not to run the company. And so when we ask for help . . . there is a give and take," with directors asking, "'have you thought about X and Y,' but it is very much in an advisory role. It's not a directing-traffic role."

Still, directors raise a range of questions about the firm's risk agendas even if they have no specific guidance to render. Drawing on our interviews, here is a sampling of questions that directors have been asking of their exec-utives about the firm's risk and response strategies:

Do risk managers and executives recognize the importance of hav-ing specified but flexible risk appetite and risk tolerance criteria, and a balancing of the two to reflect changes in the firm's external environ-ment and business conditions?

Do risk managers understand how decisions related to the firm's risk appetite impact on its risk tolerance?

Does the firm have enough capital and resources to support and manage its risks?

Have executives delegated and pinpointed responsibility and accountability for those risks across the organization?

To answer those questions, executives and managers typically synthesize data from prospective perils in their company's current portfolio and risks that may arise in its new initiatives. Sifting through the figures, they have also become savvier about the decision biases that can get in the way of a deliberative approach.

As pointed out in the prior chapter, after an adverse event, managers tend to overestimate the probability of the same event reoccurring in the near future because of availability bias. But we have learned that many managers are now more aware of this bias. By way of example, the chief risk officer of an insurance company reported that his firm had become overly cautious in the wake of the 2008–2009 financial crisis. The company imposed a con-servative regimen to ensure that the firm would not be at risk, as some had feared it might be during the depth of the crisis. That near-miss led execu-tives and managers to become very risk averse, but as a result, they slowed the firm's growth below what it was capable of and what investors were expecting. The chief risk officer and other managers worked to mitigate that mindset. "Our risk-taking appetite was more restrictive than it should have been," he recalled, "but now we have replenished our capital and our risk appetite is back to what I would call a nice healthy state."

Others whom we interviewed also warned that a personal reputation for excessive caution might be viewed inside the company as the equiva-lent of unwarranted risk avoidance in a period of promise. They feared that their firm could acquire a reputation among competitors and investors for slow growth. For this reason, some sought to position risk management as synonymous with healthy growth. Many echoed the mantra offered by the manager of one information technology company: "You can't be successful without taking a business risk."

In developing their risk-management and crisis-response strategies, chief risk officers and others keep their company's risk appetite and risk tol-erance much in mind. A food processing company, for example, had been considering entry into an African region known for instability and violence. The company considered political risks as more threatening than natural disasters since in that part of the world the former tended to be more unpre-dictable than the latter. The firm investigated whether the company could offload some of its political risk through insurance, but the chief risk man-ager concluded that the cost of such a policy was so high that "transferring that risk was not necessarily something we wanted to do on a regular basis."

In the end, the firm's limited tolerance for that risk outweighed its appetite and it scotched its African strategy.

Similarly, an automotive-parts company was considering expansion into the Central and South American markets. Before doing so, the risk manager asked for evidence on the expected profitability of this new foray. Although it was forecast to be a high-return investment, the company nonetheless opted to limit its expansion because it was concerned with the higher-than-normal uncertainty given the new terrain and its local volatility. While the company certainly sought aggressive growth, it backed off when its risk manager warned of its limited tolerance for high risk.

Another multinational company recognized that it had to invest in mitigation practices to ensure compliance with local standards of the many countries in which it operated. With its risk appetite and risk tolerance in mind, company managers pressed for the firm to exit countries where the payoffs were not large enough given the risks involved. Its chief risk officer explained: "We view ourselves as being in the risk-taking business, but one has to be prudent and only take risks that people understand and accept and are prepared to support and mitigate, not risks that you haven't quantified and measured and stressed."

Some companies, especially in financial services, noted that a shifting regulatory environment could also alter the company calculus for developing risk-management strategies. The Federal Supervisory Capital Assessment Program in 2009 began stress testing the financial strength of the nation's largest financial institutions. The federal government then required them to develop a plan for maintaining sufficient liquidity to buffer against most worst-case scenarios. The chief risk officer of a financial services firm reported that as a result, his company had altered its dividend and stock repurchase strategies.

Stimulated by new regulations, many financial institutions reported affirmative developments in both their risk-modeling practices and investment and lending policies. They extended stress testing to a wider range of risks than required by these regulations. As the chief risk officer of a bank reported: "We're actually developing capital plans based upon the outcome of the stress examinations. And we do them not just for the regulators. We do a great many of them just for our own inquiry into the portfolio's performance." He noted that the stress testing had been initiated before the

2008–2009 financial crisis, but it received "a much higher level of scrutiny and importance today."

A directive of the European Union in 2009 defined the minimum amount of capital that insurance companies must hold to reduce the risk of insolvency. The chief risk officer of a life insurance company noted that the directive, known as Solvency II, forced her firm to develop scenarios for risks that could occur with as low an annual probability as one in two hundred, and to identify the steps that should be taken now to cope with the risks should they occur later. As a result, she reported, "I started sitting down with our operations leaders across the business and walked through with them the worst-case scenarios."

LEAD THE RISK-MANAGEMENT STRATEGY

Leading the risk-management strategy is the fourth and final stage of the risk-management cycle of Figure 4.1. This, like each of the earlier stages, is vital for deliberative action. By way of illustration, Morgan Stanley's risk officer Richard Rescorla, whom we met in the prologue, became an esteemed figure for having led the urgent evacuation of his firm's four thousand employees from the World Trade Center on 9/11. And conversely, British Petroleum's then chief executive Tony Hayward was challenged after a postmortem of the Deepwater Horizon oil rig explosion in 2010 revealed that the catastrophe might have been preventable had the CEO and key decision makers opted to implement his firm's own safety strategies.[4]

For executing a company's risk and response strategies, research has revealed that front-line managers are often more acutely aware than are executives of emerging hazards and how they can be best contained. In the months prior to the financial disasters that struck AIG and Lehman in 2008, for example, we now know that many midlevel managers had voiced their growing fears that the subprime mortgages that they were massively insuring could result in catastrophic losses, but their executive overseers did not absorb or act on those early warnings to avert disaster.[5]

The same leaderless behavior was evident at Morton-Thiokol, the maker of the solid-fuel booster rockets for the space shuttle *Challenger*, in the run-up to *Challenger's* disastrous launch in 1996. The company's engineers foresaw the probable failure of the O-rings in the low temperature of the launch and conveyed their fears to Thiokol executives. Yet the engineers' warnings were discounted by the executives, who gave the National Aeronautics and Space Administration a green light for launching *Challenger* despite the near freezing conditions at the launch site. The value of front-line managers' appraisals for executing risk and response strategies was evident again at NASA in the run-up to the loss of the space shuttle *Columbia* in 2003 because of a damaged left wing. Shuttle engineers warned mission controllers about potential damage to the wing during launch, but those at the top dismissed their concerns.[6]

Leadership in the large firms studied here comes in many layers, and coordination among them becomes an all-important ingredient in a firm's enterprise's risk-management and crisis-response strategy. To that end, many companies have created a risk architecture and company culture that bring those tiers together through a common set of values, as we will see in the chapters ahead. An executive of a healthcare company outlined the importance of a shared mindset for aligning risk management across the layers in his firm:

> We live by a core set of values, and that is rigorously and consistently referred to at every staff meeting. We talk about integrity and behaving ethically and honoring commitment, providing quality service and accountability. By adhering to these values in both the short and long term, our customers feel that we are doing the right thing. Those values are well communicated and repeatedly communicated throughout the organization, and also embedded within our scorecard system for performance reviews.

RISK-ANALYSIS CYCLE

1. A firm's risk appetite is the amount and kind of risk that it is willing to accept to achieve its objectives. It is balanced against the firm's risk tolerance, a company's allowable likelihood for accepting a large loss that can disrupt the firm or the maximum loss that it is willing to incur for a given risk.
2. Many firms have developed a deliberative risk-analysis cycle. Building on past experience, management identifies and assesses the hazards faced by the firm, and then sets its risk appetite and

risk tolerance as the foundation for developing and leading its risk-management and crisis strategies.

3. A greater risk appetite requires higher tolerance for disruption. Finding the right balance between the two has become a management essential for deliberative thinking and helps explains the rise of the role of chief risk officer at many companies.

4. The company's risk-management and crisis-response strategies coupled with the firm's culture are key ingredients for more deliberative decision-making by top executives and front-line managers.

Risk-Management Praxis

Do you have enough capital to support those risks? Do you have enough resources to manage those risks? Are you able to deploy those resources to manage the risks, and have you assigned responsibility and accountability for those risks across the organization?
—Executive, *Conglomerate Corporation*

As companies have added enterprise risk management to their operations during the past decade, they have developed a number of specific practices for doing so. These are the tangible steps that executives and managers have utilized for transforming their commitment to risk management into reality.

"Praxis" is defined as the process by which a theory or principle is enacted or realized. Drawing on our interviews with the leaders of a hundred of America's major publicly traded companies, we identify here the most widely used tools for assessing and managing risk that have been devised in recent years. We begin by way of example with a brief look at Dell Technologies after Bangkok's massive flooding in 2011 that had disrupted the computer-maker's operations and as a result led to a more deliberative risk-management strategy.

A BANGKOK SETBACK

Founded in 1984 by Michael S. Dell, the company rapidly expanded to become one of the world's largest personal computer makers. Headquartered in Texas, it was included among the S&P 500 until 2013 when its founder and a private equity firm, Silver Lake Partners, took it private. Dell acquired EMC Corporation, a data storage company, in 2016, and together they generated $62 billion in annual revenue.

But five years earlier, Dell encountered an unexpected speed bump in Thailand. A historic flood in 2011 submerged much of Bangkok for two months, including the assembly plant of Western Digital, one of Dell's hard-disk suppliers. Dell announced that it would have to raise computer prices since the disks' costs had been driven up by their sudden shortage. Dell even warned that it might have to limit its now scarce supply of computers to only its higher-end customers.

Stung by the unanticipated supply-chain disaster from the flood, Dell began to track in detail the business-continuity readiness of its suppliers, identifying the risks faced by each partner. It then diversified its suppliers geographically and pinpointed management responsibility for business continuity both internally and with its suppliers. It required risk metrics with frequent updates from both its partners and its own divisions.

Dell also pressed for stronger risk management within each of its operating units by setting company-wide risk standards and benchmarking individual units against them. Its executives backed this up with warnings that risks in each component of the business could impact the enterprise as a whole. They introduced stress testing and regularly conducted a business impact analysis of plausible threats, including another inundation of Bangkok.

NEAR MISSES

Near misses and disasters experienced by others can prove exceptionally instructive by providing object lessons with compelling implications, if they are heeded. The basic precept is well captured by an article with an intriguing title, "Learning from Samples of One or Fewer." Its authors argue that organizations need to pay attention to adverse events that do not occur as well as those that do, using the airline industry as an example where both crashes and near misses are reported. Constructing such histories is a low-cost way to attend to adverse events that could happen in the future, and they can instructively warn companies of scenarios that could result in serious disruption.[1]

Prior research confirms that companies strengthen their safety performance following calamities witnessed among other firms in the same industry. As previously noted, the 1984 disaster at Union Carbide's Bhopal plant led many chemical manufacturers to strengthen their own plant safety. Similarly, the 1989 near meltdown of a nuclear reactor at Pennsylvania's Three Mile Island facility led to a reduction in the number of unplanned outages among American nuclear power plants nationwide. And accident rates at airlines and railroads are observed to decline after mishaps of others in the same industry.[2]

Directors, executives, and managers whom we interviewed confirmed the importance of learning from close calls and others' setbacks. An executive in an energy firm reported that he became more concerned with its own operational risks after BP's Deepwater Horizon explosion in 2010. The vice president for corporate strategy of an auto parts supplier reported that his firm redoubled its own vigilance after witnessing the unprecedented bankruptcies of Enron Corporation and WorldCom in 2001–2002.

The manager of disaster recovery at an electric utility reported that while her company had never experienced a serious disruption, it had suffered close calls that persuaded management to better focus on its risks and to hone its readiness: "We've had a number of power problems in our data center," the manager explained. "One time we came within less than a minute of having one of our data centers go completely dark. So that was a near miss. But now we have revised the process so that even that wouldn't be catastrophic because we can continue delivering power to our customers even if we don't have a data center."

A risk manager of a biotech company reported how his company had become more adept at running its own supply chains after witnessing setbacks experienced by others:

Sometimes, the scenario doesn't even come to mind as to what could possibly happen until you see it happen either in your competitor or you have a near miss yourself. One of the things that I've started to think about is doing business with a key supplier who no longer can meet your requirements because it has had a regulatory shutdown. The FDA or regulatory body comes in and shuts the supplier down, and it can no longer supply the product. We have seen that happen with other companies, and [we've] had that happen within our own company for a short period of time. . . . But what happens if it's a long-term key supplier? Who else is out there to help us?

Managers who have witnessed a near miss of their own or a competitor's setback report that they are more likely to have built their own practices for buffering against a direct hit. Following the Japan earthquake of 2011, for example, the CEO of an American retailer ordered every building inspected to make sure that each was earthquake-proof. An executive of a manufacturer reported that he had learned from watching a severe downturn in the telecommunications industry in 2002 to separate financial risk from operating risk. The chief risk officer of an investment bank formalized a process to define his firm's risk appetite and tolerance after witnessing the ravages of the 2008–2009 financial meltdown.

Companies also look to their competitors for affirmative guidance, at times even imitating what others have done well, actions that academics have labeled *mimetic behavior*. An executive in a chemical firm, for example, explained that the selling of one of its business lines brought it into conformity with others in the industry. To avoid transporting toxic chemicals between a plant where they were produced and another where they were used, he found that other chemical firms had reduced their transportation risks by consolidating both facilities on one site, and he followed suit.[3]

Many of the practical devices that we characterize here have emerged not only from the massive disruptions of recent years that we identified in chapter 2, but also from a company's setbacks and near misses and those of others. Business leaders have learned from what other companies have done to shore up their own risk and crisis-management strategies, adopting measures that have succeeded elsewhere.

We highlight the practical measures under the general areas of modeling risk, systematically reducing risk, improving communication, strengthening suppliers, networking with competitors fostering continuity, and imagining the next disruption.

MODELING RISK

Many companies came to appreciate from their own experience and that of other enterprises during the 2008–2009 financial crisis that they required better risk modeling to anticipate and buffer themselves from disruptions like those that had followed Lehman Brothers' bankruptcy. Acknowledging that they had been blindsided by its devastating ripple effects, company leaders vowed to prepare for their next crisis by having better risk assessment techniques and forecasts well in place.

A financial services firm reported that it not only strengthened its appraisals of specific products and individual regions but also came to model industry-wide risks. In the words of its chief risk officer, "We needed to make sure that our systems understood risk, not just at the product level, but at the overall customer level. We also started putting very high emphasis on making sure that we have industry-level understanding of risk in addition to geography." Another financial institution, acknowledging that its own model had failed to forecast the downturn after Lehman's failure, created stress tests and scenario analyses to expose hidden hazards that might be lurking in its loan offerings, investment portfolios, structured investments, and market funds. In the colorful phrasing of its chief risk officer, "In order to effectively analyze our stress testing and scenario analysis, it was the great philosopher, Clint Eastwood, who said, 'A man has got to know his limitations.' And there are no truer words than that. If you want to understand the risks in your company, you must understand your concentrations of credit and concentrations of risks."

Some firms created a risk balance sheet that quantified prospective hazards and determined where they were concentrated, including worst-case outcomes and whether the enterprise could withstand them. The chief risk officer of a real estate investment trust itemized pragmatic questions such as: "Is your balance sheet strong and flexible enough? Have you done a sensitivity analysis via different worst-case scenarios to determine whether you'd remain liquid and solvent? Are you positioning yourself in the right path of growth so that you're not too far over the cliff if things don't go the way you want?"

A risk-related balance sheet can usefully incorporate the company's risk appetite, risk tolerance, and risk readiness, and the extent to which its current capital, organization, and talent are prepared for a disruption. In the summary words of the risk manager for a multinational conglomerate:

Once you align your risk appetite, you start choosing to take or avoid certain risks. You also have to make sure that you have what I would call preparedness for the risk that you've chosen to take. Preparedness really means: Do you have enough capital to support those risks? Do you have enough resources to manage those risks?

Are you able to deploy those resources to manage the risks, and have you assigned responsibility and accountability for those risks across the organization?

Some companies, especially in the insurance industry, built sophisticated risk models and used advanced analytics to guide their investment strategy and underwriting decisions. The chief risk officer of a major reinsurer reported, for instance, that detailed vigilance was now required to determine how much exposure it faced should another earthquake devastate Japan or another Hurricane Sandy hit the United States:

> What we do is insulate ourselves to levels that we feel are appropriate and comfortable for our capital position and our structure in significant parts of the capital markets. We use the strength and security of the capital market to make sure that our balance sheet is always in a proper risk-adjustment state. Have we got the right amount of surplus for the exposure that we're carrying under any of the scenarios that we could possibly imagine within a one-in-a-hundred-year event?

SYSTEMATICALLY REDUCING RISK

Companies that experienced near misses or catastrophic events emerged with a new appreciation for practical measures that could insulate them against future disruptions. The terrorist attacks of September 11, 2001, on New York and Washington, DC, for example, made firms aware that virtually any organization could be threatened by extremism, even if headquartered a continent away, and many responded with bolstered security for their own employees. A risk manager at a communications company explained how he and his associates reacted to that calamity:

> The onset of 9/11 had us take a fresh look at the risks from terrorism, both internal disruption as well as external forces. And it got us to improve our protocols, our procedures, our processes. For example, now all of our buildings, except for our retail centers, are pretty much locked 24/7. We rely on technical aspects of entry into our buildings using card access, tracking who comes and goes from our buildings, using more electronic surveillance at our buildings for protection.

Another after-effect has been for firms to simply reduce their risk appetite. This has been particularly evident among financial firms after the crisis of 2008–2009, in part because legislation requires that they quantify, justify, and better manage their hazards. That in turn led companies to more carefully appraise the aggregate risks of their portfolio or product mixes.

A reduction in risk taking, however, also comes with downsides, as some managers were quick to learn: risk avoidance can leave a firm in the shadow of its more aggressive competitors. The chief risk officer of an investment firm explained: "You have to have good initiatives in place with respect to product development and testing to make sure that we're ready for changes in risk appetite. Otherwise you could become irrelevant to the marketplace in the long term."

Consider a practical question applied by some firms to reduce their vulnerabilities: Is the value of a given operation simply not worth the risk it imposes on the company? Recall from chapter 3 the energy company that decided to abandon its offshore exploration after the BP Deepwater Horizon accident, concluding that it was simply not worth the risk. Another energy firm terminated partnerships with other companies it deemed too small to cover the price of their own drilling disasters, again in the wake of the BP accident, fearing it could be saddled with their costs. A chemical firm concluded that it could not afford to accept the risk associated with its outputs in medical devices implanted in the human body.

Firms also transfer portions of their risk to others by purchasing more insurance. For example, a biotech company acquired a policy to cover product liability and business interruption, and even started a captive insurance company to cover some of its risks. A firm in financial services acquired insurance against the insolvency of lower-quality counterparties. A consumer products company now constructs worst-case scenarios to determine how much more insurance it requires to cover damage from extreme weather events. Its chief risk officer discovered, however, that insurers were not always ready to provide the expanded coverage they wanted, at any price.

Companies also recognized the need to diversify their operations so that no enterprise-critical resource could be lost without a ready substitute. In this regard, a company with operations in an insecure foreign location had been forced into an improvised solution following a disaster when it had failed to create a standby facility. "We had to literally move these computers and these servers on the back of tuk tuks," a three-wheeled motorized taxi, reported a senior risk manager, "and then put them on pickup trucks and in employees' car trunks and fight our way through a war zone to reset these computers."

Appreciating that disasters can make sole servers inoperable, firms increasingly back up vital data on other computers or store them remotely. A parts distributor, for instance, created an offsite location for its information systems since its main headquarters was located in an earthquake zone. One bank diversified its operating units so that even with the loss of two units, a third could at least temporarily take over vital functions. A health-care company established two mobile satellite ground stations to service call centers with both voice and data in the event of a telecommunications outage. If the firm lost service in the mid-Atlantic area, for instance, it could open a five-hundred-person call center elsewhere to serve the region within forty-eight hours.

And of course well-known protective measures are widely applied such as earthquake-resistant construction in seismic regions. A pharmaceutical company had designed one of its production facilities in Japan to withstand an earthquake of magnitude 7.0. Even though it had underanticipated the 9.0 magnitude earthquake that struck in 2011, the company's cost of repair after the earthquake was only several million dollars on a $200 million facility, and it was quickly back online. "We lost power but the plant held up very well," recalled the company's risk manager. "Within a couple of months we were able to make all the repairs to the plant and be back to full operation."

Some companies also use financial incentives and performance evaluations to discourage employees from taking unnecessary risks. For example, a real estate firm implemented a system to hold local construction managers responsible for identifying and reducing risks associated with their building projects. The chief risk officer of a bank characterized a new employee appraisal program intended to do the same: "We evaluate explicitly the top 120 leaders in the company against the following expectations for managing risk: how responsive they are in terms of proactively identifying and remediating risk, and what kind of example they set."

If they are unable to offload their risks, some firms decide to simply live with them. After a food-processing company suffered an explosion in one of its storage facilities, insurers sharply elevated their premiums and the company opted to go without coverage. An information technology firm was unable to insure its operations in emerging markets when it couldn't find insurers willing to provide protection for those locations. A manager of a pharmaceutical company explained why her enterprises had little choice but to go without coverage after a costly lawsuit settlement: "We were talking about price increases of a factor of five to ten with attachment points increasing by hundreds and hundreds of millions of dollars, and ten pages worth of product exclusions. Basically any product we sold would be excluded."

IMPROVING COMMUNICATION

After experiencing adverse events, many companies improved their communication at all levels within the enterprise. Executives and managers concluded that they had to continually assess and reassess their own risks and to make sure that everyone knew the roles that they would play in the next disruption.

During the financial crisis of 2008–2009, lower-tier managers more frequently messaged their upper tiers, sometimes even the governing board. As the turmoil receded, many directors and executives resolved that they would have to more actively report company risks and expand their definitions of potential risks far beyond the levels that they had previously felt were probable or realistic. The chief risk officer at a conglomerate stressed the point: "We have greatly increased the internal transparency and awareness of these risks for senior management. We do a lot more talking about it, modeling the risks and making sure that we spend time thinking about the unthinkable. What would our actions and contingency plans be in the case of a series of scenarios that people would have said, 'That would never happen.'"

Given the arcane nature of some risks, executives recognized the need for clarity and simplicity when going to the boardroom. "Prior to the financial crisis, it was a challenge for many of the board members to understand the complex nature of the risks that financial services firms were undertaking," explained the chief risk officer of a financial institution. "The challenge that all chief risk officers face today is to be very effective in communicating by explaining complex risks such as derivatives in very simple language."

Directors welcomed the flow of more complete and transparent information given that their firm's recovery or even survival rested in part on their shoulders. As one board member told us: "All directors are responsible for risk oversight. We have to make sure that the full board is comfortable with where the audit committee has been delegated specific oversight responsibilities."

At the same time, company executives intensified their messaging to front-line employees, especially if some of them had been personally touched by a crisis. After suicide bombers killed fifty-six people in the London Underground in 2005, a financial firm opened an online register for employees. One of its managers explained:

> The cell phone network was shut down purposely because these explosive devices were detonated via cell phone in backpacks. So it was impossible to communicate with a lot of our staff initially. We developed this "I'm okay" system, which allows employees, anytime they're impacted or involved in a natural disaster or any kind of security event, to be able to proactively reach out to us and say, "Hey, I'm okay."

The upward communication within the firm came with a cost, however, as employees were forced to take time from their problem-solving mode to brief the firms' executives who craved details on what the ranks were doing. As the risk manager of a financial company ruefully recounted: "When a crisis happens, every senior executive in New York, London, and Tokyo is calling and asking to be briefed, and you spend your time responding to these people and not managing the crisis. So you've got to establish a discipline that says, 'Look, we do a briefing at 8 a.m. and 6 p.m. You phone in for that briefing; don't bother me the rest of the time.'"

Executives and managers also ramped up their messaging to community and public sector organizations and the media during a crisis, appreciating that customers, investors, analysts, reporters, and mayors are all looking for reassurance that the company was still operating, even if at half speed, and taking steps to return to normal in short order. As the chief risk officer of one financial firm explained: "We have a very big brand and that's a risk because you're a big target, but on the other hand, it [also] protects you. You need to define yourself before others come and define you. We are now investing more in government relations and community relations so that if something happens, people don't immediately assume that we screwed up."

STRENGTHENING SUPPLIERS

Given the increasing reliance by firms on hundreds of other enterprises worldwide for components and inputs, corporations have targeted their supply chains for risk reduction. Measures range from requiring suppliers to have their own business-continuity plans in place to stockpiling one's own supplies and products in case of an outage.

Firms pressed suppliers to guard against the hazards in their own backyards, as the risk manager of an information technology company explained: "One of the things that we're doing on a going-forward basis is making sure that all of our key suppliers have business continuity and/or disaster recovery plans in place. . . . This should not be a casual inquiry; this is something that we need to hold our key suppliers to. If they don't have a plan in place already, then they need to do so." An investment management company began auditing its suppliers when it discovered after 9/11 that its own backup communication line had then been rerouted to the same location as its primary line, resulting in a momentary loss of connection after the attack.

Some companies amassed reserves of essential materials even though it can be expensive to hold them for emergency use. They also built up their inventory of finished products to ensure that they can meet customer commitments. One metal supplier, for instance, stores a four-month stockpile of copper to guard against disruptions among its major providers. Similarly, Dell maintains a large inventory of finished computers to hedge against sudden shortages or excessive pricing of components that go into its products.

NETWORKING WITH COMPETITORS

Companies have also fostered informal networks with competitors to share nonproprietary information on similar risks that they face, compare their experiences in trying to insure against business interruption risks, and discuss measures that can mitigate future disruptions. For example, international banks with operations in Tokyo asked one another what each knew about whether the Fukushima nuclear reactors were close to critical in the days after the Tōhoku earthquake and tsunami in 2011, and what actions they were considering should their employees be in danger.

Trade associations have also formalized the informal in some industries, such as pharmaceuticals, where risk managers regularly meet to share proven practices. The risk officer for a drug company explained how his association, the Drug Insurance Group, operated:

It's just risk managers of larger companies. They'll talk about common issues, things that they're seeing in the insurance marketplace. They do not talk about individual insurance programs they're placing and anything that's company confidential. Rather they talk in general about what's happening in the market.

Some informal networks have formalized across industries, allowing companies to learn what others have devised when faced with an adverse event. For one risk manager, joining one such network proved instructive:

> Since [risk management] is new to me, I've joined the Association of Contingency Planners. Last night, I actually went to a "Date with Disaster," to stay in tune with what's really going on in your area. There are things that you never even thought about, and little tips you pick up, not to mention the networking that you get from folks that have been doing this for fifteen to twenty years. It helps you envision what your command center will look like if you actually had to turn it on.

Taking that one step further, some companies in the same market have prearranged to pool their resources in case some of them are hit by a disaster. Companies in the energy industry, for example, have formed "mutual assistance crews" that they can each deploy to help another energy firm when disaster strikes. Though the dictates of the free market might view these collaborations as anticompetitive, they are held together by personal networks and the virtues of necessity, as the manager of one of those energy companies explained:

> When an event hits, we get on the phone and start trying to arrange resources. What makes the mutual assistance work is that we've developed relationships and know one another. When it comes time to start requesting that one company send their resources to another company, we're doing it out of a relationship-trust situation. I would recommend you get involved in your mutual assistance group, go to their meetings, develop those relationships, [and] understand how the dynamics work because companies don't just magically send their troops off.

Company leaders also pooled information that allows them to benchmark their risk reduction measures against others in the same industry. Some of the risk managers with whom we talked reported that they frequently joined industry-wide gatherings to share risk methodologies and better practices. Some have even looked to organizations outside their markets for guidance. As described by the vice president of health, safety, and environment in an energy company: "We think we understand the risks in our business the same way most of our competitors understand risk. What we've tried to do in the last six months is to reach outside our industry and look at how a few other people are managing risk. We've spent time with financial companies. We've spent time with large manufacturing companies. We've spent time with NASA just to understand how they view risk, and determine if we have some blind spots we're not thinking about."

Reaching out to others often extended to professional and academic consultants. For example, one energy company engaged a university with experts in cybersecurity to evaluate the firm's current protections and shortfalls. "We had a university come in and evaluate all of the hundred employees in our security division," reported the manager who had engaged the academic consultants. "I asked them to take a look at the skillset for every employee and every job compared to what their job description is and tell me what the gaps are, and then come up with a plan to address those gaps."

FOSTERING CONTINUITY

Companies have gathered many of these measures under the rubric of enterprise risk management, rather than leaving them to their operating divisions. A chief risk officer often takes primary responsibility for all and reports to a senior official, frequently the CEO, with the board of directors in turn looking over their shoulders. The chief risk officer lays out a set of metrics for tracking the firm's threats and readiness, builds relationships with the external agencies and organizations upon which the company may depend during a crisis, and readies all for the unthinkable.

The business continuity manager of a firm in the healthcare industry described how company-wide preparations for disaster enabled his firm to continue functioning during and after Hurricane Katrina:

We needed to roll out our infection control procedures, and our medical areas. Healthcare management personnel were instrumental in advising the corporate team on what those measures should be. The human resources community stepped up and helped us put in additional policies and procedures regarding taking time off when you have sick children or sick family members, or if the schools were closed. The IT department stepped up with rapid transition to our social business procedures, to spread people out so that they don't increase infection throughout the organization. We had masks on standby to be distributed in case things got worse. So, it was a team effort, and it really showed the company's commitment to our members and our employees.

While enterprise risk management can help firms avoid some crises, it certainly cannot prevent them all. Having clearly defined emergency procedures and roles in advance proved critical. During a crisis, a designated crisis leader or incident commander is readied to take charge, and that person is usually not the chief executive. Temporary authority is delegated to a temporary crisis leader, and even the CEO may be asked to take a back seat for the duration, trusting the momentary lead to function without micromanagement. The risk manager of a chemical company explained:

> I happened to be the crisis management officer during and after Hurricane Katrina. Because of the scale of the event, the CEO said, "I'd like to come in and sit in." I said, "You can sit in, but if you say a word you're leaving." Anybody I've talked to about crisis management says the hardest thing is trusting your crisis management team to do what you've trained them to do. In those moments it's a command and control structure. "You have fifteen seconds to tell me what you want to do but I'm going to decide what we're doing after that."

Central to enterprise risk management is business continuity planning, the firm's procedures for sustaining operations in the wake of a catastrophe. Many firms had found it useful to identify the capabilities it could lose during a crisis and then resolve how to operate without them, as argued by the vice president of business continuity for a health insurer: "There has been a tendency historically to focus on risk management and business continuity management as a discrete stand-alone function. [But] you have to step back and not think about what will cause the problem, but what you would lose if something happened . . . and where will I get these resources in a timely manner." Often, such plans are created division by division on the premise that they are best decentralized, as a risk manager for a financial firm reported: "Every department determines the contingencies it could face and for how long. The department then prepares for these events to ensure that it can take care of our people and get in touch with them quickly."

Early warning systems can alert firms to the onset of a natural disaster, political crisis, financial downturn, or cyberattack so that crisis protocols could be quickly invoked. A retail firm, for instance, formed a storm-tracking team that watched for potential hurricanes off the coast of Africa, giving them one to two weeks to prepare for the worst. If it appeared that the storm would strike the United States, the trackers alerted and updated a catastrophic response team as well as senior managers, store operators, and distribution centers. The risk-management team at a financial institution created a system of "trip wires" whereby it would be forewarned of any emerging threat: "These were triggers that helped to set into motion reactions that help inoculate you from some of the worst effects of that potential crisis."

IMAGINING THE NEXT DISRUPTION

After a natural calamity had damaged facilities or disrupted suppliers, many firms had plans in place to assure business continuity should the "what-if" recur. They constructed a host of worst-case scenarios and developed strategies for dealing with these threats to their operations, and created emergency handbooks on what to do in the wake of disruptions. One department store, for example, developed strategies for responding to an array of weather extremes, though acknowledging that, like warfare, the best-laid plans are often abandoned on first contact. Still, the scenario exercise provided invaluable discipline, as a store executive explained:

> We learned that processes and protocols that are designed with the intent of a high degree of precision in advance of the disaster can experience slippage due to the unforeseen and the unintended. But you can still get yourself back into business. You can determine the well-being of your employees of your customers, and damage to your property—and then recover your operations logically.

Our interviews revealed that many firms used scenario planning when their executives and managers anticipate crises they had not yet experienced and when it was especially difficult to quantify their likelihood. The CEO of a manufacturing company explained: "Proactive scenario planning is important, even when there are people who argue this is never going to happen and this is not the best use of our time. We told them that they were going to do the exercise anyway. We have learned that being prepared and being somewhat flexible is the best way to handle the unexpected."

A media company took its executives through quarterly scenario exercises on low-probability events to strengthen their readiness for them. The director of business continuity for the company reported that he had tested the arrival of a package with anthrax, and the placement of an explosive device outside a facility. "We take senior-management staff through different scenarios such as these to make certain that they pay attention to business continuity by focusing on how one can react to the situation and what can we learn from being exposed to it and what do we need to change."

Many firms performed simulations annually to identify gaps in crisis plans and continuity planning. As described by a risk manager with a financial firm: "You have to practice these tools when there isn't a catastrophe in order to make sure that they work when needed." The executive for a bank described how it vetted plans for unforeseen circumstances by rolling a pair of dice to determine which key personnel would be suddenly unavailable for the duration of the event: "Anyone who comes up odd is suddenly unavailable. Now let's see if you can run the plan if a random number of key people were suddenly unavailable."

While executives and managers at many firms reported they held a variety of exercises to imagine disruptions, the scale of the engagements varied widely. Some were limited to a small team in a crisis room for several hours, while others expanded to a wide swath of managers for several days, and many drew in the top team. An executive of a healthcare firm described his firm's daylong simulations with the executive team. "The chairman and CEO was actually at the command center interfacing with the local fire chief to discuss the impact to the building, campus, or office."

Whatever the many particulars of the risk praxis, what has been most striking from our interviews with those at the center of them is their widespread emergence out of the ashes of their own experiences, those of others, some near misses, and still others imagined. Wrapped under the banner of enterprise risk management and business continuity planning, and pulled together with deliberative thinking, the risk practices have become increasingly commonplace among large companies. While this chapter focuses on the actions taken internally by key decision makers, governing boards also play a critical role in developing risk management strategies as we will see in Part III.

RISK-MANAGEMENT PRAXIS

1. Many risk-management and crisis-response practices have emerged from large-scale company disruptions since 2000, including the terrorist attacks of 9/11 and the financial crisis of 2008–2009. Firms have also learned from their own near misses and adverse events, as well as those of others.
2. Companies are striving to prepare for and manage adverse events, disruptions, and crises in a more comprehensive fashion under the rubric of enterprise risk management and business continuity planning.
3. Some of the most widely used practical devices for planning and preparation include:
   - modeling risk
   - systematically reducing risks
   - improving communication
   - strengthening suppliers
   - networking with competitors
   - fostering continuity
   - imagining the next disruption

PART III

What Disrupted Companies Do

M any enterprises have taken steps in recent years to evolve from a limited and reactive focus on risk to more far-reaching and proactive strategies. Their deliberative protocols can serve as instructive templates for others to consider, if not to emulate.

To do so requires that directors, executives, and managers become adept at learning from their own and others' near misses and disruptive events, as well as from other firms that have more fully developed their risk-management strategies and practical measures. After-action reviews on one's own setbacks and reviews of the crisis experiences and risk reduction measures of an array of companies are also useful in developing a more deliberative approach to preparing for and managing catastrophic risks.

To appreciate those crisis experiences more graphically, part III offers accounts of how a select set of large companies have drawn upon deliberative thinking and procedures to cope with disruptions. In chapter 6, we turn to two German companies—Lufthansa and Deutsche Bank—that worked hard to recuperate from major setbacks. In the case of Lufthansa, the company sought to recover from a fatal air crash induced by one of its own pilots. In the case of Deutsche Bank, the firm sought to sustain its operations in Japan in the wake of the 2011 tsunami that overwhelmed the nuclear reactors at Fukushima and threatened the security of the entire region. We see how directors, executives, and managers in both companies developed and applied a host of practical measures for protecting against disruptions and surmounting those that could not be prevented.

Chapter 7 focuses on how the governing boards of three US firms—American International Group, General Electric, and Boeing—partnered with company executives in the face of looming hazards. Here we see the power of deliberative thinking in shaping how companies operate and the value that the board of directors can bring when proactive.

Chapter 8 chronicles how companies have increasingly striven not only to insulate themselves from catastrophic risks but also assist victims, local communities, and even nations in recovering from extreme events of their own. We see how Lawson, a convenience-store franchise in Japan, assisted its country's recovery from the Tōhoku earthquake in 2011, and how Walmart worked closely with the Federal Emergency Management Agency to distribute essential products in the wake of Hurricane Katrina in 2005. We witness a kind of turning inside out, with companies drawing on their deliberative thinking and practical measures to help others overcome their own disasters.

6

Crises at Lufthansa and Deutsche Bank

It was professional, the core group knew what to do, [and the] team profited from previous collaborative work success that established a shared work ethos. . . . Crisis management has to be proactive, not reactive.

—CRISIS TEAM MEMBER, *Lufthansa*

For leaders of large American companies, dealing with adverse events and the resulting setbacks has emerged as a priority concern. Any major firm operating internationally today is subject to numerous disruptions, and German companies face challenges similar challenges to firms in the United States. We have conducted parallel interviews with them as well, to better understand the role that deliberative thinking and practical measures have played in how they have coped with unexpected disasters. From their experience we can draw additional insights on risk measures that US firms might want to consider.

We focus on crisis management by Lufthansa, one of Germany's largest employers, with 124,000 on the payroll in 2017, and by Deutsche Bank, German's largest financial institution by assets under management, with $2 trillion in 2016. Both firms were in the DAX index, Deutscher Aktienindex, German's blue-chip stock market metric comprising thirty premier companies trading on the Frankfurt Stock Exchange.

The two companies faced very different setbacks. In the case of Lufthansa, the disruption was caused by a copilot's commandeering and crashing of a passenger flight in 2015. In the case of Deutsche Bank, the disruption came in the aftermath of Japan's 2011 earthquake, tsunami, and nuclear meltdown. Symptomatic of the global nature of company risks, the Lufthansa pilot ended his flight in France, and Deutsche Bank's crisis emerged in Japan, both outside the headquarters country.

What is striking about the disruptions is that neither would have been expected in the form that they took. Like all commercial airlines, Lufthansa had prepared for the loss of an aircraft, but not from a pilot-induced crash. According to a compilation by the Flight Safety Foundation, only thirteen commercial aircraft accidents in the history of aviation had been pilot prompted, a very low-probability event.[1]

Similarly, while all financial institutions fear a market meltdown, Deutsche Bank had never anticipated a direct threat from a nuclear meltdown. In each instance, the value of a host of practical measures for catastrophic risk management becomes graphically evident.

PILOT-INDUCED CRASH AT LUFTHANSA AIRLINES

On Monday, March 24, 2015, the pilot of Germanwings flight 9525 lifted an Airbus 320 off a runway at Barcelona's El Prat airport in Spain at 10:01 a.m. on a routine two-hour flight to Düsseldorf, Germany. Thirty minutes later, copilot Andreas Lubitz locked pilot Patrick Sondenheimer out of the cockpit and plunged the aircraft into a fatal nosedive, slamming ten minutes later into a remote mountain range. Among the 150 passengers and crew members on board, eighteen were students or teachers from a single high school in Germany. No one survived. As a wholly owned subsidiary of Deutsche Lufthansa AG, Europe's largest airline group, the Germanwings accident, the first fatal crash for Lufthansa in twenty-three years, would severely test the parent company's readiness for dealing with catastrophe.[2]

Lufthansa had launched the low-cost subsidiary in 2012 to service European passengers at all German airports except its two premier international hubs at Frankfurt and Munich. With greater efficiency than its parent, Germanwings offered better prices—and yielded higher profits. And it benefitted from the secure brand of its owner. Lufthansa had built a stellar reputation as a reliable carrier and was rated Europe's second-safest major airline after KLM. But it was not without turbulence: in the months before the crash, Lufthansa had engaged in a contentious dispute with its pilots over retirement policies, and only a week prior to the accident, a labor strike had grounded 220,000 Lufthansa passengers on 1,600 flights.[3]

Germanwings would learn after the crash that copilot Andreas Lubitz had a history of depression and anxiety, and had been referred to a psychiatric clinic just two weeks before the crash. Yet none of this had come to the attention of the airline before the loss, in part because of the then prevailing privacy policies. An agency parallel to the US National Transportation Safety Board, France's Bureau d'Enquêtes et d'Analyses (BEA), would later conclude that "no action could have been taken by the authorities" or the airline to keep Lubitz "from flying that day, because they were informed by neither the copilot himself, nor by anyone else, such as a physician, a colleague or family member." The BEA investigation noted that Lubitz's "professional level was judged to be above standard by his instructors and examiners" and that "none of the pilots or instructors . . . who flew with him in the months preceding the accident indicated any concern about his attitude or behavior during flights."[4]

Still, in the three days following the crash, Lufthansa's stock dropped 8.5 percent. As the human cause of the crash was becoming public—investigators announced that it had been the copilot's "intention to destroy this plane"—shares of airlines around the world plummeted, as seen in Table 6.1.[5]

Table 6.1. AIRLINE STOCK PRICE PERCENTAGE DECLINE
ON THIRD DAY AFTER GERMANWINGS AIR CRASH

Air Berlin	−2.4
AirFrance/KLM	−2.6%
Delta	−6.5
Japan Airlines	−2.1
Lufthansa	−3.3
Qantas Airlines	−3.6
Ryanair	−2.6
Singapore Airlines	−2.4
Virgin	−3.9

SOURCE: Neilan, 2015.

On confirming the cause of the crash, BEA investigations recommended that Lufthansa require additional medical evaluations and support for pilots who show signs of depression or psychotic episodes, no matter how minor. Of course that might not suffice if a pilot disclosed little or nothing to medical examiners or coworkers, and in any case German doctors could still face a fine or even imprisonment for breaching patient confidentiality. BEA argued that while pilot privacy must still be honored, the airline must also ensure against malfeasance by the crew, since it carried final responsibility for the well-being of all on board. In the wake of the disaster, the German aviation authority set up a database to include information from pilots' medical exams, and it revised its own procedures to more effectively detect emergent psychiatric issues among its pilots.

On its part, the European Aviation Safety Agency recommended that "airlines should ensure that at least two crew members, including at least one qualified pilot, are in the cockpit at all times of the flight or implement other equivalent mitigating measures." After the crash, Lufthansa instituted a requirement that two crew members remain on the flight deck at all times as a "precautionary measure." Israeli airline El Al had already addressed the cockpit vulnerability by installing a separate toilet within the secure area of the flight deck, but of course that measure stemmed from fear of an external attack on the cockpit, not one from within.[6]

INSIDE THE AIRLINE

Lufthansa vice president Peter Andres—a senior member of the firm's crisis management team—learned of the disaster within minutes of the crash. Andres had joined Lufthansa upon completing a university business degree, decamped for a period, and then returned to the airline in 1994, working in flight management ever since. His management responsibilities had grown at one point to include three thousand personnel and all flight operations at the airline's premier airport at Frankfurt, and, later, all ground services for the airline worldwide. Andres had served on Lufthansa's crisis management team with responsibility for the system's operations from 1994 to 1997, where he held the role of "housekeeper" for all crisis issues and served as acting head of the team during several disruptions. He had rejoined the crisis management team after 9/11.

Lufthansa's chief executive turned to Andres in 2005 to oversee the airline's security. Andres now reported on the firm's risks and their mitigation directly to the company's top management team, including the chief executive and his four direct reports. Andres' mandate required him to be a keen judge of everything from ground safety to political instability. Ground safety came to a head in the spring of 2011, when Lufthansa's flight operations in Japan were significantly affected by the meltdown of the Fukushima nuclear reactors in the wake of the earthquake. Political instability came to a head in 2014 when a violent upheaval in Libya shuttered Lufthansa's operations in Tripoli, damaging some 90 percent of the airport facility and destroying twenty aircraft on the ground, though Lufthansa had fortunately halted its flight operations three months earlier.[7]

After the Germanwings flight slammed into the mountain at 10:41 a.m. on March 24, 2015, the head of the crisis management team, Werner Knorr, executive vice president for flight operations, convened his team by 11:15 a.m. as part of a pre-established protocol, and minutes later he called four hundred predesignated employees into action as a special assistance team. The team would come to work around the clock at the accident site, in the call centers, and directly with the victims' families. In all, more than nine hundred served on the team, including a number from Lufthansa's Swiss subsidiary, who brought a much needed fluency in French.

Lufthansa opened a call center for public inquiries at 11:41 a.m., just an hour after the crash; created a family assistance center at 12 noon; established a liaison with the German Ministry of State by 1 p.m.; briefed German chancellor Angela Merkel at 2:30 p.m.; held a press conference featuring its chief executive at 3 p.m.; and dispatched its "go-team" to the accident site at 5 p.m. The Lufthansa CEO arranged to fly over the crash site with the German Minister of State at 6 p.m.

Everybody was "absolutely stunned," Andres reported. For his frequent updates on the accident site, family losses, and the cause of the crash, Andres had earlier come to appreciate that his advice to the internal parties and securing action from them was only as good as their pre-established trust in the crisis team managers. To that end, Andres had long adopted a personal precept that he would never mislead or underinform any Lufthansa manager, and that he would have to be individually known to each of them. "It is a personal relationship" with those inside the firm that counted, he explained, and also with a select circle on the outside. He had built direct ties over the years, for instance, with his counterparts in United Airlines,

British Airways, and other major carriers, a network from which he could draw experienced counsel during a crisis. He had also established ties with the German police and security agencies and with the Ministries of Interior and State. A crisis is not a moment for exchanging pleasantries and business cards for the first time.

The confidence of others in the crisis management team, constructed over many years, proved essential in the first days after the Germanwings crash, a reminder that familiar and trusting relationships are best created before they are needed. This was especially true in this instance since nobody had prepared for or even anticipated a loss of this kind. Airbus-380 pilot Werner Knorr, executive vice president for flight operations and head of the crisis management team, briefed the CEO and his top executives at headquarters. The crisis management team designated a senior manager to remain on site as company liaison with the local mayor, recovery team, and victims' families.

Many volunteers outside the company assisted as well. Local residents, regional police, and rescue crews engaged in the painstaking process of retrieving items that could be connected with a victim and sent them to the family, a teddy bear among them.

The crisis-management moment then morphed into postcrisis mode. Lufthansa had early anticipated that assistance for the affected families would have to continue for years, ranging from organizing anniversaries to financing the education of children whose parents had perished. The years ahead would be managed by a "postemergency" group which had been set up only days after the accident. Its director reported to one of the airline's top five officers, and she would work collaboratively with Lufthansa's passenger service center and the accident recovery team. Given the nature of the disaster, the postemergency group expanded its roster to include medical, legal, and other specialists while dropping others whose expertise was no longer essential, including, for example, a flight-operations specialist.

CRISIS COMPLEXITY

The unanticipated complexity of the Germanwings crisis called for intricate management of it. The crash's 150 victims represented eighteen countries, including the United States and Germany. In cooperation with the German government's own crisis management team, all available data on the passengers' identities were gathered. Dozens of embassies requested information on whether their citizens had been on board. Numerous languages were required for counseling victim families. Multiple authorities in France, Germany, and Spain demanded information on the crash site. More than a thousand family members came forward, many insisting on a pilgrimage to the remote mountain crash site, and in response, Lufthansa temporarily rented an entire hotel in Marseille, the nearest major city. Besides securing rooms for victims' families and the Lufthansa special assistance team, venues for clerics to console and relatives to mourn had to be found as well.

The crash site's remote location added to management complexity. One hundred miles from Marseille, and with hardly any hotels nearby to accommodate victims' families let alone the response teams, local villages were not prepared for the huge influx. Organizing transportation and accommodations became a continuous task for the special assistance team managers in Marseille.

With only forty-eight hours of lead time, Lufthansa also had to take over protection of the accident site, and in response Andres contracted a firm to provide 24/7 security in a mountainous area accessible only by four-wheel-drive vehicles. Close cooperation with local police proved to be critical for Lufthansa's managers as they also had to organize recovery of more than fifty tons of wreckage at the crash site by helicopter.

At the same time, the crisis management team was working with still fragmentary data for an explanation of the crash. Was it adverse weather, a technical malfunction, or a terrorist attack? Within two days of the event, however, the team turned to the possibility of pilot malfeasance after *The New York Times* disclosed stunning information. Its reporters had learned from an unnamed source in the French investigation that the cockpit voice recorder had revealed the intensifying sounds of a person knocking on the cabin door—with no response from inside the flight deck. One of the two pilots had evidently stepped out of the cockpit, and "what is sure is that at the very end of the flight," the source reported, "the other pilot is alone and does not open the door." The airplane's descent was steady, suggesting no technical failure, and there were no adverse weather conditions. Lufthansa had not yet received direct communication from the French investigators, but when alerted to *The New York Times* article by a midnight call, Andres concluded the worst, and the crisis management team arranged for the copilot's family members to evacuate their home before reporters found them.[8]

Later, the crisis management team reflected on their handling of the crisis with an eye to strengthening their readiness for catastrophic risk management in the future. Its members singled out three capacities that proved vital, summarized here in the form of suggestive guidelines for other companies facing a major but unanticipated disaster of this magnitude: 1) pre-establish leadership and organization with a readiness to act, 2) act fast in the wake of a disruption, and 3) give primary attention to those most adversely affected.

CRISIS-MANAGEMENT CAPACITIES

A first capacity is a *pre-established leadership and organizational readiness to act*. In the case of the Germanwings disaster, it began with the Lufthansa chief executive, Carsten Spohr, an engineer by training and a pilot himself, who still held a license to fly an Airbus A320. Saying that the loss was "the darkest day for Lufthansa in its sixty-year history," he personally oversaw the company's response. Germanwings had its own crisis management team, but as parent CEO, Spohr took charge of the recovery, and with a watchful eye, he and his executive team delegated authority directly to Werner Knorr and his ten-person crisis management team for doing so.

The crisis team itself had been premolded into an action-ready, mission-critical band. "You have to have a relationship with the members before you can solve the problems together," offered Andres. When Germanwings 9525 plunged into the mountain, crisis management team members were able to quickly assemble for action. "It was professional, the core group knew what to do, and we knew each other," recalled Andres. "The team profited from previous collaborative work success that established a shared work ethos. A larger number of industrial actions and weather-related traffic disruptions had given the team numerous challenges in the months before the accident to perform."

A second capacity from the Germanwings flight disaster, identified through Lufthansa's after-action reflection on it, is a primacy on *taking fast action* after a disruption. "Crisis management has to be proactive, not reactive," offered Andres. "You have to generate capacity to be more proactive than reactive." The board had explicitly empowered the crisis-management team, for instance, to act without further formal approval, including the liberal use of company credit cards and an on-the-spot authorizing of contracts for recovery services.

Though a comprehensive crisis handbook—the Lufthansa Emergency Response and Action Plan—had been compiled well before the crash, the crisis management team nonetheless had to creatively address many emergent issues. In deciding on an immediate cash payment to the victims' families, for example, the crisis team was initially constrained by airline approval procedures that would normally require three days for any international disbursement. But as information on the prospective payment had become public, family expectations and media pressures dictated faster action. The crisis team asked for—and received—a suspension of standard procedures, allowing families to receive the money within hours. "Don't hesitate to decide," Andres concluded, because "you'll never recover the time." The moment "is precious," and, as a result, "all execution has [to be] extremely fast." The role of media as enforcer here could not be overestimated, eager as it often is to bring the faintest sign of company tardiness or self-interest to public attention.

A third capacity is to give *primary attention to those most adversely affected* by a catastrophe. "We have promised the families that we are there for them as long as necessary," said Lufthansa chief executive Spohr, and we "shall stick to that promise." In addition to the immediate cash payment to families, private counsel for the families, and a fund for ongoing loss-related expenses of the families, the airline also reached out to others who had also been directly affected, including people near the crash site who had volunteered so much of their time. Lufthansa later arranged for eight hundred local-area residents to visit Paris at its expense, and for its CEO to join them personally, witnessing together a French-German soccer match.

The experience of Lufthansa is also a potent reminder that catastrophic events often come in ways almost completely unanticipated by company managers. The very best preparations are essential for the imaginable, but they can fall short in the wake of the unimaginable. Until it actually transpired, who would have ever expected a commercial pilot to deliberately take down an aircraft with 150 people on board? In its terrible aftermath, the airline has taken tangible steps to prevent a recurrence, and tactical improvements continue. But what Lufthansa had already put in place—a crisis team that had prepared for rapid response whatever might befall the airline—was the deliberative side of the equation. One can only imagine the chaos and costs in the days after the crash if the airline had no disaster protocol, no incident commander, no crisis team. We see again the value of pre-established leadership and organizational readiness, prepared for the expected but also the unanticipated.

NUCLEAR THREAT AT DEUTSCHE BANK

The largest financial institution incorporated in Europe, Deutsche Bank employed more than a hundred thousand people in more than seventy countries, and in 2010 generated $43 billion in annual revenue, ranking just behind Citigroup Inc. and ahead of HSBC Holdings among the world's largest banks. It maintained significant presence in Japan, concentrated mainly in Tokyo, where most of its 1,500 staff members were based. That operation serviced customers in Japan—the world's third largest economy after the United States and the People's Republic of China—and also served as the franchise hub in northern Asia, managing everything from corporate credit lines to private banking for wealthy customers throughout the region.[9]

Within twenty-four hours of Japan's 9.0 magnitude earthquake and tsunami in 2011, Victor Meyer, the bank's global head of corporate security and business continuity, had confirmed that all of the bank's employees were safe and secure. Though a great relief in itself, this would provide only momentary respite for Meyer and the firm. Minutes after the earthquake, an enormous wall of water swept along the northeast coast of Japan toward the Fukushima Daiichi nuclear power plant, one of the world's fifteen largest atomic power complexes with six nuclear reactors at water's edge.

Japan is a famously active seismic area, and protection from hazards associated with earth tremors had been engineered into the Fukushima plant. Under regulatory oversight, Tokyo Electric Power Company Incorporated (TEPCO), the plant's owner/operator, had earlier constructed a twenty-foot barrier to protect the plant against a tsunami resulting from an 8.0-magnitude earthquake. But the Tōhoku earthquake was thirty times more powerful, and it sent a forty-five-foot wave crashing over the barrier, flooding a set of backup generators programmed to kick in if the plant's power supply was interrupted and if several hours of reserve battery power were also exhausted. The wave also cut off all external power for the plant, and although the reserve batteries worked as designed, when they were depleted, and without the backup generators, the plant's main water pumps were soon without power to continue cooling the reactors' cores and fuel rods.[10]

PREPARING FOR THE WORST

When Meyer joined Deutsch Bank in 2004 as head of corporate security and business continuity, he was already familiar with dire threats and large-scale disasters. A graduate of the US Naval Academy, he had served for more than fifteen years as a US Navy SEAL before attending business school. He was responsible for security in the recovery of the USS *Cole* in Aden, Yemen, in 2000 and had risen to be chief of counter-terrorism and contingency plans for the US Navy for the European and African regions. Just prior to joining the bank, he had served on a task force to track and seize terrorist finances.

Well before the events of March in Japan, Meyer and his staff had built a crisis management training program that inculcated swift response into the firm's DNA, not only for operational events like natural disasters, but for financial risks as well. They focused on countries where the sovereign risk rating was weakest, natural disasters most frequent, or headcount the largest. The way in which the exercises were incorporated into the risk division's flagship development program for managing directors was particularly distinctive. Its crisis management exercise was designed to assess candidates' ability to make decisions under pressure with incomplete information. Candidates participated in a two-day crisis simulation in which they were called to formulate a response to major crises, such as a pandemic or hurricane passing in close proximity to a large city. Senior observers from external companies and service providers were added to enhance realism.

Meyer built the company's crisis management training program on several premises that had emerged from recent company experience: specific blueprints will be of less use than an ability to develop an impromptu plan; partnerships are essential for intelligence and resources, but partners will be pulled back by their own constraints in a crisis; and, while catastrophic risks are increasingly global by virtue of greater degrees of interconnectedness, local readiness is also vital.

Victor Meyer was in Hong Kong on the afternoon of Friday, March 11, when he learned of the deadly events unfolding in northeast Japan. He watched in horror, as did so many viewers, when CNN repeatedly broadcast video clips of the tsunami sweeping inland. Within three hours, he had confirmed that the earthquake and tsunami had not, so far, destabilized the financial markets or damaged company networks. He confirmed as well that there were no employees reported missing or injured. As he boarded a flight to London, it appeared that there would be minimal impact on the bank's operations and little danger to business as usual for its Monday opening. For a global bank, it seemed that the events in Japan, as terrible as they were, would cause little more than a momentary pause. The most critical problem at the moment was to ensure that stranded employees reached their homes safely.

By time Meyer landed in London, however, reports from Japan were turning ominous, and he began to appreciate the potential ramifications of the earthquake and tsunami's impact. Colleagues in Asia were already signaling apprehension. They warned, for example, of rolling blackouts that could disrupt the power supply to the bank's data centers. Meyer realized that he could not yet quantify the risks, but he intuitively understood the growing potential damage from the crisis.

Deutsche Bank's disciplined approach to risk management, built over many years under the leadership of chief risk officer Hugo Banziger, had served the bank well, particularly when compared to most of its peers. But now Meyer faced a potentially catastrophic event, the full implications of which were just beginning to emerge. It appeared increasingly possible that the events they were witnessing would cascade to create a threat to the bank's operations in Japan.

The loss of generating capacity from the Fukushima plant was already disrupting Japan's electrical grid, with some reports suggesting that there could also be some form of meltdown and release of nuclear material. If radioactive debris spread to Tokyo, the bank could conceivably be confronted with the prospect of a sudden evacuation of its staff. At the least, it could limit the ability of much of the bank's staff to access their offices and trading floors, and to support the most vital operations in Tokyo, including the bank's main data center. Meyer had no real-time information on the rapidly worsening condition in the Fukushima plant's reactors, but the situation seemed to be, at best, highly uncertain. Recalling one of the worst nuclear disasters in history, he wondered, what if the overheating nuclear complex degenerated into a situation similar to the Chernobyl meltdown? He initiated a daily briefing of Deutsche Bank's CEO Josef Ackermann and chief risk officer Hugo Banziger.

By March 17, six days after the earthquake, the Japanese government had ordered the evacuation of 200,000 people who resided within twelve miles of the Fukushima plant, and the US Department of Defense authorized family members of military personnel stationed on Honshu—Japan's largest island where the damaged power plants were located—to evacuate. The Department of Defense also suspended travel of families of military personnel into Honshu. Meyer learned that CNN—whose crews routinely reported on the ground from the most risky places worldwide—was pulling out of Tokyo. The government of France recommended that its nationals leave Tokyo. This was viewed by many as a particularly strong signal, given France's deep knowledge of nuclear technology since the country derives more than three-quarters of its electricity from nuclear energy.[11]

As daily reports from Tokyo offered increasingly apocalyptic scenarios for the nuclear power plants whose cooling had now been completely compromised, Meyer began daily briefings of Deutsche Bank's management board, the most senior executive group. It was the first time since he had joined the bank that Meyer had confronted a disaster serious enough to call for daily crisis briefings of the top executives. Meyer also dwelled on whether his team was ready for what was shaping up to be a high-intensity ongoing crisis. And he worried about the possible necessity of evacuating Deutsche Bank's employees and their families at a time when Tokyo's 13 million residents would all be trying to do the same thing. "Was he ready to order an evacuation?" he wondered. "What should be the final trigger, and did he have a realistic, executable plan?"

EVACUATION

Several concerns dominated Meyer's report to the top executives on the sixth day after the earthquake. First, he had paid close attention to announcements by the Japanese government, and, at the moment, the government was not recommending a widespread evacuation. As a supplementary source, Meyer also monitored disclosures from the US Nuclear Regulatory Commission (NRC). It was initially reassuring to Meyer that Japanese regulators were still stressing business as usual, but as NRC administrators and Japanese reporters began to suggest that the situation was deteriorating, the government's reticence became increasingly worrisome.

Second, Meyer was concerned that the Tokyo Stock Exchange might suddenly shut down, though authorities were thus far silent about this possibility. Third, he considered a scenario where power and other critical infrastructure in Tokyo would be disrupted, severely affecting the bank's ability to operate. Fourth, he tracked information on the compromised Fukushima plant's containment vessels and monitored the weather, as the direction of the winds could potentially send a radioactive cloud toward Tokyo. Fifth, he was concerned that the German media would confront the bank's executives about the company's plans to protect its employees in Japan, especially as the crisis appeared to worsen by the hour.

Finally, while the German media was likely to focus on Deutsche Bank's thirty-eight German nationals in Tokyo, the Japanese media would be far more concerned about locally hired staff. Meyer believed that the bank's expatriates and locals would have to be supported equitably, but also distinctly since their needs differed. He knew, for instance, that local staff would be reluctant to leave extended family members behind if offered relocation options, while the expatriate staff would be more ready to leave.

After conferring with the bank's regional management in Tokyo, top executives decided to authorize temporary relocation of any expatriate families who opted to evacuate. And, as a precaution, the bank was already moving staff members and their families abroad to assure their safety, dispersing its traders to Singapore, Hong Kong, Mumbai, Sydney, and London, and its operations staff to Manila.

Deutsche Bank rented six hundred hotel rooms in various cities in southern Japan. Fukuoka, one of the largest Japanese cities most distant from Tokyo, was the destination preferred by planners at several companies, and Deutsche Bank found itself competing not only with other firms but also with a local sport tournament. Even when it offered $100,000 to one hotel for the option of reserving all its rooms over the next twenty days, the request was denied. Chartering a Boeing 747 aircraft to fly employees and their families from Tokyo to Hong Kong would have cost approximately US $1.3 million per flight—a price that fluctuated daily, and sometimes hourly, as both charter companies and potential buyers monitored the media coverage.

POTENTIAL LOSS OF TRADING

Given the high volume of the bank's Japan-based sales and trading, Meyer knew that the business flow could not be interrupted without dire consequences for the company. "If we lose a trading floor for an extended time,"

Meyer warned, "we are in a worst-case scenario that requires activation of our secondary trading floor, redeployment of staff, and dynamic management of open risk positions." Worldwide, the company executed more than one million transactions per day and cleared more than $1 trillion in euro/dollar exchanges, the lifeblood of the bank. A Japanese regulatory authority had deemed Deutsche Bank to be one of the most systemically important banks in the world. If its Tokyo operations were suspended, it could disrupt sales and trading in Hong Kong, Seoul, and other capital centers.

Deutsche Bank's primary trading floor was adjacent to the Imperial Palace in Tokyo, and Meyer reasoned that it was least likely to suffer blackouts if power supplies fluctuated or were compromised altogether. But other centers did not enjoy the same protective geography. Meyer concluded that he may have to move some trading and operations activities outside of Japan, and he and his staff readied themselves to brief senior managers about this contingency.

As Meyer and his colleagues were escalating their crisis management activities, they determined that they required an independent assessment rather than relying on appraisals from TEPCO on whether the disaster at the Fukushima plant complex could spin out of control as the core meltdowns intensified. Were emergency crews still battling to stabilize the stricken plant on-site or had they been evacuated due to excessive radiation levels? How low were the water levels in the reactors and over the fuel rods? What were the forecasts by independent experts? Could a fire in one of the damaged reactors waft radioactive isotopes into the atmosphere? Which way were winds likely to prevail in the days ahead? When would electrical power be established to the cooling pumps, and how badly had they been damaged by the tsunami? Meyer quickly gathered information from a network of experts on nuclear safety and the management of nuclear accidents. Yet, he had to draw his own conclusions about the looming threats on which to base risk-management decisions for the bank.

KEY RISK INDICATORS

Meyer and his team established and monitored a set of key risk indicators (KRIs). "When we put these KRIs in place," he said, "we would start every morning by going through our intelligence, culling that information, going risk by risk, and talking about each. Is it getting better? Is it getting worse? Is there no change?" Then, when Meyer briefed top executives later in the day, he began the update by highlighting what had occurred the evening before. "This is what happened overnight," he explained. "This indicator is trending up, this indicator is trending down. This is why we take this view, this is what we don't know, and here are the gaps in our information."

Information provided by counterparts at rival banks proved especially valuable. Meyer participated in frequent conference calls with them where he learned that their public declarations were not always in accord with their private actions. While some banks were publicly asserting that they were operating their business as usual, Meyer learned that they were covertly evacuating employees out of Tokyo and had already booked hotel rooms in southern Japan.

Because of the bank's global footprint, Meyer ran his intelligence gathering around the clock. As night fell in Japan, the process continued in Singapore, then Frankfurt, and then New York so that he had up-to-the-minute information for his daily briefings. In one of these briefings, for instance, he reported that the Fukushima plant had suffered explosions resulting in radiation leakage and the evacuation of nearby residents but that it still wasn't clear what Deutsche Bank should do. The Japanese government was urging companies to stay, while the German government recommended that its nationals go.

GLOBAL STRATEGY AND LOCAL ACTION

Meyer decided to devolve tactical decisions to bank managers in Tokyo, and for this he depended heavily on the local chief executive and chief operating officers, who held formal roles as crisis managers in the bank's crisis management organization. The chief of security, responsible for operational risk and business continuity in the region, reported to Meyer, was also based in Tokyo. Relying on the local network made sense, because its members were better positioned to appraise the risks on the ground. It was their own operations that would be most affected, not to mention their own health and safety. They had the greatest stake in reaching optimal decisions for the bank.[12]

Still, since this was a crisis with global consequences for the company, strategic oversight remained at headquarters. And despite the evident advantages of a local approach, Meyer also believed that the crisis managers on the scene would need help and that they could be misdirected by the local situation, intuitive responses potentially prevailing over what should have been deliberative actions. The Japanese government appeared to be downplaying the crisis and its prospects, suggesting that the power plants were under control while other sources were suggesting the contrary. Meyer wondered if the local managers might be affected by local calls for patriotic stoicism and thus underestimate the gravity of the moment. Local managers were also eager to get back to business as usual. Since the company policy was to apply most of the costs of the crisis to the budgets of the affected local business units, perception of a less severe crisis could result in lower costs for the local operations, albeit less preparedness. Accordingly, Meyer warned the local risk managers, "not to go native, succumb to groupthink, or give in to stress and fatigue."

When the German government recommended that companies evacuate their German staff from Tokyo, German reporters asked the bank whether it would do so. Meyer and his team decided to respond in a limited way by noting that three expatriate German managers were evacuated. They gave non-German expatriate staff the option of moving their families out of Japan, and thirty foreign employees who had been in Japan on business travel were evacuated. In all, a hundred bank employees were moved offshore.

CRISIS PREPAREDNESS

By the end of March, TEPCO was gradually regaining control over the leakage of the Fukushima plant's reactors, and though modest levels of radiation continued to spread through the region and work their way into the food chain, it became evident to Meyer that a mass evacuation and business closure in Tokyo was increasingly unlikely. The company had suffered from rolling blackouts at some of its facilities, and fear-fueled distraction had been widespread among both employees and customers. Meyer estimated that the bank's productivity in Japan was down to about one-third of what was considered normal, but it was now climbing back to precrisis levels.

Meyer suspended the daily briefings with top management, and the company dispatched a top executive to visit the Japanese operations, signifying that inbound traffic was once again safe enough to authorize. "We're committed to the franchise," Meyer paraphrased the executive's message to the

Tokyo staff. "This has been a traumatic event, but it's time to look forward. The best way to put this behind us is to get out there and generate more business."

There was much to be learned from these events. Meyer concluded that Deutsche Bank had to construct and prepare for future worst-case scenarios. "If anybody had told us to anticipate the collapse of the [World Trade Center's] Twin Towers or a meltdown of four nuclear reactors," he said, "I would not have worried about it before, but now I do."

Meyer also better appreciated how difficult it could be to obtain reliable and actionable information in the middle of a crisis. Much of the essential real-time technical data on the evolving conditions at the Fukushima plant were either not released to the public or altered to appear less disastrous. Securing the kind of information that was vital for the biggest decision that he faced—whether to evacuate bank employees and their families from Tokyo—was difficult, and the information he had obtained depended on preexisting relationships. The media, he believed, had overstated the risks and provoked anxieties, while the government downplayed the risks. Meyer learned that it was critical for risk managers to secure informed and accurate appraisals from their own experts.

Meyer also knew that Deutsche Bank, like most financial institutions, was sensitive to market and regulatory perceptions and conscious of the interests and concerns of policy makers. Taking actions that suggested that the government of Japan was being less than forthcoming in its reporting on the crisis could only be undertaken covertly.

A final lesson of the Fukushima plant experience for Meyer was the importance of global dependency. Though the bank was headquartered in Germany, an earthquake on the other side of the world had sent Meyer, his team, and company executives into crisis mode for more than a month. He knew that intercontinental dependency was likely to become even more prominent as the bank's footprint became more extended, with larger offshore staffs and satellite operations.

Even before the Japanese crisis of March 2011, Deutsche Bank had been moving toward greater catastrophic risk preparedness. In the wake of the Indian Ocean tsunami of 2004, the Haiti and Chile earthquakes in 2010, and massive Pakistan floods in 2010, the company, in the words of an internal planning document, "became convinced of the need to better clarify the bank's response to catastrophic events in locations with a presence and/or travelers." The agenda, the company stated, was to "better define the bank's legal, reputational, operational, and ethical responsibilities during a large-scale catastrophic event." This meant emphasizing the firm's commitment to each of its country operations; constructing a command and control system all the way from front-line managers to top executives; placing a priority on the security of employees; ensuring uninterrupted clearing, settlement, and payment services; adjusting liquidity; and creating a global coordination group that had the ability to make deliberate decisions during a crisis.

The Tōhoku events served as a real-life stress test of the catastrophic risk-management system that Meyer and his staff had built. Like all such trials, it reinforced current practices, such as training simulations for extreme risks, and called for new ones, such as creating a means for better intelligence gathering during a crisis. It also reinforced Meyer's long-standing emphasis on strategic planning and tactical flexibility that allowed him to, as he stated, "make decisions very, very quickly."

CATASTROPHIC RISK-MANAGEMENT ABROAD

Our colleague Burkhard Pedell, a faculty member at the Institute for Business Administration at the University of Stuttgart in Germany, interviewed executives at twenty large German firms in industries ranging from manufacturing, automobile and telecommunication to pharmaceuticals and information technology. The companies included Bayer, Daimler-Benz, and Siemens, companies similar to the major American firms featured in this book.[13]

Many of the same underlying drivers and pitfalls in catastrophic risk that we have found among the American firms were evident among these German corporations. About half of the German executives and managers reported that the top three sources of risk for their firm were regulatory and political events, natural disasters, and financial and economic crises. Many also cited a rising number of other hazards that are difficult to forecast or even anticipate. In light of the increasing threats, some reported that the flow of upward reporting to the top governing body had intensified. And many indicated that their firms had added risk criteria explicitly into their operating cultures and job descriptions. At the same time, however, risk appetite, risk tolerance, and risk mitigation had generally not yet been fully incorporated into the firms' strategic planning.

The experience of these firms offer additional guidance for those in the United States and elsewhere in preparing for adverse events and managing them. Three risk-management developments emerged through the interviews with the executives and managers of the German companies:

• Accelerating the cycle time for crisis response, including the drafting of business continuity plans, scenario planning, and management training
• Changing operations in response to emergent risks
• Bringing risk management more directly into company planning

When asked to define the top leadership competencies for managing risk, the German executives and managers singled out the importance of strategic thinking in foreseeing and averting a crisis, communicating persuasively during a crisis, and a readiness to foster a culture of individual responsibility for risk and its management both before and after a crisis. One other notable theme from the German companies, certainly evident among the American firms as well, was the growing interdependencies among the major sources of risk. One of the German firms had thus come to annually appraise the correlations among all the risks that faced its individual business units and across the entire firm.

THE PRACTICE OF CATASTROPHIC RISK MANAGEMENT

The actions taken by the executives and managers of Lufthansa and Deutsche Bank in the aftermath of their unanticipated crisis suggest several additional management practices for companies to reduce and cope with future setbacks. We conclude with three of the most prominent and, in our judgment, most providential.

CRISIS AT LUFTHANSA AND DEUTSCHE BANK

1. When disaster strikes, if directors, executives, and managers have already put in place a risk management culture and architecture enabling them to take comprehensive action in response, companies

will be better prepared to recover from disruption and remain aligned with the firm's core values.

2. Personal familiarity and mutual trust between a company's crisis team and its business leaders serve as a facilitating foundation for rapid mobilization when a crisis strikes.

3. Critical to a firm's recovery are a leadership and organizational preparedness, a readiness for fast action, a set of key risk indicators, and real-time data on the potential threats at hand.

From Reactive
to Proactive Boardrooms

All directors are responsible for risk oversight; audit is responsible for the process, but really, all directors are responsible for the oversight.

—CHAIR OF THE BOARD'S AUDIT COMMITTEE, *Chemical Company*

"Corporate risk-taking and the monitoring of risks" are "front and center in the minds of boards of directors," warned governance advisor and attorney Martin Lipton and colleagues in 2015. Their concern was fueled by a host of factors ranging from financial instability to anger and resentment at corporate influence. Whatever the sources of discontent, directors who fail to monitor company risks do so at their own peril: "The reputational damage to companies and their boards that fail to properly manage risk is a major threat."[1]

At the same time, Lipton and others urged directors to stick to their oversight role rather than trying to micromanage company risk: "The board cannot and should not be involved in actual day-to-day risk *management*," they warned. Directors instead ought to stick to their "*oversight* role," shaping executive action but not detailing it. This chapter is focused on that shaping as it has emerged in recent years, drawn from our direct observation of governance practices at many of America's largest firms.

Several decades earlier, Lipton's warning would have been out of place as boards were exerting little oversight or influence on the company in any area. Back then, whatever the exhortations for directors to act, many were simply too disengaged to do so. Today, governing boards increasingly partner with management in a host of arenas, from company strategy to executive leadership, a development that we have chronicled elsewhere.[2]

This transformation of the governing boards of America's largest firms from somewhat disengaged to full partners has come at a time when company risk management has come to the fore, as chronicled in this book. Just as company executives have increasingly focused on risk management, so have company directors. They are adding value to company risk management in ways that would have been inconceivable in their earlier, less-engaged era.[3]

What we find is that the company's governing board is ideally positioned to bring deliberative thinking to catastrophic risk management, while leaving the firm's risk practices to company executives and division managers. The board's dozen or so members are charged now with working hand-in-hand with their top executives in stage-managing the firm's longer-term performance—but not charged with its day-to-day enactment. In focusing on what companies actually do—our agenda in part III—we see management taking special responsibility for developing measures for risk reduction and the board bringing a deliberative mindset to the process.

To appreciate the place of risk management in the boardroom, we turn to a survey of 884 directors of large public companies in 2016. The survey asked them to indicate the areas of director expertise that should be represented in the boardroom. More of the directors deemed financial expertise as important (93 percent) than any other capacity, but two-thirds identified operation expertise (69 percent), industry expertise (68 percent), and *risk-management expertise* (63 percent).[4]

Moreover, company boards have become confident that they are now devoting the right amount of attention to risk management. More than 90 percent of the directors surveyed in 2016 stated that they spend enough time with their executives to "sufficiently understand business risks," and that as directors they were indeed concerned with longer-term risks stemming from economic, technological, geopolitical, and environmental trends. Half of the directors also reported that their firm's key risks are now on the table at every board meeting. The risks most often described by the directors as posing the greatest governance challenges are strategic and

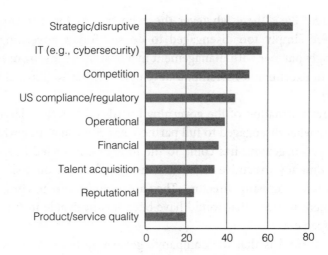

Figure 7.1 The Risks Posing Greatest Oversight Challenges to Company Directors, 2016
SOURCE: PricewaterhouseCoopers, 2016. Percentage affirmative response to the survey
question, "Which of the following risks pose the greatest oversight challenges to your
board?"

disruptive trends, information technology, competition, compliance and
regulation, and operational issues, as shown in Figure 7.1.[5]

Some boards, however, had not engaged more deliberatively in risk
oversight, as was evident when examining the implosion of the American
International Group triggered by Lehman's failure on September 15, 2008.
We begin with a brief look back at AIG's boardroom just before the disaster,
a moment when directors fell short in their supervision, to better appreciate just how far many governing boards have moved toward active risk
management—and also how consequential a failure to do so can be. To see
what active engagement looks like among those boards that have advanced,
we then chronicle how directors have become more involved at one large
enterprise, General Electric.

Building on these accounts and our interviews with executives and directors of publicly traded companies, we characterize key features of deliberative board engagement in catastrophic risk management. With greater
engagement comes added value, not just risk avoidance, as we will see in the
case of Boeing directors overseeing the firm's high-stakes bet on a new aircraft technology. The chapter concludes by turning to the role of the board
in defining guidelines for dealing with extremely unlikely events that can
threaten a firm's very existence.

A GOVERNANCE RISK FAILURE AT AIG

American International Group's Financial Products division (AIGFP), based in London, had become a premier insurer of packets of home mortgages in the 2000s, at one point backing $1.7 trillion in such bundles, roughly the equivalent of Russia's gross domestic product at the time. Employing less than 1 percent of the firm's workforce, AIGFP was producing more than 17 percent of its parent's income, and it helped AIG emerge as the world's largest insurer. Given AIG's scale and performance, Dow Jones included it in its renowned blue-chip stock index, the Dow Jones Industrial Average, in 2004.[6]

Despite the many outward signs of success, regulators, raters, and advisors began to warn AIG directors in the mid-2000s that its AIGFP portfolio, with its vast credit default swaps on massive blocks of subprime mortgages, looked increasingly troublesome if market conditions were to change and negatively affect those transactions. The US Office of Thrift Supervision, serving as AIGFP's primary Washington regulator, told AIG directors in 2005 that it had found "weaknesses in AIGFP's documentation of complex transactions, in policies and procedures regarding accounting, in stress testing, in communication of risk tolerances, and in the company's outline of lines of authority, credit risk management and measurement." On the eve of the Lehman-sparked financial crisis in September 2008, the federal regulator warned AIG again of what it deemed unwarranted risk-taking in its underwriting of subprime mortgage pools, urging directors to force executives to improve AIGFP's controls and risk management. AIG's outside auditor, PricewaterhouseCoopers, also warned of accounting weaknesses. A governance rating agency gave the AIG board a barely passing grade of D.[7]

Despite external admonitions, there is no public evidence to suggest that the AIG directors had taken steps to rein in their excessively risky but enormously profitable London division. A likely factor was the view of its mortgage practices voiced by company executives. AIG's chief risk officer stressed on August 5, 2007, that the danger in the credit default swaps "is very modest and remote." The top executive of AIG Financial Products himself told investors on December 5, 2007, that "this is a money-good portfolio." AIG's chief executive decreed that the risk-analysis models of AIGFP were "very reliable," giving him and the company a "very high level of comfort."[8]

Yet when a credit rating agency in the wake of Lehman's failure on September 15, 2008, downgraded AIG's debt from AAA to A——a huge blow to AIG's model of low-cost insurance premised on an impeccable credit rating—the company was suddenly forced to post collateral to back its AIGFP insurance guarantees, resulting in a loss of $61 billion during the next three months, the largest quarterly loss of any company in American business history. As its losses ballooned further, the United States stepped in with the Troubled Asset Relief Program to save AIG from certain bankruptcy, by injecting $182 billion into the company.

Remarkably, though, with that infusion saving the enterprise, a new management team and a new governing board nursed the company back to health. Returning from the brink of bankruptcy, AIG repaid the $182 billion with an extra $23 billion in interest to the United States by 2013, a part of the story probably less known to the general public.

The most intriguing question in retrospect is why AIG directors had opted to ignore the warnings from regulators and even some of the firm's own managers. Criticism and complaints are part of the normal upward flow to anybody in authority, and the challenge for the AIG board was to separate predictable static from genuine warnings. While several elements might have been at play, it is arguable that AIG's revenue growth and earnings success in the years running up to the 2008 debacle fostered a boardroom assurance that shaded into hubris, lessening director readiness to press executives to think more strategically about the mounting risks their managers were shouldering.

By savoring AIG's short-term gains, AIG's directors appeared to have abandoned the kind of deliberative thinking for which more boards now carry special responsibility. As noted earlier, psychologists and behavioral economists have provided evidence that overconfidence coupled with availability bias can lead individuals to project today's success into tomorrow. When things are going well there is a natural tendency not to question the factors that may have led to positive returns, and to assume that the trend will continue. AIG's directors may thus have downplayed the warning, their attention drawn to the firm's current gains rather than the mounting concerns.[9]

GOVERNANCE RISK PRACTICE AT GENERAL ELECTRIC

If AIG directors had been too inattentive, General Electric directors pressed company executives to be more vigilant, to identify their risks and to explain and justify the measures taken. The difference, we believe, was due to the directors' deliberative mindset that they brought to the boardroom.

One of the world's largest enterprises, General Electric in 2016 operated in more than 170 countries with more than 330,000 employees. *Fortune* listed GE as one of the best corporations for leadership development, and it regularly included GE among its globally most-admired companies. General Electric's $120 billion in revenue in 2016 came from a broad portfolio of businesses in infrastructure, healthcare, and industrial products. The company's demanding management style can be traced to a succession of strong-willed chief executives, but crisis recovery over the years had added impetus to well-thought-out strategic planning. John F. Welch, who had served as GE chief executive from 1981 to 2001 and had faced his share of setbacks, bluntly concluded, "You'll never have a great company until you have a near death experience." The financial maelstrom of 2008–2009 furnished something close to that.[10]

GE Capital, which provided close to half of the parent's earnings at the time, had been exposed to subprime mortgages and credit defaults just like AIG after Lehman failed in September 2008. GE Capital's earnings declined by 38 percent in the third quarter of 2008, pulling down the parent's income by 22 percent. The market price of insurance on GE bonds soared, close to a junk bond rating. GE's stock traded for less than half of what it was a year earlier, stripping more than $200 billion from the firm's value. Chief executive Jeffrey Immelt, appointed in 2001, scrambled for a private bailout, raising $18 billion in emergency cash through a $15 billion stock offering and a $3 billion infusion from Warren Buffett. That proved enough to enable GE to make it through the financial crisis, but once stabilized, the company opted to rid itself of a major risk driver, selling or spinning off much of what had constituted GE Capital.[11]

General Electric executives and directors were also no longer content to assume that their autonomous business units, each with its own profit-and-loss requirements and their offsetting markets, would somehow naturally guard against risk. They sought outside guidance, and they pursued a two-pronged strategy: divisional and functional risks were still best managed within the separate business units, such as GE Aviation or GE Energy, and by the separate corporate functions, such as legal or finance, since each faced dramatically different threats. At the same time, the company would have to become savvier about companywide threats as well.

With prodding from GE directors, Immelt and his lieutenants moved to create a more long-term framework for tracking and managing risk. In 2009 they appointed a veteran GE manager, Mark Krakowiak, as the company's first chief risk officer. Krakowiak set out to heighten risk awareness across the company, strengthen frameworks for identifying and managing short- and long-term risk within each business, and expand director and executive engagement in overseeing both. His objective was not to avoid risks, but to better understand whether they were managed well enough to ensure that the gains in taking them outweighed their downsides. "If you manage the risk better," Krakowiak explained, "you should be able to deliver better shareholder value than companies that are strictly defensive about risk."

General Electric's governing board and top management directed each business unit to make its willingness to accept risk explicit and, in doing so, help set the boundaries of its strategy by examining the relevant trade-offs between risk appetite and risk tolerance. GE's medical business, for instance, defined its boundaries with a simple statement: "We're not going to go into anything that goes inside the body." If the business had a compelling rationale for crossing that line, it would have to convince the directors and CEO that doing so not only made strategic sense but also that the added risks would be acceptable.

At the same time, Krakowiak created the corporate risk committee, chaired by GE's chief risk officer and populated by the CEO, vice chairs, general counsel, and audit director. It appraised each business's appetite for risk and their management of risk, reporting on hazards across the business and how they might become correlated and thus pose systemic risk to the company.

To guide the work of GE executives and the corporate risk committee, its directors created their own risk committee. With director encouragement, for instance, Krakowiak set forward metrics for identifying and measuring risk—division by division and function by function. Hazardous terrain included low-probability but high-consequence events. "It is the one-in-a-hundred event that can kill you," Krakowiak warned. "To not figure out how to mitigate it, or how you're going to react if it does happen, is unacceptable."

The GE board's experience in managing risk points to five areas for directors' deliberative engagement in risk oversight, leaving the risk practices to company executives: 1) ensure that risk management is both centralized and decentralized in its appraisal and oversight; 2) identify a leader of risk management who has extensive experience in the company and widespread relationships with executives; 3) build a board's capacity to appraise the tradeoffs between risk-taking and risk appetite, along with a comprehensive set of metrics for both; 4) establish a company risk committee with the CEO, other top executives, and the chief risk officer; and 5) direct special attention at long-term, large-scale risks, since executives may otherwise tend to gloss over them with the demands of day-to-day management. Taken together, these can provide guidelines for operating principles for board vigilance and executive action.

BRINGING IN THE BOARD

In parallel with the greater engagement of company executives in managing catastrophic risk at General Electric, company directors whom we interviewed generally reported that their governing boards had become substantially more involved in risk management in recent years. When asked when their board had significantly increased its deliberative engagement, two-thirds said that the up-tick had come within the last seven years.

One insurance firm, for instance, had elevated risk responsibility to the full board, and an energy company had done much the same, sparked by the Deepwater Horizon oil spill in the Gulf of Mexico. Now, the directors of the energy firm annually reviewed the firm's risk-management practices in its exploration, production, and retail functions, including oversight of its reputational risks. Directors played an active role when the firm evaluated its risk appetite and tolerance, and when the enterprise was confronted with a crisis.

The audit committee at a chemical company asked that the board's appraisal of risks be elevated from the audit committee's purview to oversight by the entire board. As the chair of the audit committee explained: "All directors are responsible for risk oversight; audit is responsible for the process, but really, all directors are responsible for the oversight." Thus, when the company considered a major acquisition, all directors wrestled with the integration risks before sanctioning the purchase.

Still, structuring the board's greater engagement in catastrophic risk remains a matter of judgment, with no commonly preferred formal arrangement. The chief risk officer of an energy company asked, when he joined the company, where best to position the function: "The role of the board obviously is protecting the shareholders and making sure we bring about wise use of the investment, and so they're very engaged in overall risk management, especially around things that could hurt us." But when he began, he was not sure how risk reporting to the board should be structured. "Would it be an audit committee function," he wondered. Or did they need a risk committee? If so, how should its reporting to the board best be arranged?

Executives more frequently communicated their company risks to their directors, and vice versa. The chief risk officer of a steel maker reported that he now informs the board every month about one or more of the firm's most salient risks, for example, a threatening trend in raw material prices, or a sagging demand for its finished products. At the same time, directors themselves were increasingly communicating the risks that they saw down to executives. The steelmaker's board, for example, often cited operating and political uncertainties that were not yet fully comprehended by company executives.

Directors and executives have also routinized their exchange of information and insight. At the steel company, they discussed the annual risk management plan at the start of the new year, with special reference to the risks that could possibly derail the plan, and whether those risks were acceptable. Midway through the annual cycle, they projected five years ahead, with special attention to the strategic, market, operational, regulatory, and legacy risks that could upset the steel company's best intentioned long-range plans.

Many catastrophic risks remain unique to a company's industry, so directors often ask executives to identify potential calamities distinctive to their sector. In the airline industry, for instance, extreme swings in fuel prices, disease epidemics, and airplane crashes are among the market-specific hazards. Even with executive diligence, however, some risks, such as the terrorist attacks of 9/11, cannot be readily anticipated. Or consider the personal tragedy that twice befell one of the S&P 500 companies where we interviewed. Its chief executive died while attending a sports event, and then just three years later, the CEO's replacement also passed away unexpectedly. The directors had no fully developed succession plan in place to anticipate either of the sudden losses.

Directors bring useful insights to the risk dialogue with their executives by having served on other company boards or as top officials of firms in other industries that had actively managed their risks. The director of a chemical company observed that although her fellow directors did not have specific risk experience in the industry, many had served as senior managers of substantial enterprises, and they consequently brought personal experience with risk management to the boardroom. Another director who had served on a number of boards reported that the risk measures at each company informed her guidance at the others. A third director had served as an executive with a major commodity trader, bringing an expertise to a chemical company that faced large risks in securing raw materials. In this way, better practices in risk management are informally conveyed from one firm to another.

The heightened state of director involvement was expressed by a person who had served on the board of a major airline for a decade. "I didn't know what ERM stood for at some point, eight, nine, or ten years ago," he confessed. "I think American corporations and American boards have just made vast strides in the last five years on risk management," he said, including his own firm and its board. "It's just radically different than what it used to be." The chief risk officer of a financial institution offered much the same: "The whole function of operational risk management" that was not on the board's agenda two decades ago has become very much so, with board reviews every quarter. Company directors, he explained, are "much more involved in terms of knowing what's going on and providing guidance where necessary."

To round out the picture, however, it should be noted that some company boards have long been involved in risk management. The chief executive of a chemical company, for example, reported that ever since joining the company twenty years earlier, he could "not remember a time when the board wasn't engaged around risk management or catastrophic risk management." Still, director engagement has generally become more vigorous, the executive reported, in part because of his personal insistence. "I send notes and updates a couple times a month on what's going on in the company," reported the CEO. Directors, he observed, have become "very concerned about the ability to operate the company or [even a] plant" in the wake of disaster. And as a result, "open two-way communication" between executives and the directors had become de rigueur in recent years, though director interest in risk management dates back many years.

RISK REPORTING

Given the complexity of the risks, some boards have formed a directors' risk committee as a stake in the ground. Still, the fraction of boards with risk committees among the S&P 500 remained relatively modest in recent years, though an upward tick has been evident. Among the S&P 500 companies in 2004, for instance, just 2 percent of their boards had formed a risk committee, but by 2016, the fraction had risen to 11 percent. Of the discretionary committees that some boards maintain—ranging from an executive or finance committee to a strategy or science committee—risk committees were notably the most rapidly growing of all during the past decade.[12]

The boards of all publicly traded companies are already required to maintain audit, compensation, and nominations/governance committees. The Dodd–Frank Wall Street Reform and Consumer Protection Act of 2010 went further in the financial services industry, mandating a risk committee for the board—composed entirely of independent directors—at bank-holding companies with at least $10 billion in assets and other publicly traded financial services companies supervised by the Federal Reserve. For other sectors, however, a board risk committee remains discretionary.

Among the primary duties normally assigned to the risk committees of boards that have established them, according to an appraisal by professional-services firm Ernst & Young, are defining the company's risk tolerance and risk appetite and then overseeing the management of both. For the vast majority of S&P 500 companies that still lack a risk committee, however, the New York Stock Exchange requires that those functions are lodged in the board's audit committee. Still, the audit committee generally concerns itself more with financial than operational threats.[13]

At an insurance company, the board created its own risk committee in the wake of the 2008–2009 financial crisis. In parallel with it, executives now meet monthly on risk management, up from a quarterly cycle. The board's audit committee continued to focus on controls and compliance, but the board's new risk committee stepped back to appraise the company's hazards more comprehensively. Building that perspective can be a challenge, as some one hundred people in the company are now directly involved in risk management, and as a result, reported another risk officer, executives worked to ensure that the directors did not become "bogged down in a lot of detail."

Other variants emerged as companies have grappled in recent years on how best to orchestrate risk oversight at the board level. A bank-holding company created a combined executive *and* risk committee with a charter of overseeing all hazards for the company. To guide the committee's work, the board expressly stated its appetite and tolerance for risk, setting forward the firm's strategic thrusts and the level of risk it was willing to incur in each area. The committee's mandate was to evaluate the company's actual risk profile against the directors' stated goals.

Many firms reported that their board's audit or risk committee included a specialized subset of directors who had a better grasp of the risk-related issues facing their industry. This was especially true among financial institutions where risk issues can be especially knotty and require financial experience for understanding the relevant issues. It should be noted that in a third of the companies, the risk managers did not meet with the board at all and reported only through one of its committees. While that made for more technically informed discussions in committees of specialists, it also reduced the issue's visibility to the board as a whole.

More generally, among the hundred companies where we interviewed, a majority of the directors, executives, and managers indicated that their senior risk managers reported to their board about company hazards at least twice a year, either directly or through executive sessions. In doing so, they worked up through one of several channels, as seen in Figure 7.2, with two-fifths connecting through the board's audit committee, a fifth through a risk committee, and two-fifths through a finance committee, executive committee, or other conduit.

Whatever the specific reporting arrangements, however, the emergent prescription is for all directors to embrace responsibility. Speaking for many directors on this point, a diversely experienced director, serving on nine company boards, made the point: "I am an advocate for the entire board handling risk matters—because the entire board is held accountable."

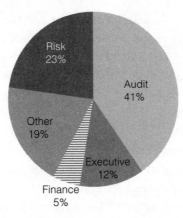

Figure 7.2 Board Committee through which Risk Managers Report to Company Directors
SOURCE: Company interviews.

That said, director understanding—and thus oversight—of the sometimes arcane issues in risk management can still be limited, as a risk manager of a major financial institution cautioned. "We have to be very effective communicating the right subject for the right decision," she said, and then warned that "some of the board members are . . . not competent" in the eyes of the regulators to understand the hazards.

Engagement of the entire board in risk oversight as a preferred practice is consistent with research findings. In a study of 296 publicly listed companies in 2011–2013 across twenty-eight countries, half in the United States, two academic researchers found that companies that had assigned risk oversight to the full board exercised stronger oversight of their risk-management functions, and that in turn correlated with stronger risk management, operating performance, and share price.[14]

ATTENTION DRIVERS

The directors' heightened attention to risk has often been driven by disasters at other firms. The underlying premise: much can be learned from other companies' misfortunes before they strike one's own enterprise.

"Every event is something we try to learn from," said a risk officer at a consumer goods company. The firm conducts a "correction-of-error" exercise to appreciate what the company should work to improve, turning for guidance to such events at Johnson & Johnson's Tylenol recall of 1982, Toyota's defect recalls of 2010–2014, and Japan's earthquake and tsunami in 2011. In looking over their shoulder at the 2010 oil spill disaster in the Gulf of Mexico, for instance, both directors and executives of the consumer goods company asked, "All right, what can we learn? What can be done better? And how does that compare to what might be truly catastrophic in our industry?" The board worried that a company of its size faced so many risks that the accumulation of many small mishaps might lead to a major calamity. Thus, the disastrous experiences or even small setbacks among other companies proved useful illuminations of the dangers with which the directors should be concerned.

When explaining heightened director engagement, some whom we interviewed referenced one or more of the great catastrophic events of the era, such as the terrorist attacks in 2001, Hurricane Katrina in 2005, or the financial crisis of 2008–2009. Others pointed to the influence of a director who sat on the board of another company that had undergone a crisis of its own. Short of such external triggers, those interviewed reported that some of their directors had remained more intuitive than deliberative in thinking about risk. In those cases, greater board engagement had sometimes been instigated by a request from below, the chief risk officer playing a prominent role here.

Sometimes the timing of unanticipated disasters moved boards to engage in the moment. One executive reported in an interview that he had been a director of a major airline that happened to be in the middle of a board meeting when the events of September 11, 2001, unfolded. The board recognized immediately that the attack would have a major impact on world affairs, and an especially damaging impact on the industry. Though not a direct target, the hijacking of four airliners, the closing of airspace for three days, and the sharp contraction in air travel all came as unanticipated shocks to the company.

The board promptly jumped into crisis mode with management, concluding that the carrier and other airlines would have to secure federal assistance if the airline and others were to survive. Directors asked the CEO of the company to step forward as a crisis leader for the industry, mobilizing for political action to press for public assistance for all airlines. The chief executive helped bring airline leaders to Washington to make their case for a US bailout, resulting in congressional approval of $10 billion in loan guarantees and $15 billion in emergency aid. Later, a fatal crash at another airline brought the board back into direct dialogue with management on catastrophic risks. Directors again counseled executives, working through the airline's policies on pilot inexperience and fatigue, both identified as contributing factors in the crash.

Governing boards have served at some companies as a deliberative partner with management, as we have seen at General Electric. Boards at other companies have played a more passive role, as we saw in the run-up to AIG's collapse during the 2008–2009 financial crisis. This points to a leadership principle advocated early in these pages. All parties—company directors included—embrace a proactive posture, delving into risks and their mitigation before a debacle materializes.

MORE OVERSIGHT AND STRATEGY

When the board does weigh in on risk management, most directors express broad concerns but usually offer little specific guidance. As an executive of an online travel agency explained, the "primary role of the board is to ask really smart questions and ensure that the proper due diligence of the business is being done. So I think the role of the board has been to ask the tough questions. Are we prepared? What are we thinking about long-term business? What happens if we continue to have these problems? What are the implications?"

As in all aspects of corporate governance, drawing a sharp line between *overseeing* company risk and *managing* company risk is like learning to spell the word *banana*: you have to know where to stop. Many companies have developed decision protocols that explicitly delineate which decisions must go to the directors for final review and which can stay within the executive team. And most firms have in any case evolved a culture of governance with shared norms on which issues and risks should be vetted by the directors. Obviously, anything that touches on catastrophic risk is board-bound; protocols on lesser risks are more ambiguous.[15]

The challenging oversight questions from directors tended to focus on company strategy, including its appetite and tolerance for risk. The executive of a financial services company explained: "Our board adopted a statement of risk appetite, which articulates . . . business strategies and how much risk we're willing to take in pursuit of those strategies." As a result, management worked to keep the board informed about any gaps between the company's actual risk profile and the risk appetite that the board had proposed.

Some executives cautioned that directors are sometimes underinformed about the firms' risks. Even more problematically, without a developed capacity to think deliberatively about the long-term risks facing their firms, director guidance can be nonstrategic or even misleading. The chief executive of a discount retail chain faced just this issue, reporting that there was a cost in taking too many hazards to the board. When the firm was building a more robust risk-management system, the CEO carried a lengthy list of its risks into a board meeting. But both directors and executives soon concluded that, in the CEO's words, "There is no way the board can ever deal with all those issues."

Several million customers passed through the discount retailer's stores every day, making more than 2 million purchases. Shoplifting would obviously not be elevated to the board agenda, but privacy protection for 78 million credit card holders should be. The directors thus posed a sharp-edged question to the CEO and themselves, "What issues do we really want to find out about and be able to control?" Protecting against a break-in to the Social Security numbers of its employees was certainly one of those issues. Prioritizing was thus key, concluded the CEO. "If you try to worry about a thousand items on the risk list, I guarantee you that nothing is going to get attention." As a result, in his experience, "you have to pick those fifteen to twenty items that are really important and zero in on them."

In the same spirit, members of the audit committee of an agricultural products company was asked by both its directors and executives, "What risks should be brought to the board's audit committee for review?" Committee members responded that they wanted regular data on the company's trading risks and anything that could significantly disrupt the firm's ability to move massive agricultural stocks from one region to another.

By way of a tangible illustration, 40 percent of the world's cocoa is produced in the Ivory Coast, but after that country's president refused to vacate his office in 2011 following an electoral defeat, European countries imposed trade embargos. Since the agricultural products company depended heavily on that one country for supplying cocoa to the makers of baked goods, breakfast cereals, and dairy products worldwide, the crisis quickly escalated up to the board's audit committee. At issue were several key questions: Should its facilities in the Ivory Coast be shut down? If the answer was yes, then how to safely evacuate several hundred employees from the country? If the answer was no, what aspects of the firm's operation should be covered by insurance?

The board's audit committee asked company executives to consider purchasing political risk insurance, but the risk manager reported that coverage was now too expensive and that the company should instead be more explicit up front about the political risks of investing in a given country. Directors affirmed the point, saying that executives should avoid the need for political-risk insurance by simply avoiding highly volatile regions in the first place. Company directors proved a useful analytic partner for company executives as they worked to create far-reaching and long-term solutions. In the end, the company decided to shut down its facilities in the Ivory Coast.

A common thread running through the varied practices of the company boards is the directors' collaboration with executives in thinking more deliberatively to surmount the decision biases and shortcomings identified in chapter 3. It is evident from our company interviews that directors are becoming more threat-attentive and more decision-deliberative, serving as more dedicated counsel for executives as they evolve their risk-management and crisis strategies.

CYBERSECURITY IN THE BOARDROOM

One area of enterprise risk that increasingly looked potentially catastrophic for companies during the mid-2010s is cybersecurity. Massive breaches of company firewalls that exposed a huge amount of confidential customer records—at Target (40 million records, as we discuss in chapter 9), Anthem (80 million records), Equifax (143 million customers), eBay (145 million records), and Yahoo (3 billion)—have led some directors and executives to place cybersecurity explicitly on their board's agenda.

The US Senate's proposed Cybersecurity Disclosure Act, introduced in March 2017, would require companies to reveal in their SEC filings "information on whether any member of the company's Board of Directors is a cybersecurity expert, and if not, why having that expertise on the Board of Directors is not necessary because of other cybersecurity steps taken by the publicly traded company." The definition of "expert" would be left to the National Institute of Standards and Technology. Industry groups have resisted the concept of Congress mandating a specific expertise for a board member that might result in excluding another director with an equally or even more vital expertise. But the emergence of the legislative proposal was symptomatic of the external pressures on directors to focus on this area of risk.

The proposed legislation stemmed from a public perception that company boards were underprepared to grapple with the risks of cybersecurity, and directors tended to agree. A survey of 245 company directors in 2015 revealed that only a third said they were knowledgeable about the issues, and a fifth did not even know if their firm had ever been breached. When asked about whether their cybersecurity governance practices were effective, three-fifths of the board members affirmed they were. Yet when the same question was asked in a separate survey of 409 information technology professionals, only a fifth concurred. An informal survey of twenty-two major companies and organizations in 2015 may help explain the disparity. Many of the IT professionals affirmed that their company board received a report at least annually about the enterprise's top risks, but that the reporting time itself typically occupied less than an hour of the board's time. It comes as no surprise then that company directors would increase board attention on information technology risks: among 884 company directors surveyed in 2016, three-fifths recommended expanding their board's time on the topic.[16]

In fact, company directors have come to devote substantial discussion to cybersecurity. Of S&P 500 firms in another survey in 2015, 89 percent reported that within the past year their directors had reviewed the company's plan for preventing and responding to a major information security breach. And 69 percent had assigned cybersecurity oversight to one of the board's standing committees—primarily the audit committee—for hands-on director attention.[17]

MANAGING RISK AT BOEING

With the board organized and an architecture in place for it to oversee risk, we turn to a more extended illustration of how engaged directors can add value to a company's risk management strategy. We will see how directors of the Boeing Company contributed to the design, pricing, and building of their company's most important new product of the era and one that could put the company itself at risk if the new product failed in the market.

The board of aircraft-maker Boeing had become deeply involved in the creation of the 787, an extraordinarily complex product that relied on untested engineering. The board had, of course, kept a hawklike eye on the company's earnings and its stock price. But just as critically for the company's long-term financial future, directors had helped Boeing develop this new aircraft, avoiding a host of potential pitfalls along the way, in what was, in the words of Boeing chairman Lewis Platt, a "bet-the-company decision."[18]

Individually, none of the design decisions in which the board was involved was a make-or-break proposition, but together, they could mean the difference between the 787's success and failure. And with billions of dollars on the line and Airbus formidably on its heels, none of this could be done passively. Yet neither could directors be peering over the shoulder of those involved in the aircraft's design. To facilitate deliberative guidance by directors but not neck-breathing oversight from them, Boeing executives broke the production process into distinct phases so that directors could weigh in at three critical junctures in the development of the aircraft.

First, the board reviewed a multibillion-dollar budget and a timeline for the aircraft's development—a task that required directors to accurately appraise the future of airline travel generally. Boeing's largest competitor, Airbus, had already cast its lot with the double-decker A380 on the premise that a superjumbo aircraft would be more appealing than ordinary jetliners to airlines that relied on crowded hub-and-spoke airports. Boeing believed that the traditional hub-and-spoke system was breaking down, as passengers increasingly demanded direct service between two airports.

The two aircraft giants were making enormous wagers on what their customers would want a decade later. Boeing's management team began by presenting the directors with its vision for the 787—the aircraft's cost, its capacity, and why it would be appealing to the company's airline customers. The directors challenged the executives' numbers and the assumptions on which they were based. Was the hub-and-spoke scheme really destined to disappear? Was the point-to-point scenario economically feasible for airlines? In response, the management team returned with refined forecasts, finally convincing the directors that the 787 would find a profitable niche.

Second, management asked the board to rule on whether the time was right to allow sales managers to present the aircraft's specifications to the airlines. This, too, was a risky call. To authorize sales presentations, the board had to be confident that Boeing could manufacture the 787 with the promised performance at the agreed price and delivered by a specified date.

The proposed airliner would be built with a higher percentage of the lightweight, high-strength composite materials that Boeing had pioneered on earlier commercial jet programs, such as the 737 and the 777. These composites would allow for lower costs and increased creature comforts, like higher humidity since the composites would not corrode with greater moisture, but the directors were not entirely sure that the company could successfully mold the composites into the larger, more complex sections—including entire fuselages—required for the 787. Directors asked executives to present compelling evidence that the 787 could indeed be built with composites and priced competitively against what Airbus was expected to offer. Once their concerns were addressed, the board authorized the sales team to communicate the aircraft's projected performance and price to their customers, the commercial airlines.

Third, directors were asked to give the final go-ahead for production of the aircraft, which would require Boeing to commit additional billions of dollars to the project long before its customers had committed any cash. They had to be persuaded that customers would in fact like what they saw, after which the sales team would be unleashed to secure the written orders upon which the big bet rested. Once signed, those orders called for stiff penalties if Boeing failed to deliver as promised. The directors pressed management for a detailed production plan and proof that anticipated engine suppliers General Electric and Rolls-Royce could create the required thrust at an acceptable price.

After board meetings over a decade on the 787's design and viability, Boeing's directors finally voted to authorize the formal product launch. They had sought tangible evidence to support each of management's major assumptions and their uncertainties. Their deliberative engagement in appraising and mitigating the new aircraft's risks did not prove sufficient to prevent repeated delays in the 787's delivery to its customers, with the first aircraft entering service several years later than expected. Still, in playing a counseling role in the product's creation, the board helped control the large risks inherent in a venture of this scale. If Boeing had miscalculated the risks, it could have morphed into a self-inflicted disaster. But it did not, and by the November 2017, Boeing had secured 1,283 orders for the 787, well more than Airbus's 317 orders for its A380.[19]

Drawing on Boeing's creation of the 787, we extract several additional guidelines for directors' deliberative engagement in risk management: 1) for high-stake decisions on products or services, engage directors at key points in reviewing, modifying, and ratifying the decisions; 2) encourage directors to press executives with detailed questions about the assumptions underlying the risks in the decisions; and 3) embolden directors to ask executives for compelling evidence on the anticipated risks and shortfalls in the service or product development.

EXISTENTIAL RISKS

If directors have one unequivocal role to play in catastrophic risk management, it is to ensure that their company does not face an existential threat. These include extreme events that are the lore of science fiction—an explosive virus, an asteroid strike, or artificial intelligence run amok. Although the executives we interviewed contended that they were focusing on worst-case scenarios, many had also concluded that they could ignore very low-probability events. Extreme threats fell below the firm's threshold of concern, and the companies would not have the budget in any case to protect against them.

Still, massive climate change occasioned by a rise of more than two degrees centigrade over the next several decades could have a life-threatening effect on a number of companies, especially fossil-fuel producers. Advocates of moving companies away from coal, oil, and gas and toward wind, solar, and other sustainable sources increasingly pressed companies like Exxon Mobil, the world's largest energy producer, to start the transformation—or face public protests, stockholder resolutions, or disinvestment campaigns. The environmental advocate, 350.org, reported that some five hundred organizations had already opted to sell their shares in fossil-fuel producers, an aggregate disinvestment of more than $3 trillion in holdings.[20]

The international climate accords negotiated in Paris in 2015 within the UN Framework Convention on Climate Change called for "holding the increase in the global average temperature to well below 2°C above preindustrial levels." Climate advocates and political protestors both outside and inside the annual meeting of Exxon Mobil in May 2016 promoted the cause. A proposal calling for the company to report how climate change will affect its business drew 38 percent of the voted shares, far from a majority but a large faction of the affirmative votes compared to that received by most social resolutions on company proxy statements.[21]

Investor pressures on boards to confront this and other existential risks are still relatively modest, but we anticipate that they will likely intensify in the decades ahead, and credit rating agencies are already beginning to appraise climate-related risks that companies are facing. Whether welcomed or not, directors are likely to find existential risks thrust on their governance agendas in years to come. Shareholders of Occidental Petroleum, a major oil and gas company, voted at the 2017 annual meeting to ask the company to appraise the impact of climate change on its long-term prospects. Blackrock, the world's largest institutional investor, voted for the proposal.[22]

A McKinsey report on risk and governance focused on just this issue. Drawing on its consultants' experience, it found that boards are more likely to miss "large company-wide" risks, to underestimate the drivers of such hazards, and to underappreciate correlated risks. McKinsey urged directors, executives, and managers to devote explicit attention to five "big bets" that each enterprise depends upon for its growth and survival that may vary across companies, and then to consider the threats to each of these bets.[23]

Big bets should indeed be the province of directors, urged the Business Roundtable, an association of the chief executives of 140 of America's largest companies with $7 trillion in annual revenue and 16 million employees. Among a set of ten prescriptive guidelines issued in 2016, it devoted two to risk and resilience, urging directors to guard against a firm's "major risks" and ensure that executives have plans in place to recover rapidly from disaster.[24]

AN EIGHT-FOLD WAY FOR GOVERNANCE AND RISK

It has been suggested by some observers that directors may bring neither the essential expertise nor the necessary time to add real value to the way that executives manage risk at their company. While onlookers are wise to cast a skeptical eye on whether a company board can make a difference in this area, it is evident from our interviews that many directors have become far less skeptical, seeing value in actively and explicitly partnering with executives to bolster company risk practices. Arguably, directors add more deliberative thinking to the equation, and they bring fresh approaches from other companies where they have seen them in action. And by concentrating executive attention on risk, whatever the specific guidance, directors can play a critical role in protecting the firm.[25]

Building on the tangible experience of the directors of the S&P 500 companies, including that of AIG, Boeing, and General Electric, we identify eight principles for guiding directors who serve on the boards of large publicly traded companies. In identifying these, we have extracted the emergent practices that are arguably most common and most consequential for directors' deliberative guidance of companies as they construct their risk-management strategies.

FROM REACTIVE TO PROACTIVE BOARDROOMS

1. Boards have become more directly engaged in company strategy and leadership, with directors taking a more deliberative role in guiding risk-management strategies, helping to define risk appetite, risk tolerance, and risk readiness.
2. Bringing directors with prior executive risk-management experience on to the board can strengthen its deliberative oversight.
3. Directors carry special responsibility for identifying hazards in company operations that can become disruptive or even disastrous if not detected and mitigated.
4. Alerting directors to company operations can help prioritize risk management in the boardroom and encourage directors to probe for risks in company decisions.
5. Directors can guide and appraise company risks in the development of new products and services, posing critical questions and challenging executive assumptions.
6. Directors can also play a special role in pressing executives to justify their forecasts, anticipated results, and identified risks—without at the same time micromanaging them.
7. Catastrophic risks deserve the attention of all directors, not just specialists on one of the board's committees.
8. Directors are advised to draw a bright line between risks where they should play an active role and those over which executives should exercise delegated authority.

Corporate Giving for Disaster Relief

WITH LUIS BALLESTEROS

We are part of a system. If the . . . government cannot [effect a recovery], we need to rebuild.

—EXECUTIVE, *Coca-Cola Company*

In prior chapters, we have focused on how low-probability but high-impact disruptions have been changing director and executive mindsets. Large-scale risks are also changing company practices for the relief of others hit by disasters—and in so doing are reshaping the nonmarket actions of companies. Any picture of how business firms are coping with their own calamities will thus be incomplete without the dual image of their increasing outreach to others in crisis.

US firms have a long history of engaging in relief and recovery in the aftermath of disasters. Reports of business organizations giving cash to fund reconstruction, donating products or services, and assisting debris removal date back to the early 1900s. In recent years, public demand for that private largesse has further intensified, pressing business leaders to become ever more socially engaged. As a result, corporate giving has undergone unprecedented growth during the past several decades, with most large companies now committed to providing at least some kind of relief when disasters strike others, especially in regions where the companies operate. By one estimate, the fraction of the largest 500 US corporations engaging in some form of disaster giving worldwide rose from less than 20 percent in 1990 to more than 95 percent by 2014.[1]

Due to the increasingly multinational operations of large American companies, more than two-fifths of the revenue of the S&P 500 companies in 2015 came from abroad. At the same time, calamities themselves are increasingly multinational in impact, so corporate giving for disaster relief has not surprisingly become more global. Consider the recovery of Chile and Japan from two of the strongest earthquakes ever recorded and the recovery of the Philippines from a category 5 typhoon.

In the wake of Chile's 8.8-magnitude earthquake in 2010, which destroyed close to 20 percent of the country's gross domestic product (equivalent to the financial losses of twenty Hurricane Katrinas in the United States), business firms provided more than half of the international aid—more than from foreign governments, multilateral agencies, nongovernment organizations, and private individuals combined. Similarly, in the aftermath of Japan's 9.0-magnitude earthquake in 2011, companies accounted for over half of all aid coming from abroad. When category 5 Typhoon Haiyan battered the Philippines in 2013, killing more than six thousand and causing more than $2.5 billion in damage, corporate donations furnished half of the relief that flowed into that country.[2]

NATIONAL IMPACT OF DISASTERS

This unprecedented rise in corporate disaster giving comes at a time when the social need for additional sources of disaster financing has become larger than ever. The average annual inflation-adjusted economic loss associated with earthquakes, floods, hurricanes, and other natural calamities rose by a factor of nearly six from 1980 to 2016, from $54 billion to $314 billion. National losses have at times even exceeded a nation's gross domestic product. Hurricane Mitch in Honduras in 1998 and Hurricane Ivan in Grenada in 2004 produced damages several times greater than their country's entire GDP. In 2017, Hurricane Irma's sustained winds of more than 150 miles per hour virtually destroyed several Caribbean islands; Hurricane Maria left Puerto Rico without power for weeks.[3]

At the same time, the value of traditional sources of disaster response and recovery—local governments, foreign governments, multilateral agencies, nonprofit organizations, and private insurance—have grown more slowly in low-income countries. The United Nations reported that never before had the long-standing forms of humanitarian aid in response to catastrophic events "been so insufficient" for meeting increasing disaster needs in 2015—a shortfall of some $15 billion—despite the fact that international aid for all humanitarian action had reached its highest dollar amount ever, $24.5 billion.[4]

During the past three decades, traditional disaster-assistance sources aside from insurance have been estimated to cover just 5 percent of the cost of natural calamities worldwide and less than 1 percent for disasters in high-income countries. Our own database reveals that foreign-government and multilateral-agency assistance in the aftermath of national calamities averaged less than 3 percent of the total cost of disaster damage.

Moreover, insurance against losses remains very limited. In the case of large-scale disasters in low- and medium-income countries, for instance, less than 3 percent of their costs in recent years have been insured. And even in countries with higher insurance penetration, such as Japan, only a small portion of disaster losses have typically been covered. Of the estimated $210 billion in damage in the wake of the 2011 earthquake and tsunami in Japan, for example, only $38 billion had been insured, leaving more than 80 percent of the country's economic loss uninsured. Overall, high-income nations are found on average to finance just a quarter of their disaster recovery through insurance. This is true even in the US, the world's largest insurance market. About 43 percent of the damage caused by Hurricane Katrina in 2005 was insured by the private market and the federally run National Flood Insurance Program, the main source of residential flood insurance. Only 20 percent of NYC households in the area inundated by Hurricane Sandy had flood insurance at the time of the disaster. Analysis reveals that the growth rate of disaster losses worldwide during the past forty years has outpaced the growth rate of insured losses by more than two percentage points per year.[5]

High-income countries that might appear financially resilient to a major disaster are often not. When the Tōhoku earthquake rocked Japan it was the world's third-richest economy, but by other metrics it was in fact underprepared for a ready comeback. Its public debt stood at more than twice the level of its GDP, and its real interest rates had gone negative. In the months after the disaster, national production faltered, Japan's supply of goods contracted by an estimated 20 percent, and the country's stock market and credit rating plunged. We have seen similar scenarios in other high-income countries, such as Italy after the L'Aquila earthquake in 2009, and New Zealand after the Christchurch earthquake in 2011. Most experts assumed that local governments in these well-developed nations would be able to self-finance much of their comeback. Yet each suffered deeply when the costs of recovery outstripped country and community capacities to respond quickly. Billions of dollars in national government assistance eventually flowed into affected areas, but in the disasters' immediate aftermath, emergency relief resources were in very short supply.

In a separate study of these and other disasters, we have found that businesses have increasingly come to fill those short-term deficits even in the most advanced economies. After five of the world's largest natural disasters over the period 2010–2015, companies gave more aid than foreign governments, multilateral agencies, nongovernmental organizations, and private individuals combined.[6]

CORPORATE PRESENCE EXPEDITES DONATIONS

Because of their local presence, firms can often identify and respond to the immediate needs of disaster-affected communities more effectively than can foreign governments and multilateral agencies.[7]

Donors are called upon to quickly ramp up and deliver assistance, and companies can often do so more swiftly than public and international agencies. A manager at Coca-Cola explained his own company's philanthropic engagement in Japan after its 2011 earthquake: "We are part of a system. If the [Japanese] government cannot [effect a recovery], *we* need to rebuild." And that is because as a company we "need the market to recover."[8]

In countries where firms have a significant manufacturing or sales presence, company donations in the wake of a disaster can bring benefits to the giving firms as well. In this sense, prosocial company behavior not only helps the disaster-stricken community but also the company itself, by generating higher returns for the company. Companies in effect help cushion their own financial shocks by focusing on disruptions in localities where they already have major operations or large customer bases, such as Walt Disney Co. when its Tokyo Disneyland and Disney Sea resorts were shut down by Japan's 2011 earthquake. Studies of corporate giving have confirmed that the share of a firm's income from a given market is a strong predictor of its willingness to make donations to that market.[9]

Business executives can bring exceptional expertise for pinpointing where relief is most needed in markets that they already serve. By way of example, logistics companies like FedEx [company name changed in 2000] and DHL Express are well informed on how best to donate delivery services for disaster relief in affected areas where they have pre-existing ground operations. Telecommunications companies like AT&T and Vodaphone are well positioned to ramp up emergency communication in regions where they already had a footprint.[10]

The allocation of corporate giving across countries affected by disasters is not evenly distributed, though. Companies donate funds and goods for disaster relief most frequently in wealthier nations: some 85 percent of corporate giving for disaster relief over the last fifteen years has gone to high-income economies. In contrast to the overwhelming business response to Japan's 2011 earthquake, corporate disaster giving accounted for less than 5 percent of Nepal's international assistance following its 7.8 magnitude earthquake in 2015. Such disparities naturally raise a question about whether corporate disaster relief is targeted where it is most needed.

CORPORATE ALLOCATIONS

To address the question of whether corporate disaster giving is optimally allocated from the standpoint of global needs, not just those of the donors, we traced corporate monetary and in-kind gifts to country relief and recovery from natural disasters during the period from 2003 to 2013. We found that 87 percent of the 150 natural disasters with the largest shortfall in a government's capacity to respond occurred in medium- or high-income countries rather than the most poverty-stricken nations.

We also examined international contributions by business firms, private foundations, nonprofit organizations, foreign governments, and multilateral agencies to relief and recovery for all major natural disasters worldwide during the same decade. Here we found that corporate giving is most likely to be allocated to countries whose governments are least able to restore essential services following a disaster. In other words, corporate dollars are directed at countries that are most vulnerable in the wake of a disaster, not necessarily the least affluent.[11]

When corporate giving constitutes at least 5 percent of total international aid after a disaster—implying that companies are taking an especially active interest in a country's recovery—recipients receive 37 percent more aid during the first four postdisaster weeks than they do when corporate intervention is less than 5 percent of total aid. This is significant because most experts on disaster management conclude that the time between the occurrence of a natural shock and the provision of essential goods—water, food, medicine, housing, communication, and transportation—largely determines the speed and scope of a nation's recovery. Whether a natural shock morphs into a full-fledged catastrophe or not depends on the rapidity of the response. The impact of Hurricane Katrina on New Orleans in 2005, for instance, was made far worse by the government's initial inability to deliver food, shelter, and care to victims.

Another measure of companies' ability to meet local needs in the wake of a disaster is the extent to which in-kind corporate disaster giving—removing debris, donating materials, or rebuilding schools—affects recovery. The ratio of in-kind to monetary contributions varies considerably across industries and countries. Our analyses revealed that when at least 30 percent of postdisaster business assistance to a country comes in the form of in-kind giving, recipients receive disaster assistance 65 percent faster than in similar countries with lower levels of corporate in-kind donations.[12]

COMPANY GIVING AND ECONOMIC DEVELOPMENT

The society-wide impact of corporate donations in the wake of a natural disaster can be gauged by a widely used index developed and calculated annually by the UN Development Program for most countries. The index uses national data on health, education, and living standards of the population, including life expectancy at birth, the number of years of schooling, and gross national income per capita. While the index does not capture other important social benchmarks, such as a nation's inequality, poverty, or insecurity, it provides a reasonably broad measure of a country's social well-being.[13]

The index in 2015 ranged from a low value of 0.35 for the Central African Republic to 0.92 for the United States and 0.95 for Norway. During the period from 1990 to 2015, the index for all 188 countries combined grew by three-quarters of a percent annually, rising from 0.60 in 1990 to 0.72 in 2015.

Building on data for major natural disasters from 2003 to 2013, we focus on the years before and after those calamities. Going back fifteen years, we find that the Human Development Index had risen from 0.60 to 0.66 on average in the years prior to the disaster—but then sharply declined in the years after the disaster—to a level not seen since some ten years earlier. In other words, a large natural disaster can wipe out a decade of a nation's human development.[14]

What becomes especially striking are the recovery trends when we break the international corporate assistance into two subgroupings. The first subgroup consists of disasters in which at least 10 percent of the international postdisaster giving came from companies with operations in the affected country. Those companies had a direct interest in assisting recovery, could quickly provide needed supplies and equipment, and had local knowledge of how best to distribute it. The second subgroup consists of disasters in which less than 10 percent of the international postdisaster giving came from companies with a substantial local footprint.

An example of the first subgroup was international postdisaster assistance to Chile in the wake of its 8.8-magnitude earthquake in 2010, where companies like American Airlines and Walmart had local operations and gave $1.6 million and $4.0 million, respectively. An example of the second was postdisaster assistance to Nepal after its 7.8-magnitude earthquake in 2015, where very little international corporate aid flowed in from companies with local operations since so few had any presence there.[15]

We graph trends in the Human Development Index from fifteen years before a disaster to nine years after in Figure 8.1, broken down by these two subgroups: the lighter line is for disasters where companies had a substantial local presence, and the darker line is for the other set of disasters where companies did not have a local presence. There is a substantial and enduring gap in our metric for social development in the years following a national disruption. Nine years after the calamity, the Human Development Index for countries without much of a corporate footprint stood near 0.67—but for countries with a substantial corporate presence, the index had risen to 0.70, a statistically significant difference. When companies are locally affected and step forward with private assistance, countries recover more quickly.[16]

To summarize these and other findings from our data, corporate giving is more likely to be allocated to countries in the wake of natural disasters 1) whose governments are least able to provide essential goods and services

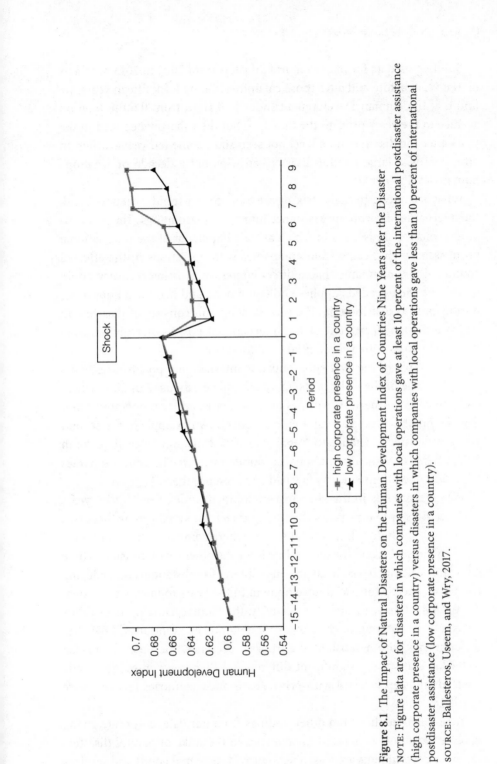

Figure 8.1 The Impact of Natural Disasters on the Human Development Index of Countries Nine Years after the Disaster

NOTE: Figure data are for disasters in which companies with local operations gave at least 10 percent of the international postdisaster assistance (high corporate presence in a country) versus disasters in which companies with local operations gave less than 10 percent of international postdisaster assistance (low corporate presence in a country).

SOURCE: Ballesteros, Useem, and Wry, 2017.

in the aftermath of the disruption, 2) where companies already have an operating presence, and 3) to which foreign government and multilateral aid is also flowing.

The analysis also reveals that corporate giving 4) goes more quickly to countries when business is giving relatively more of the relief; 5) does not crowd out aid from other sources, but rather complements it; and 6) substantially enhances a country's social comeback where companies already had a local operating presence. Taken together, the observed patterns of corporate giving benefit both the most afflicted countries and the companies doing the most business in them.[17]

PARTNERSHIPS FOR DISASTER RELIEF

Given the rise of corporate giving in the wake of disasters worldwide, international assistance after disasters can increasingly be expected to include business firms alongside traditional donors. The joining of their postdisaster giving agendas can facilitate recovery in ways that neither party can achieve alone, directing business assistance where it is most needed and where it best supplements public aid.

Consider Lawson Inc., Japan's second largest convenience-store franchise with more than 10,000 outlets. It has a long-standing practice of working to remain open in disaster zones, no easy task given Japan's perch along the Pacific ring of fire. Lawson conducted extensive scenario planning and created a protocol for keeping its stores staffed and stocked in even the most calamitous moments, with twice-annual drills to field-test its practicalities.

Just five minutes after Japan's 9.0-magnitude earthquake in 2011, Lawson executives invoked the emergency protocol among its convenience stores and distribution centers in the affected region: first a check on employee injuries and safety; then a damage appraisal of the storefronts, distribution centers, and supply chains; and finally, dispatch of extra fuel, merchandise, and support teams into the afflicted region.

Of Lawson's more than nine hundred stores in the Tōhoku region, some 60 percent managed to remain open, and 90 percent of the rest reopened within six weeks (twenty-six others had either been totally destroyed or were in the Fukushima nuclear evacuation zone). The company did not wait for customers to walk in—difficult for many in the worst-hit areas—and instead delivered free food and water to evacuation centers. As many roads were impassable, Lawson sent truckloads of motorcycles to deliver its supplies. When motor fuel ran out, it dispatched a gasoline truck to deliver it. Lawson responded in many stricken areas where public authorities could not, playing a complementary role at a crisis moment when the timely intervention by both public and private agencies was greatly valued.

In anticipation of Hurricane Katrina in 2005, Walmart had similarly prepared itself for the worst through its emergency operations center, a centralized communication, coordination, and response hub. When the tropical storm that eventually became Hurricane Katrina gathered force, the emergency center expanded its staffing to sixty, borrowing from more than thirty company departments, and carefully tracked the storm's power and direction with its own weather-modeling software. It warned Walmart stores in the likely landfall zone to stock up with a host of emergency supplies from eight disaster distribution centers, which had been stockpiling $5 million in such goods just in case.

Based on its past experience with disasters, Walmart had also come to appreciate the importance of pre-established relationships with state and city officials, and then incorporating them into the company's planning and communication process. In its local stores, for example, emergency preparedness included coordination with local police, safeguarding employee records, and shielding facilities against physical damage. Walmart also sought to support employees and their families through a hotline to report any personal concerns and to receive disaster-related updates and guidance. Walmart's emergency operations center also worked with the US Department of Homeland Security's operations center to assure the availability of essential goods. Local stores froze prices on such items as flashlights and bottled water, and they arranged distribution of 1,500 truckloads of products and 100,000 free meals to hurricane victims at a time when government provisions were still scarce. They also worked with local police to assist with search-and-rescue efforts and, later, safe travel to and from work. They also collaborated with the American Red Cross in searching evacuation centers for unaccounted-for employees.

Other firms did much the same in the aftermath of other disasters. Following the 9.2-magnitude earthquake in Alaska in 1964, for example, Safeway stores lowered their prices on orange juice and other items in high demand, and limited the number of units that a customer could purchase.

In the aftermath of Chile's earthquake in 2010 and Japan's in 2011, some retailers froze essential-product prices for months.[18]

During Chile's rescue of thirty-three miners trapped by a cave-in in 2010, several American companies stepped forward in complementary partnerships with public officials. While the country's Minister of Mines concentrated on drilling rescue shafts to extract the stranded miners, Aramark gave food, Apple donated phones, Pennsylvania drillers contributed equipment, and UPS delivered the drills to the remote site of the entrapment.[19]

The Siam Cement Group, Thailand's third-largest private enterprise and a sprawling conglomerate in not only building materials but also chemicals, hotels, and property management, took comparable action in 2011. When the Chao Phraya River inundated Bangkok in 2011, where so many of the company's operations were concentrated, its top executives took on the role of crisis managers, working to rescue thousands of employees from the rising waters and moving hundreds of offices and products to drier land.[20]

Siam Cement booked a thousand rooms in nearby hotels for stranded staff; instructed 6,000 employees to work from home; dispatched teams to help employees whose homes had been flooded; distributed 20,000 relief kits along with life jackets, mobile toilets, and small boats; and delivered more than a million sandbags to the Bangkok region. Later, as relief turned to recovery, Siam Cement mounted training programs for home repair, discounted construction materials, and helped reconstruct three hundred day-care centers and schools.

In the wake of the Ebola outbreak in West Africa in 2014, other companies did much the same. Henry Schein Inc., an American supplier of healthcare products, for instance, gave a million dollars' worth of masks, gloves, gowns, coveralls, sanitizers, and other protective gear to thwart the epidemic's spread. Firestone built a treatment center when a nearby hospital would not accept Ebola patients, Unilever gave several million bars of soap, Coca-Cola used its distribution network to dispense medical supplies; and FedEx delivered urgently required medical supplies and protective equipment. Companies acted informally alongside public agencies in the wake of a calamity, each providing what it was most capable of delivering and complementing the others.[21]

The multipronged disaster response by Siam Cement, Henry Schein, UPS, and other companies worldwide should actually come as no surprise since, as we have seen, the trend lines in hazard frequency, severity, and costliness are rising worldwide. The disruptions are directly affecting more company operations, and traditional sources of relief and recovery are increasingly falling short.

Businesses will face increasing pressure for donations and partnerships as the funding gap widens even more in future years. It is likely that directors, executives, and managers will seek to become even more involved in disaster recovery and will want to learn more about how to do this efficiently, especially where their companies operate and their employees and customers live. The result should be of value to the giver and the recipient, benefitting both the enterprise and society. Business leaders have indicated that their contributions are not just about their own reputation but also reflect their desire to help those most in need.[22]

CORPORATE GIVING FOR DISASTER RELIEF

1. Corporate giving is likely to play an increasing role in the disaster relief and recovery of communities and countries, given that the costs of calamities are likely to continue to grow and further outstrip traditional sources of disaster assistance in the years ahead.
2. Firms concentrate their financial and material donations in the aftermath of a public disaster on regions where companies already have operating footprints, local knowledge, and established partnerships.
3. Compared with disaster assistance from traditional sources, financial and material aid from business is likely to come more quickly, be more aptly targeted, and thus be more consequential for those most in need.
4. As more companies are bolstering their own catastrophic risk-management mindsets and practices, they are simultaneously learning how to build their capacities to more effectively assist others facing disruptions of their own.

PART IV

Reaching Vital Stakeholders

We have witnessed how large American and European firms have dealt with and learned from catastrophic events. We have seen how they have expanded their deliberative thinking and developed enterprise-wide risk-management practices, from the governing board to front-line managers, to better anticipate, mitigate, and recover from a growing number of high-consequence events.

It has been a long and ongoing march. As firms have become more adept in the art of anticipation and comeback, disruptive forces have also been expanding, with corporate risks becoming more costly and more impactful. And crises are likely to emerge more rapidly, making fast reaction a necessity. The process is likely to resemble a game of cat-and-mouse, firms adopting measures in the wake of one shock only to be challenged anew by the next, making companies more resilient but never entirely secure.

In this repeated cycle of setback, learning, and mastery, companies have focused on strengthening their management mindsets and practices. Executives and their boards have given greater attention to defining their risk appetite and risk tolerance, communicating their preferences to division managers. They have also directed more attention to their relationships and reputations with outside constituencies, including customers, regulators, creditors, and investors. We thus turn in part IV to how firms have worked with external stakeholders concerned with and affected by company disruptions.

First, risk disclosure has become a standard for publicly traded companies since the US Securities and Exchange Commission added a requirement that they do so annually. This move toward more risk transparency is one of the DISRUPT drivers we discussed in the opening chapter. In chapter 9 we study the annual risk disclosures of the hundred S&P 500 firms where we interviewed directors, executives, and managers. We find that their risk reporting has doubled in length during the past ten years. And companies warn of a surprising source of disruption: governmental actions took top billing among all the risks that they disclosed to their shareholders.

Second, we look at the role the government plays not only as a source of risk to firms but also as a risk manager. In chapter 10, we report that public regulations often stress business leaders. Inadvertently failing to comply with regulations cannot only damage their company's reputation but even shut down its operations. At the same time, government has become an important risk manager, working to reduce the perils companies face by lowering their exposure to external shocks, providing data to help them build resilience, and aiding the recovery process when disaster strikes.

Third, we consider institutional investors and the impact of company risks on the value of their company holdings. Chapter 11 looks at how adverse events have depressed company value among all firms in the S&P 500. Investors seek to be informed of the risks that companies in their portfolio confront, and company directors and executives have often warned them of the major risks facing their enterprise. Deliberative thinking and management practices have become more important for companies, and investors have become less forgiving when directors, executives, and managers revert to simplified heuristics and behavioral biases in reaching decisions. Restoration of company value for investors in the wake of a catastrophic stock price setback can take several years or longer.

We conclude *Mastering Catastrophic Risk* in chapter 12 by categorizing an array of shortcomings that business leaders have exhibited in dealing with extreme events, and then proposing steps to reduce the likelihood and the impacts of large-scale disruptions in the future. We then provide a practical checklist for action that should be of interest to those in charge of leading some of the world's largest corporations—and virtually any enterprise or organization facing an increasingly uncertain and turbulent environment.

Disclosing Threats

The data breach we experienced was significant and went undetected
for several weeks.

—TARGET CORPORATION, *following a massive cyberattack in 2013*

Black Friday, the day after Thanksgiving, has long been deemed the beginning of the holiday shopping season when major retailers open their doors
early for discounted offerings. Next comes Cyber Monday, the largest online
shopping day of the year. The cash flowing through retail registers can be
enormous: upward of $50 billion or more over the four-day shopping spree.

A nightmare haunting all retail stores is that something goes terribly
wrong, crushing the firm's holiday revenue or even damaging its reputation. For those running Target Corporation in 2013, that nightmare became
reality.

One of America's premier retailers, Target opened its first store in
Minnesota in 1962, and by 2012 it was drawing annual revenues of more
than $70 billion from 1,800 locations in the United States alone. *Forbes* mag-
azine had ranked Target, the second largest American store-system behind
Walmart, as one of the world's most valuable brands.

As with any firm operating on such a scale, Target faced an array of
potential disruptors of its business. Cybersecurity was not necessarily one
of its major concerns in 2013, but that was about to change. Hackers had
installed malware—software intended to damage, disable, or access a firm's
computer system—in Target's security and payments system to launch what
would become at that time the largest retail cyberattack in US history.

Target had earlier engaged a contractor to work on the heating, ventilation, and air-conditioning of its many stores, and the retailer had given the contractor access to its computer network so that the outside firm could remotely track the temperature and energy consumption of Target's stores. That interdependency, one of our DISRUPT drivers, came with a significant downside. The contractor had inadvertently opened an unsecured back door into Target's computer network, allowing hackers to roam freely. Unfettered, they installed malware that copied customers' credit card information from store registers whenever a purchase was scanned and the card was swiped for payment.

The company was not entirely blindsided by the breach. Target had already invested $1.6 million in malware detection, hiring a team of security specialists in Bangalore, India, to keep a twenty-four-hour watch on Target's network. They had standing instructions to notify security at the company's operations center in Minneapolis if anything looked the least bit suspicious. During Black Friday weekend, the hackers began uploading their malicious software. With its installation, they copied company-held credit card data initially to outside servers, first in the United States, and then to Russia, where the credit data was peddled on the black market. The Bangalore team spotted something amiss in the system on Saturday, November 30, 2013, and alerted the security team in Minneapolis.[1]

But then, nothing happened. The Minneapolis security team did not react, nor did it inform company executives of the breach. Nearly two weeks later, on December 12, the US Justice Department warned Target of what looked like suspicious activity in its credit card files. Company executives met with Justice Department and Secret Service officials the following day, and they brought in a team of outside experts for an independent investigation. Yet it was not until December 15 that the firm finally excised the malware from most of its registers in US stores—and by then, the damage had been done.[2]

A staggering number of Target's Black Friday shoppers had been compromised. The hackers had extracted the credit card information of some 40 million customers, and quickly moved several million of those accounts to the black market for a going rate of $100 per card. The 40 million stolen cards could ultimately fetch as much as $4 billion.[3]

In additional to reputational issues, the financial losses were significant. The company would spend $60 million over the next two months mopping up the breach, and litigation predictably followed. The company reached a $67 million settlement in 2015 with a number of financial organizations led by Visa; a $39 million settlement with MasterCard; and a $10 million class-action settlement, requiring that the firm hire a chief security officer.

Congress summoned Target executives to testify, where they publicly admitted that they and their staff had simply missed the warning signs. Some of the executives themselves would not survive the crisis. Beth Jacob, the company's most senior technology officer, resigned in February 2014, and Gregg Steinhafel, the chief executive and board chair, followed suit three months later. According to Target's 2017 annual report, the company incurred $292 million in cumulative expenses since the data breach, partially offset by insurance recoveries of $90 million.[4]

Congress feared that another nightmare-cum-reality could happen again to millions of retail customers at Target or elsewhere, and it turned its spotlight on company security risks more broadly. Six separate committees scheduled hearings, and legislation was introduced that would increase the power of the Federal Trade Commission to oversee company data security and require companies to notify customers when their identity had been stolen, although that bill did not pass.[5]

TRANSPARENCY

Target's cyberbreach spawned both public demand and private determination not only to improve digital security but also to provide greater transparency into the nature of the risks and what companies were doing in response. Customers, creditors, and investors wanted to know more about risks to which they were subject from the companies where they buy, lend, or invest. This increasing demand for corporate transparency, another driver of DISRUPT, had also turned into regulatory reality.

The United States had already been pressing for greater customer-focused visibility in financial services. The Consumer Financial Protection Bureau, for instance, was established in 2011 to foster greater "transparency for mortgages, credit cards, and other consumer financial products and services." It publishes the number of consumer complaints it has received about commercial banks, credit unions, debt collectors, and other financial firms.

It named names, cautioning consumers who cared to visit its public website about underperforming companies.[6]

Greater investor- and creditor-focused transparency had come to all business sectors in 2005, at least for publicly traded firms, brought to the fore by the federal government. That year, the US Securities and Exchange Commission required companies listed on a stock exchange to disclose their current and potential risks in their annual 10-K report. Distinct from the glossy annual reports to stockholders, the 10-K must include a summary of a company's business results, how its directors and executives are paid, and an audited financial statement. In the newly required section 1A of the 10-K filing, companies must also disclose details on the company's hazards—defined as the most significant factors that make the firm's stock offering speculative or risky. While one might expect that investors and creditors would like to know not only about such risks but also what companies are doing about them, companies have almost universally opted to describe the risks with little reference to any risk-mitigation measures that they may have undertaken.[7]

Consider Target's 2012 official 10-K disclosure in section 1A, early in 2013, before the security breach:

> We have a program in place to detect and respond to data security incidents. To date, all incidents we have experienced have been insignificant. If we experience a significant data security breach or fail to detect and appropriately respond to a significant data security breach, we could be subject to costly government enforcement actions and private litigation and our reputation could suffer.

Though Target's formal disclosure here clearly turned out to overstate its detection and response capabilities, its reference to the litigation and reputational threats were prescient. Investors and creditors were cautioned, even though at the time the company correctly stated that "[to] date, all incidents we have experienced have been insignificant."[8]

A year later, Target disclosed the enormity of its Black-Friday-weekend nightmare:

> Until the fourth quarter of 2013, all incidents we experienced were insignificant. The Data Breach we experienced was significant and went undetected for several weeks. We experienced weaker than expected

U.S. Segment sales immediately following the announcement of the Data Breach, and we are currently facing more than 80 civil lawsuits filed on behalf of guests, payment card issuing banks and shareholders. In addition, state and federal agencies, including State Attorneys General, the Federal Trade Commission and the SEC, are investigating events related to the Data Breach, including how it occurred, its consequences and our responses. Those claims and investigations may have an adverse effect on how we operate our business and our results of operations. If we experience additional significant data security breaches or fail to detect and appropriately respond to significant data security breaches, we could be exposed to additional government enforcement actions.[9]

DOUBLING DISCLOSURES

The company risk disclosures required by the SEC in form 10-K provide a useful window into corporate transparency for not only external stakeholders but also for the curious public, even if the disclosures may not fully capture the many hazards that can abound. To peer through that window, we studied the 1A sections in the 10-K reports of the one hundred S&P 500 firms where we interviewed directors, executives, and managers, and analyzed the data for both 2007 and 2014.[10]

We asked how companies prepare their disclosure in section 1A, and we learned that the reported risks are typically assembled through collaboration among the firm's legal staff, led by the general counsel, the risk manager, and company executives. They reported that the disclosure had forced them to think not only about their firm's well-known hazards but also its more nascent risks. The 10-K filing has spurred more deliberative thinking over a fuller spectrum of a firm's risk.

In fact, companies almost doubled the length of their annual 1A sections from 4,300 words on average in 2007 to 8,500 words in 2014. To appreciate the nature of the increase, an average book page such as the one you are now reading contains some 400 words. The typical company risk report in 2014 was equivalent to about twenty book-length pages, almost double the number in 2007.

At the extreme, consider the disclosures of a financial institution and a chemical company. The financial institution's 1A disclosure had 15,000 words in 2007. The company found reason to lengthen it in 2011 to 22,000 words, and by 2014 to 28,000. But even at the low end, texts have grown markedly. The chemical company used just 300 words in 2007, but had expanded to more than 1,500 by 2014. And symptomatic again of how setbacks can be the incubator of deliberative invention, Target Corporation's 1A disclosure a year after its historic cyberbreach doubled in length compared to a year before the disaster.

Indirect evidence suggests that greater company disclosure is indeed valued by investors—if not necessarily serving consumers who presumably devote fewer hours to reviewing company 10-Ks before buying from them or giving credit card numbers to them. One study, for example, reported that companies with higher-quality risk disclosures enjoyed higher returns and greater share value than firms that were less revealing.[11]

On the other hand, another study found that more risk disclosure is in fact correlated with more company hazards. Drawing on predisclosure proxies for company risk, the study's authors reported that the higher the imputed actual risks, the greater the company's risk disclosures. And then, the authors confirmed that the greater disclosures of the risks led to greater volatility in the companies' stock prices. This finding implies that investors do indeed find meaningful signals in such disclosures, despite the challenge of translating qualitative information into investment decisions. The 1A reports, for instance, normally include no estimate of the amount of expected impact of a given risk on the firm's earnings, nor the likelihood that a given risk will become an actual disruption during the coming year. Still, the evidence indicates that investors do make use of the disclosed information in ways that make sense.[12]

A SURPRISING SOURCE OF RISK

With several hundred 1A risk disclosures in hand, we set about classifying company risks into twenty-one buckets, ranging from capital structures and intellectual property to operational threats and international hazards (our procedure is described in Appendix 2).

Since natural disasters, terrorist incidents, and cyberattacks have been among the most visible and most documented sources of company hazards in recent years, we anticipated that these events, grouped under the category *disaster risk*, would be mentioned with the greatest frequency. However, in reviewing the contents of section 1A disclosures, a surprising factor emerged as the top risk.

Government action—defined as public policies, regulations, and decisions that affect the way a company conducts its business—is the most extensively referenced source of company risk. And this holds true not just among financial service firms where it might be expected but also among companies in most other sectors as well. Moreover, it prevailed in 2007, just before the financial crisis, and in 2011 and again in 2014.

Other, more expected sources of hazard also appeared in many of the 10-K reports, just less extensively than government actions. In 2007, the other sources included legal issues, at 12 percent of what companies reported; international threats and capital structures at 10 percent; competition and accounting hazards, both at 7 percent; and disasters and reputational threats at 6 percent. Fewer than 5 percent of the reported dangers fell in a host of other domains, including perils associated with operations, suppliers, acquisitions, intellectual property, credit risk, capital expenditure, labor, customers, investments, and key personnel.

Of the twenty-one separate sources of risk-related measures that we tracked in the 10-K reports, government action is also the only source that firms reported as significantly increasing from 2007 to 2014, from 15 percent of the cited threats to 20 percent. Other sources moved around more modestly, some down and some up. Legal risks decreased, from 12 percent in 2007 to 6 percent in 2014. International threats and capital risks both increased, from 10 to 12 percent and 8 to 11 percent, respectively, over this seven-year period, keeping in mind that the overall length of the 1A section had doubled over this period.

Firms in the financial sector were especially likely to cite risks related to government actions, such as the additional regulations that emerged in the aftermath of the 2008–2009 financial crisis. New legislation in the United States—the Dodd–Frank Wall Street Reform and Consumer Protection Act of 2010—and abroad, the tightened capital requirement issued by the Basel Committee on Banking Supervision in 2011, required banks and to some extent large insurers to increase their liquidity and decrease their leverage. Yet government actions are the number-one target of risk identification for companies in all ten major industry sectors we looked at except for consumer staples, where it ranked second, and telecommunications, where it stood third among the twenty-one categories of risk. Finally, it is noteworthy that calamities—including natural disasters, terrorist attacks, and technological accidents—play a relatively modest role in what companies report that they most worry about, despite occasional headlines to the contrary.

Government as a company-cited risk factor is not due to just the hazards that come with public regulations. According to those we interviewed, it also stemmed from the government's own riskiness. Several executives whom we interviewed expressed a fear about the federal government's solvency: Might the United States itself be at risk? Standard & Poor's had lowered its long-term sovereign credit rating on the US government one notch, from AAA to AA+ in 2011, and Moody's Investors Services and Fitch both moved their US ratings to a "negative" outlook in 2011. These downgrades by the premier credit rating agencies stemmed from the relatively high level of government debt and the continued inability of Congress to reach an agreement on spending measures, revenue streams, and debt limits. A further downgrade could radically affect financial markets and economic conditions, and impair the value of US debt obligations held by many of the large corporations. Like long-term climate change, a further downgrading of the government's creditworthiness—or, heaven forbid, a default—could not only threaten company operations but even imperil the firm's existence.

RATING AGENCIES ON ENTERPRISE RISK MANAGEMENT

Just as section 1A of company 10-Ks opened the door for corporate risk disclosure, and just as companies have increasingly availed themselves of the opportunity to do so, rating agencies have also ramped up their independent appraisals of company risks for investors and creditors who worry not only about company returns and repayment but also the management and governance features that can harm both. One of the more prominent and influential agencies to have done so is Standard and Poor's itself.

Standard and Poor's set forward a risk-appraisal framework for evaluating companies in 2012, building on an assessment of enterprise risk management of insurance companies launched earlier as a pilot. Its Management and Governance Credit Factors for Corporate Entities and Insurers introduced a set of nonfinancial qualitative metrics to rate corporations on their risk-management capabilities on the premise that these factors have become important for assessing an enterprise's creditworthiness. Today, they are part of how S&P determines a company's rating: firms that are seen as more capable of overseeing and managing their risks are deemed more creditworthy.[13]

To calculate a company's management and governance risks, Standard and Poor's metrics include strategic direction, risk appetite, and execution capability. With each factor rated positive, neutral, or negative, S&P classifies companies in one of three risk categories:

1. A positive score if management has successfully instituted comprehensive policies that effectively identify, monitor, select, and mitigate key risks, and has disclosed its tolerances for each to key stakeholders.
2. A neutral score if management has a basic set of standards and tolerances in place but may not have fully developed its risk-management capabilities.
3. A negative score if management has few defined standards and little risk-management capability.

Standard and Poor's also questions whether the company's risk measures meet several risk-management benchmarks:

- Does the enterprise regularly identify and assess the impact of critical strategic risks?
- Has the enterprise determined limits for acceptable levels of risk, and if so, how are they enforced?
- Does the enterprise hold accountable specific individuals for oversight of the most critical risks the enterprise faces, and if so, what are the rewards (consequences) for success (failure)?
- Does the enterprise employ an effective risk-based approach to strategic decisions?
- Has the enterprise effectively communicated to employees, owners, and other key stakeholders its tolerance for risk and commensurate expectations for earnings volatility?

Standard and Poor's extended its appraisal to the governing board itself. To what extent do directors provide oversight of the firm's risks, risk appetite, and risk tolerance? Is the board independent of management in ways that allow it to exercise vigilant oversight of company risk-taking? The rating agency offers two overall classifications of companies that fall short of ideal governance practices:

A neutral score if the board provides appropriate oversight of key enterprise risks, compensation, and/or conflicts of interest; the board is supportive of management but retains control as the final decision-making authority for strategic matters.

A negative score if the board provides limited oversight and scrutiny of management, as evidenced by compensation practices that promote outsize risk-taking or that tolerate unmanaged conflicts of interest and/or inadequate succession planning for senior management.

While Standard and Poor's and other credit raters such as Moody's and Fitch speak primarily to major lenders, two governance raters, Institutional Shareholder Services and Glass Lewis & Co., speak more to institutional investors, and they too have introduced criteria for appraising company riskiness. Institutional Shareholder Services, for instance, rates companies' overall "governance risk" relative to other publicly traded companies, taking into account whether members of the board's audit and compensation committees are independent of management. Glass Lewis rates a number of comparable factors, including whether the board discloses how it oversees company risk and whether directors had indeed monitored a significant environmental or social risk faced by the firm. When companies fell far short of these and other governance-risk criteria, both Institutional Shareholder Services and Glass Lewis have recommended voting against their directors at the annual shareholders meeting.[14]

Overall, expanded risk disclosure has become more of a norm among large publicly traded firms in America. For over a decade now, the US Securities and Exchange Commission has furnished a formal vehicle for doing so, and credit and governance raters have amplified and evaluated not only what threats companies do in fact disclose but also what companies have in place to manage them.

DISCLOSING THREATS

1. Improved risk disclosure practices by publicly traded companies have led to greater corporate transparency and reduced asymmetries in the information available to company managers, customers, creditors, and investors.

2. Companies across virtually all industry sectors have shared more information about their risks in recent years, doubling the reporting of enterprise hazards in the risk section of their annual 10-K reports.

3. Of the twenty-one different sources of risk discussed in the 10-K reports, government actions have received significantly more attention across industry sectors than any other risk area.

4. Rating agencies now offer independent appraisals of how well companies are capable of thinking deliberatively and their risk practices in place to prevent or surmount setbacks. While those appraisals are not quantitative in nature, they shed light on good practices and top performers, and indicate those companies whose risk practices are not up to par.

A Two-Edged Sword

Any changes in regulations, the imposition of additional regulations, or the enactment of any new or more stringent legislation . . . could adversely affect our business and results of operations.

—Guess Inc., *10-K Report, 2015*

We now take a closer look at the roles of government both as a source of perceived corporate risk and also as risk manager. Our analysis reveals that companies give more space in their risk disclosure statements to government actions than any other source of concern. A substantial percentage of section 1A in the 10-K filings is devoted to the risks associated with public regulations and other actions by government.

But while the government can be viewed as a disruptor, it plays a role in mitigating future risks. It requires companies to commit time and money to comply with new rules or enforcement of existing regulations, but these same regulations have prodded companies to be more transparent about their risks and to take actions to reduce them.

The rules faced by large companies are many, and the costs of compliance can add up. The annual 10-K disclosure by clothing retailer Guess Inc. in 2015 referenced the multifaceted perils of government relations felt by many business firms:

Any changes in regulations, the imposition of additional regulations, or the enactment of any new or more stringent legislation including those related to health care, taxes, transportation and logistics, privacy, environmental issues, trade, product safety or employment and labor, could adversely affect our business and results of operation. . . . In addition, if we fail to comply with applicable regulations, particularly wage and hour laws, we could be subject to government enforcement action and class action civil litigation, which could adversely affect our results of operations.[1]

Yet public policies can also level the playing field, stimulate deliberative thinking, and otherwise reduce the hazards that a firm faces. We begin our exploration of government as a two-edged sword with a brief chronicle of the destabilizing elements of government regulation, as identified by many S&P 500 firms in their publicly available 10-Ks, and then discuss examples of legislation and government programs that protect companies against some of the most extreme risks.

THE PRICE OF NEW REGULATIONS

Though intended to reduce company risks, regulatory measures that emerged out of large-scale disasters like the 2008–2009 financial crisis are sometimes perceived by companies as only adding to their risks. The burden of complying with the new rules is deemed to outweigh the purported business benefits.

A vice president for risk with a pharmaceutical company highlighted the challenges his organization faced:

What we continue to be concerned about . . . is unintended consequences of this change, of legislative or procedural changes where folks in the regulatory or governmental arena make a change that's supposed to do one thing and they can't see the negative impact that it's going to have elsewhere. So we spend a lot of time trying to be very careful about articulating with our government partners—and with all of our partners—[that they] think about it carefully this way because "here are some elements that maybe you're not seeing."

Company reactions to several of the most consequential legislative interventions of recent years, including the Sarbanes–Oxley Act of 2002, the Dodd–Frank Act of 2010, and the Affordable Care Act of 2010, illustrate the point. It should be noted, however, that one or more of these acts may be revised or even rescinded in future years.

FINANCIAL DISCLOSURE

Arguably one of the most impactful pieces of federal legislation—requiring more corporate disclosure than any since the 1930s—has been the Sarbanes–Oxley Act of 2002, formally termed the Public Company Accounting Reform and Investor Protection Act by its Senate proponents, or SOX for short. Intended to strengthen the accuracy and reliability of company reporting to investors, the act required firms to disclose more facts and assure less fraud. That might seem like a no-brainer for most—after all, who could disagree with the premise that it is fair for investors to know what they are investing in—but the close-up application of SOX would prove vexing for many firms.

Numerous business executives had opposed the bill before its passage, asserting that compliance with its many rulebooks would be difficult technically, time-consuming in practice, and could not help much in protecting investors from company malfeasance. Market reactions to the passage of SOX implied that there was some truth to the claims of more downside costs than upside benefits, at least among smaller publicly traded firms. The stock prices of young high-growth companies declined after the legislation's passage. More generally, the stock prices of firms that were slow to comply with SOX rose after passage while the stock prices of companies that appeared to have been managing their reported earnings before SOX fell after the legislation's passage. Former Federal Reserve Chairman Alan Greenspan articulated widely expressed company angst: "Sarbanes–Oxley has decreased U.S. competitive flexibility," he said, and was "proving unnecessarily burdensome" to regulated firms.[2]

Despite reservations by Greenspan and firms about the disruptive effects of SOX on company performance, Congress doubled-down after the financial crisis of 2008–2009. It authored the Dodd–Frank Wall Street Reform and Consumer Protection Act of 2010, commonly referenced as Dodd–Frank, imposing the most far-reaching disclosure rules since the Great Depression of the 1930s. It touched virtually every facet of the nation's financial services industry, and many companies asserted that the nearly four hundred new regulations stipulated in the act's 2,300 pages actually increased their performance risks, the opposite from of what Congress had intended. Among the complaints from financial service companies: new rules were promulgated with too little warning, the act was excessively enforced, liquidity requirements were too high, and limits on banking practices were too constraining.

The Bank of New York Mellon spelled out such risks in section 1A of its 2011 10-K report:

> U.S. regulatory agencies . . . cause changes that impact the profitability of our business activities and require that we change certain of our business practices and plans, including those relating to cross-selling our products and services. These changes could also expose us to additional regulatory costs and require us to invest significant management attention and resources to make any necessary changes, all of which could impact our profitability.[3]

In the view of other companies, the Dodd–Frank regulations had the potential of significantly negatively impacting on their ways of doing business. The investment management firm Legg Mason Inc., for instance, warned in section 1A of its 10-K report:

> The federal government has made, and has proposed further, significant changes to the regulatory structure of the financial services industry. . . . Any of these revisions could adversely affect our liquidity asset management business and our results of operations.

Even nonfinancial companies criticized Dodd–Frank for generating risk rather than reducing it. The forced changes flowing from this and other legislation, in the eyes of company managers, induced instability and hence more uncertainty. Retailer Macy's Inc., for instance, warned of such impacts in its 10-K in 2011: "Litigation or regulatory developments could adversely affect the Company's business or financial condition. The Company is subject to various federal, state and local laws, rules, regulations and initiatives, including laws and regulations with respect to the credit card industry including the Credit Card Act of 2009 and the Dodd–Frank Wall Street Reform and Consumer Protection Act of 2010."

THE AFFORDABLE CARE ACT

Among firms in the healthcare industry, whether making therapeutic products or selling medical services, health-reform regulations dominated their risk disclosures, especially those stemming from the Patient Protection and Affordable Care Act (ACA) of 2010. Many companies cited the heightened uncertainties associated with implementing the act. Aetna Inc., which markets healthcare insurance plans and related services, cautioned in its 10-K in 2011 of the risks it faced with ACA's becoming law the previous year:

> The federal and state governments continue to enact and seriously consider many broad-based legislative and regulatory measures that have materially impacted and will continue to materially impact various aspects of the health care system and our business. The political environment in which we operate remains uncertain. It is not possible to predict with certainty or eliminate the impact of additional fundamental public policy changes, including changes to health care reform that could adversely affect us.

Even non-healthcare companies viewed the Affordable Care Act as adversely impacting their business. For AutoZone, the nation's second largest seller of automotive parts and accessories, with more than 5,000 stores, the ACA might have seemed a secondary source of uncertainty, but its 10-K in 2010 warned: The Affordable Care Act "as well as other healthcare reform legislation being considered by Congress and state legislatures may have an impact on our business," and it "could be extensive."

COMPLIANCE DEFIANCE

Many companies, health and nonhealth alike, stressed the risks of inadvertently failing to comply with the new regulations. Most companies we interviewed reported that a reputation for integrity is regarded as critical, and that if a company did not freely and fully comply with regulations, its brand could suffer and its product sales and stock price could decline. AutoZone disclosed its anxieties along this line in its 2010 10-K report:

We believe our continued strong sales growth is driven in significant part by our brand name. The value in our brand name and its continued effectiveness in driving our sales growth are dependent to a significant degree on our ability to maintain our reputation for safety, high product quality, friendliness, service, trustworthy advice, integrity, and business ethics. Any negative publicity about these types of concerns may reduce demand for our merchandise. Failure to comply with ethical, social, product, labor and environmental standards, or related political considerations, could also jeopardize our reputation and potentially lead to various adverse consumer actions. Damage to our reputation or loss of consumer confidence for any of these or other reasons could have a material adverse effect on our results of operations and financial condition, as well as require additional resources to rebuild our reputation.

Failure to comply with regulations may not only damage company reputation but in some instances even shut down company operations. Oversight and action by the US Food and Drug Administration (FDA) posed one such brand threat. As an executive at a large healthcare company explained: "If we get into a situation where we have a product for which the FDA believes we have not done our due diligence or put the appropriate control measures or labeling in place, they wouldn't hesitate to shut that business down. They wouldn't hesitate to stop us from shipping that product. So when it comes to dealing with the FDA for us, they have pretty much carte blanche over us."

Actions by public regulators, such as the FDA, can also result in indirect risks to enterprises that depend on well-functioning supply chains. With just one weak link within a network of sources, for instance, production can grind to a halt. As an executive with a biotechnology firm stated: "If one of your suppliers is shut down by the FDA for safety issues, you can no longer supply your product. This might be fine for a short period of time, but what happens if it's a long-term key supplier? What else is out there to help us? Those things are typically not planned." Nor are they normally covered by business-interruption insurance.

Executives and managers with manufacturers and retailers dependent on sprawling supply and distribution chains outlined the many risks inherent in the multiple sources of regulation—from municipal zoning rules to antitrust laws—to which they and their networks were subject.

Many S&P 500 firms generate a significant portion of their revenues outside of the United States, and they and their partners are also subject to regulations of foreign jurisdictions. Third-party regulatory risk is of special concern, as failures by joint-venture and alliance partners abroad can result in business interruptions, and even direct costs if a multinational firm is penalized for the misbehavior of its partners. Moreover, the US Foreign Corrupt Practices Act of 1977 prohibits bribery of foreign officials for company gain. This too can translate into company concerns, since it is often difficult to monitor the activities of all suppliers a large corporation contracts with across a large number of countries, as warned the upscale retailer Abercrombie & Fitch in its 2011 10-K report: "As our business becomes more international in scope and we enter more countries internationally, the number of laws and regulations that we are subject to, as well as their scope and reach, increases significantly and heightens our risks."

Not surprisingly, those with responsibility for regulatory compliance have taken on an elevated stature in the company pyramid. A survey of eight hundred companies worldwide in 2016, for instance, found that their chief compliance officer reported directly to the chief executive or board of directors in nearly half of the firms. Four out of five companies reported that public regulation could have an adverse impact on their company strategies. The governing boards of a fifth of the firms had created an oversight committee on compliance and ethics. In a separate survey of some 1,400 chief executives in 2015, four out of five singled out public regulation as the foremost threat to their growth, exceeding political and social instability, exchange-rate volatility, cyberthreats, and climate change.[4]

The depth of concern was summarized by an executive of a large financial institution whom we interviewed:

[The] lack of coordination among the multiple regulators and the multiple regulatory streams is causing a significant challenge for the whole industry. It's one thing to cope with lessons learned after the financial crisis: we have to change the balance sheet; we have to change liquidity; we have to change capitalization; we have to change the way that we take risks. That's completely understandable. But it's another thing for five or six [or even] ten regulators to each say, "Okay, so here's my twenty conditions." And if you add up more than a hundred of the conditions we have to live with, there's a significant possibility that [they can turn out to] be mutually exclusive.

In summary, many firms see government regulations as a premier source of risk. This was true before the financial crisis of 2008–2009 and became even more so afterward. Though many directors, executives, and managers whom we interviewed applaud well-thought-out and effectively implemented regulations to protect consumers, many opposed other regulations. They were especially concerned with the uncertainty that comes when new regulations are created, old regulations rescinded, and ongoing regulations revised. As already noted, they also expressed a fear about the federal government itself, that is, whether the United States might itself be at risk.

THE SWORD'S OTHER EDGE

The US government, to its credit, was the first to alert Target about its massive cyberbreach; it did again with Yahoo and several other corporations that had been attacked without realizing it. In myriad other ways, public officials and policies have reduced rather than exacerbated company risk. The Clean Air Act of 1963, intended to strengthen programs for the prevention and abatement of air pollution, has improved the quality of health for all, including company directors, executives, managers—and employees.[5]

Despite the time and resource risks associated with the introduction of additional financial regulations from the Sarbanes–Oxley and Dodd–Frank acts, their new rules were targeted at preventing company malfeasance and excessive riskiness that would benefit all parties if well implemented. Investors, for example, had lost an estimated $900 billion from accounting frauds from 1997 to 2004, including enormous losses from the bankruptcies of Enron Corporation and WorldCom in 2001.[6]

More generally, well-enforced regulations may be essential in reducing the likelihood of another financial crisis that would again add to the downdrafts facing virtually all companies. By constraining excessive risk-taking of some reckless enterprises, government policies can reduce the risks for all. As captured by Michael Lewis in his book *The Big Short*, debt traders in the mid-2000s were anticipating that only a fraction of homeowners would default on their mortgages that had been bundled and sold to others, as normally happens. Their own rational calculus helped create systemic risks when the number of defaults by all traders rose far higher than expected. Those we interviewed said that the government should intervene to limit such correlated risks. And with that protection, companies can then better calibrate their own risk-taking. As explained by the chief risk officer of an investment bank:

> What we have done voluntarily is recognize more precisely the types of systemic risk to which we as an industry are subject, and the various manifestations of that, and the various ways that systemic risk occurs throughout the business and across its products. . . . We have become more attuned to the factors contributing to systemic risk and more determined that we will insulate ourselves to the extent possible from those factors, but also that we will attempt ourselves not to contribute to it. And that desire not to contribute to it may mean different decisions with respect to what products we would participate in than would have been the case precrisis.

Or consider large-scale terrorist attacks, nuclear accidents, and natural disasters. None of the directors, executives, and managers whom we interviewed even hinted that government agencies such as the Department of Homeland Security, the Federal Emergency Management Agency, or the Nuclear Regulatory Commission should not intervene when such calamities strike. And nobody found fault with government provision or guarantees of corporate insurability for the kinds of extreme events that private insurers avoided.

Disaster insurance financing has emerged as an exercise in public-private risk sharing for good reason. In the aftermath of the terrorist attacks in 2001, for instance, most insurance companies refused to continue to provide coverage against terrorism, unless required by law to do so, as in the case of workers' compensation. As a result, many corporations could not secure insurance against another attack at a price they believed reasonable for nearly a year after September 11, 2001. In 2002, the federal government established the Terrorism Risk Insurance Act, where private insurers cover the first layer of losses from a terrorist attack and the federal government then assists with higher claims, a public-private partnership that provides companies in the United States with up to $100 billion in insured coverage. The Terrorism Risk Insurance Act has been renewed several times, most recently in 2015 for another seven years. Now, the US Treasury is responsible for losses from a terrorist attack that exceed $60 billion.[7]

Similarly, in the aftermath of both Hurricanes Katrina and Sandy, the US Congress created special funds to assist recovery from uninsured losses (more than $150 billion from these two storms combined), and provided significant disaster aid again following Hurricanes Harvey, Irma, and Maria in 2017. A large portion of that public money went to rebuilding public infrastructure that corporations depend on to operate their business.

If a nuclear meltdown akin to the Fukushima disaster struck an American nuclear facility tomorrow, company leaders are likely to support analogous interventions. And indeed, the United States has shared the financial burdens of an accident with owners and operators of nuclear facilities for upward of sixty years. The Price-Anderson Nuclear Industries Indemnity Act of 1957 compensates nuclear power owners and operators for liability claims stemming from nuclear accidents. Congress has extended the act several times, making significant alterations, most recently in the Energy Policy Act of 2005, which extended the legislation through 2025. It established no-fault insurance in which the first $12 billion (as of 2017) is funded by the private sector, with the federal government coming to the rescue when claims run higher. Without this guarantee, utility companies had balked at building nuclear power plants.[8]

In any number of other areas as well, company directors, executives, and managers would applaud the government's reduction of corporate vagaries. Scientific research and development, for example, is inherently costly to firms since massive investments may not necessarily pay off. Offsetting that risk, a host of federal agencies support, conduct, and share the fruits of research and development, including the Army Corps of Engineers, Centers for Disease Control and Prevention, Department of Homeland Security, National Institutes of Health, National Science Foundation, National Aeronautics and Space Administration, National Oceanic and Atmospheric Administration, and Office of Naval Research. Government is thus seen from the corporate perch as a two-edged sword, a source of downside risks in some areas but a risk mitigator in others.

A Two-Edged Sword

1. The government is viewed by companies as a leading source of business risk.
2. Company failure to comply with regulations can damage not only a company's reputation but even shut down its operations.
3. Business leaders also view the government as playing a critical role in mitigating some risks their firms would not want to handle on their own.

Safeguarding Value

Character is much easier kept than recovered.

—Thomas Paine

Institutional investors seek as much as anyone to understand the risks that the companies in their portfolio face. After all, catastrophic risks can, overnight, destroy a huge fraction of a company's value—that is, investors' assets—and an existential risk can lead to the loss of the entire enterprise. Thus, among the many obligations of company directors and executives is to transparently inform investors of any speedbumps or serious roadblocks that may lie ahead. But what risks or events are likely to have a negative impact on the market value of a firm? And then, how long will it take for the stock price to bounce back, if ever?[1]

A UNITEDHEALTH SETBACK

Consider UnitedHealth Group Inc., one of America's largest healthcare companies, with revenue topping $189 billion in 2016 and employing more than 230,000 people in 2017. Some 1,300 institutional investors held shares in the company, valued at more than $190 billion in 2016. The ten largest holders each have multibillion-dollar stakes in UnitedHealth, as seen in Table 11.1. The ownership of the top shareholder alone, Vanguard Group, stood at $9.6 billion, more than enough to rivet its portfolio managers' attention on any disruptors that could reduce or destroy that value.

Table 11.1. Ten Largest Institutional Investor Holdings
in UnitedHealth Group, 2016

Institutional Investor	% Shares	$Billion Value
Vanguard Group Inc.	6.33	9.64
Fidelity Management & Research	5.86	8.93
State Street Corporation	4.69	7.14
Capital World Investors	4.36	6.64
Wellington Management Co.	4.16	6.33
Price (T. Rowe) Associates Inc.	3.46	5.27
BlackRock Institutional Trust Co.	2.85	4.33
Capital Research Global Investors	2.68	4.08
JP Morgan Chase & Company	2.55	3.88
ClearBridge Investments, LLC	2.38	3.61

SOURCE: Yahoo Finance; value as of December 30, 2016.

Large investors in UnitedHealth had plenty to cheer about in 2016–2017. During the twelve months ending on May 3, 2017, when the S&P 500 Index had risen 19 percent, UnitedHealth's stock price soared by 41 percent. But if sanguine then, the premier holders had far less to applaud a decade earlier, when company value had cratered.

New York attorney general Andrew Cuomo announced in February 2008 a wide-ranging investigation of health insurance companies to determine whether they had systematically overcharged patients for using doctors and hospitals outside their insurer's network. He issued sixteen subpoenas to the nation's largest insurance companies, including Aetna and Cigna. He also announced after a six-month investigation that he would be taking legal action against Ingenix, a subsidiary of UnitedHealth. Ingenix managed a database used by most major health insurance companies to set reimbursement rates for out-of-network medical expenses. The subsidiary had allegedly manipulated data in determining the rates for which insurers reimburse their clients for doctor and hospital visits. Insurers, as a result, paid out substantially less than they would otherwise have been obligated.

UnitedHealth executives dismissed the allegation at first, saying that Ingenix was using state-of-the-art data, drawn from more than a hundred health plans across the industry and based on more than a billion transactions. For investors, so far so good: UnitedHealth's share price did not budge.[2]

But on March 6, 2008, the New York attorney general issued new subpoenas to UnitedHealth and other insurers, now invoking the Martin Act, which authorizes both civil and criminal enforcement actions against publicly traded companies. UnitedHealth's stock plunged the next day and then nosedived. In just one ten-day trading period, the company's value contracted by more than a quarter. The failure of Lehman in September 2008 and the ensuing financial crisis did not help, and UnitedHealth shares that had traded as high as $49 in early 2008 could be acquired by March 2009 for less than $20.[3]

UnitedHealth reached a settlement with New York State in January 2009 that required the company to invest $50 million to create a new, independent database managed by a nonprofit organization. In the attorney general's words, "Our agreement with UnitedHealth removes the conflicts of interest that have been inherent in the consumer reimbursement system. This has been an industry-wide problem, and it demands an industry-wide reform. We commend UnitedHealth for leading the industry on this issue, and we encourage other insurers to follow suit." Two days later, UnitedHealth settled a class-action lawsuit for $350 million, with the funds distributed to physicians and patients who had been affected by the out-of-network payment system.[4]

UnitedHealth's market value had declined by three-fifths from $65 billion in late 2007 to $26 billion at the end of December 2008, thus removing $39 billion from investor portfolios, a catastrophic setback. Institutional holders lost 60 percent of the assets that they had been entrusted to grow for their customers. They no doubt wondered if they could still trust UnitedHealth with their clients' money. The reputational ripples ran deep, and it would take more than three years to restore investor confidence. It was not until April 2011 that UnitedHealth's stock price rebounded to its predisruption value.

Professional money managers who have come to dominate shareholding at most of the S&P's 500 companies do not look lightly on wealth-destroying surprises such as witnessed at UnitedHealth. Shareholders are unforgiving in their reactions to downward jolts in company value unless there is a persuasive plan for recovery and prevention in the future. This has had the effect of magnifying penalties for deficiencies in a company's deliberative thinking and risk practices.

Some disruptions emanate entirely from within the firm, with no one else to blame but its employees. This was evident in the wake of any number of management stumbles, as happened at United Airlines in 2017 when it forcibly removed a passenger already seated on a departing flight to make room for a flight-crew member. Shocked by the incident and the resulting firestorm of public criticism magnified by social media, investors swiftly removed more than a billion dollars from United's $20 billion market value. Actions perceived as small by the firm at the time can later result in alarming drops in its market value.[5]

VOLKSWAGEN'S DECEIT

Self-inflicted damage can also be the result of management malfeasance. Though some executives and directors may not know of the improper actions until they are made public by investigators, investors can still hold everyone at the top accountable. This was evident in the crisis that erupted in 2015 at Germany's Volkswagen Group (VW), one of the world's largest automakers.

VW admitted that it had installed "defeat devices" on some 550,000 vehicles with diesel engines sold in the United States since 2009. The illicit software detected when its vehicles were being tested for emissions—and then activated engine equipment to reduce their emissions of nitrous oxide, a well-known cause of respiratory disease. Once back on the road, the software instructed the engines to return to their normal levels of effluence, far exceeding legal limits. Volkswagen later admitted that it had installed similar software on 11 million other vehicles sold in Europe and elsewhere.[6]

The company promoted its diesel vehicles as both cost effective and environmentally sound, but in fact they gave off some forty times more nitrous oxide on the road than in a lab, far exceeding environmental regulations. Catalytic converters had been used to reduce nitrous oxide in regular gasoline engines for years, but they simply could not be made to succeed with diesel fuel. Studies estimated that VW's excess emissions from 2008 to 2015 would result in at least sixty premature deaths in the United States and 1,200 in Europe.[7]

When the deception came to light, company CEO Martin Winterkorn denied that he had authorized or even known of it. "It's incomprehensible why I wasn't informed early and clearly," he asserted during a public hearing in Berlin. "I would have prevented any type of deception or misleading of authorities." He attributed the deception and misdirection to "the terrible mistakes of a few people." A leading German newspaper reported that "a few people" might actually be more than two dozen, that at least thirty VW managers had known about the deceit for years (a claim the company denied). The head of VW for America, Michael Horn, was even blunter: "We have totally screwed up," he said to a New York gathering. "Our company was dishonest with the EPA, and the California Air Resources Board and with all of you."[8]

Under siege, Volkswagen's chief executive resigned in September 2015, and then in July 2016, state attorneys general from New York, Massachusetts, and Maryland challenged VW's initial defense that the emissions deception had been engineered in secret by a few midlevel executives. They termed VW's decision, in the words of a reporter, an "orchestrated fraud that lasted more than a decade, involved dozens of engineers and managers and reached deep into the company's boardroom."[9]

Drawing on newly revealed VW documents, *The New York Times* wrote that "the emissions issue was the main agenda for a 2007 meeting attended by Matthias Müller, the current chief executive. . . . A presentation for the meeting detailed plans to conceal excess emissions of diesel cars in the United States, including the so-called defeat device at the center of the crime."[10]

Board members denied their own culpability. VW director Olaf Lies, who also served as the economy minister for the German state of Lower Saxony, which owned 20 percent of the corporation asserted that company executives and managers "who allowed this to happen, or who made the decision to install this software" had acted criminally—but that he and his fellow board members had only learned illegal actions "shortly before the media did." He plaintively asked why the board wasn't informed earlier about the problems.[11]

The replacement CEO, Matthias Müller, remained at the helm through 2017 despite further regulatory, media, and legal accusations. But he removed seven of the company's top ten executives, and dismissed or suspended a number of engineers and managers, including the head of brand development and several directors of research and development where the illicit software had been engineered.

In the wake of the disastrous revelations, the company posted an annual loss of $1.8 billion, the worst-ever financial performance in its eight decades of operations. It set aside $18 billion to resolve customer claims in the United States, and it announced that it would repurchase or repair all of the affected vehicles by 2018.

The crisis took an immediate toll on the carmaker's market value. VW's stock price plunged 17 percent on the first trading day after the existence of the defeat device became publicly known, and on the next trading day, by another 17 percent. In the eighteen months after the deception first became publicly known in April 2015, VW's share price declined by nearly half, from a high of €250 on March 16, 2015, to €92 on October 2, 2015, as seen in Figure 11.1.

In aftermath of the self-inflicted crisis, Volkswagen converted production from diesel-drive power trains to electric vehicles. Its "Together—Strategy 2025" called for the launch of more than thirty battery-powered models over the next ten years, anticipating that green models could sell 2 to 3 million vehicles annually, up to a quarter of the firm's passenger cars. It committed more than €10 billion to focusing on environmentally friendly technology. And it appointed former German constitutional judge Christine Hohmann-Dennhardt to serve as its director of "integrity and legal affairs."[12]

Despite the recovery efforts, investors had lost €60 billion that they had yet to recover more than two years after the company's self-inflicted

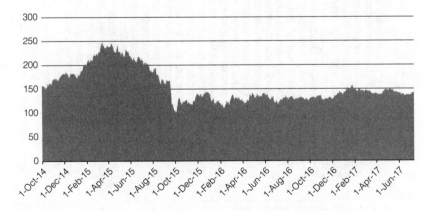

Figure 11.1 Volkswagen Share Price on the Frankfurt Stock Exchange, 2014–2017 (in euros)
SOURCE: Google Finance.

catastrophe. And though the board survived, the VW chief executive and others did not. Investor reactions to unexpected downdrafts of this magnitude extend not only to massive selloffs but also to executive ousters. Rarely are directors so penalized, but executives have seen their careers cut short, even if they have plausibly claimed that they had not been aware of the malfeasance of their subordinates. Disruptions can hit the top line first.

EXECUTIVE AND DIRECTOR REMUNERATION

Executive compensation has come to increasingly depend on the continuous growth of investor value. When a company's share price plummets in the wake of a great setback, market value and executive pay will decrease significantly. Conversely, when share price soars, investor wealth and executive income will follow suit.

As a result, company executives have become more directly attuned to disruptions that can cut into their own personal income. This can be seen in the changing composition of pay for the top seven executives of forty-five large American manufacturers from 1982 to 2016, as displayed in Figure 11.2. Until 1998, a majority of their compensation had been in the form of a fixed salary, but for the past two decades, most executives have become focused

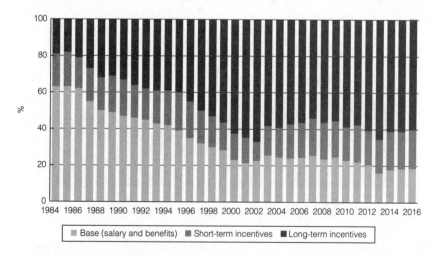

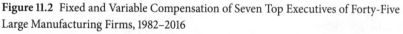

Figure 11.2 Fixed and Variable Compensation of Seven Top Executives of Forty-Five Large Manufacturing Firms, 1982–2016
SOURCE: Aon Hewitt, 1982–2017, and the authors; benefits not in 2013–2016 data.

on long-term incentive pay, largely in the form of stock options, that depend much upon a company's share price. Without a perilous setback, executive remuneration goes up as company value goes up. When a setback cuts that value, executives can end up with a significantly smaller paycheck.

It should be noted, however, that an unintended side-effect of stock-option-based executive pay is to treat huge setbacks as little different from lesser crises, a product of the asymmetry built into stock options: If the value of an option has sunk to zero, as likely would have happened to executive options in the cases chronicled here, then additional disruptions have no additional adverse impact on executives' pay. Their stock options are worth zero whatever the further setbacks.

It should also be kept in mind that since many managers outside the executive suite are also compensated partly in stock, catastrophic risks will be personally felt by them as well. The same is true of corporate directors, who are increasingly compensated in shares, not just fees, for their service. Three-quarters of the directors of the S&P 500 companies in 2016 received a majority of their compensation in stock-based pay, though largely via grants of stock rather than options to purchase stock. Across the S&P 500, just 38 percent of director compensation was in cash, while 54 percent came in the form of stock grants and 6 percent in stock options. This has the fortunate effect of incentivizing directors more symmetrically than executives: a hazard that leads to a 20 percent drop in a company's value cuts into the directors' own wealth twice as much as does a 10 percent setback. Directors thus have greater financial inducements than in the past to help prevent events that can severely depress a firm's market value.[13]

SEVERE STOCK PRICE DROPS

Given the gearing of pay for directors, executives, and managers around company disruptions, business leaders have become more incentivized to give greatest attention to the disruptions that have the greatest impact on their firm's market value. Knowing the sources of the largest setbacks can thus serve as pragmatic guidance for those most responsible for avoiding them.

To that end, we studied stock prices of S&P 500 firms focusing on disruptive events that resulted in a value loss of at least a fifth more than their industry generally experienced immediately after the disruption. We identified 20 percent–plus changes in stock price for individual companies over a short ten-trading-day period relative to changes in their overall industry average.[14]

We focused on daily movements in stock prices for all firms in the S&P 500 over the period January 1, 2000, to December 31, 2011. For industry groupings, we followed ten major-sector classifications of companies in the S&P 500 index and the twenty-one risk categories that we have already discussed in chapter 9 on risk disclosure. Across this decade we identified 2,110 instances of price drops of 20 percent or more compared with industry peers among the S&P 500 firms, and we have sought to identify their immediate causes. In conducting this analysis, we learned that more than 28 percent of the losses—599—came in the immediate wake of quarterly or annual earnings announcements without evidence that they stemmed from any specific risk factor, and we excluded these from our analysis.

The three most frequent drivers of the precipitous losses in company value were reputation and marketing, operations, and acquisitions. *Reputation and marketing*: risks related to the firm's brand, reputation, image, product pricing, and market share (they represented about 12.6 percent of all price drops); *operations*: risks associated with mismanagement or unforeseen shortfalls in the internal operation of a business, including production and manufacturing (12.2 percent of the price drops); *acquisitions*: risks stemming from all phases of a major acquisition (9.9 percent of the price drops). The adverse stock-price disruptors are clustered in a relatively small number of risk sources: the top three account for a third of the 20-percent-plus downdrafts, the top five for half, and the top ten—including personnel events and changes in capital structure and government actions—were responsible for nearly four-fifths of sharp price declines. Here we also find that the number of large downdrafts in stock prices of the firms where we interviewed rose five-fold from 2000–2006 to 2007–2011 as a result of government policies or actions.

What was most notable from our analysis was the relative paucity of sharp declines in stock prices in the wake of natural disasters, terrorist attacks, and technological accidents. Of the twenty-one risk factors considered, this category—labeled *disasters* for simplicity—ranked sixteenth during the twelve-year period. Natural disasters did not account for any of the 20-percent-plus price drops of firms relative to the performance of their peers.

It may be the case that the impacts of natural calamities on a given company are not manifest for weeks or even months. It may also be due to the wide geographic dispersion in the operations of large companies: even though some operations may be severely impacted by a hurricane or earthquake, the value of the company as a whole is normally little affected.

An exception can be found, outside of our American companies, in the calamity that struck the Tokyo Electric Power Company's nuclear power station at Fukushima in the wake of Japan's 2011 earthquake and tsunami. The firm was later charged with management negligence both ahead of and during the crisis when three of its reactors melted down and spewed radiation. Its share price had traded at more than ¥2,100 before the crisis, but declined to just ¥190 several months later, a loss of more than 90 percent of the company's value. By 2017, more than five years later, the share price had still not recovered, trading below ¥500.

Although we used a 20-percent-plus change in stock value over ten days compared to industry peers as our criterion for this analysis, lesser movements in the wake of an adverse event can also be distressing. The stock price of an insurance company, for example, lost more than 10 percent of its value within a month after a disaster. That destroyed several billions of dollars in the firm's value to investors that would not be restored for a year. Similarly, an energy company saw its value increase by 5 percent after Katrina when oil prices spiked, but then witnessed it plunge by 13 percent the following month as lasting damage to the oil industry in the Gulf region from the hurricane became evident. As one of its executives explained: the "return to normal operations following damage caused by Hurricane Katrina at our Louisiana facility was more complex and time consuming than anticipated." It would be nine months before the stock price returned to its pre-Katrina levels.

Large-scale disasters can also depress the entire stock market, as did the terrorist attacks of September 11, 2001. Anticipating emotional reactions after the attack, executives of the New York Stock Exchange and the Nasdaq Stock Market closed trading until September 17, the longest shutdown since 1933. On the first day after NYSE reopened, the stock market fell more than 7 percent, a record for the largest one-day loss in exchange history. The Dow Jones Industrial Average declined more than 1,300 points, a drop of some 14 percent, and the S&P 500 index dropped more than 11 percent. During the first five trading days after the attacks, companies lost $1.4 trillion in value for their investors.

Natural disasters have never triggered such a staggering loss in company value, and the exchanges have taken actions to guard against that happening. With the approach of Hurricane Sandy in 2012, for instance, the NYSE, Nasdaq, and Bats Global Markets (the operator of several exchanges) all shut down trading for two days, the first multiday weather closing for NYSE since the great blizzard of 1888 that paralyzed the Northeast. Sam Stovall, then chief equity strategist for Standard & Poor's Capital IQ, forecast the market's view as Sandy made landfall: "The hurricane would most likely not have a lasting effect on market performance," and later noted that the S&P 500 stock index actually rose 4 percent in the three months after Katrina. "History says that hurricanes in the US typically don't trigger market declines," he concluded. "Equities are more likely driven by wider-reaching global events than localized natural disasters." And in fact, the S&P index remained stable at about 1,200 points in the month prior to and the month after Hurricane Katrina made landfall in August 2005.[15]

HOW QUICK A COMEBACK?

Enterprise resilience, a firm's readiness to come back from adversity, can be measured by the time it takes for the full restoration of its market value. Disruptions of the kind we have chronicled here are generally large enough to cause deep damage, but not so deep as to impose lasting damage, as least as indicated by the time required for an enterprise's full recovery.

Both industry sector and risk source affect the recovery time. Information technology firms required on average some 132 weeks—more than two and a half years—to fully recover after a severe setback. Utilities and healthcare companies also required more time than the average, with 131 weeks for utilities and 102 weeks for healthcare (Table 11.2).

Risk sources also had a major bearing on recovery times: for increased competition, 62 weeks; industry trends, 137 weeks; acquisitions, 121 weeks; government actions, 61 weeks; and disasters, 58 weeks, as displayed in Table 11.3.

Another more graphic way to view the recovery time is displayed in Figure 11.3. It provides a visual summary of the time required for stocks to recover after a significant drop, categorized by the type of risk. The average recovery period ranges from just four months to more than three years.

Several messages for directors, executives, and managers of large publicly traded companies: (1) firms in information technology, utilities, or healthcare require longer time for recovery; (2) for those disrupted by competitive

Table 11.2. STOCK PRICE RECOVERY TIME OF FIRMS FOLLOWING A 20%+
DECLINE RELATIVE TO INDUSTRY PEERS OVER 10 TRADING DAYS, BY INDUSTRY
SECTOR, RANKED BY RECOVERY TIME

Industry	Mean Recovery Time in Weeks	Number of Events	Standard Deviation in Weeks
Information technology	132	494	200
Utilities	131	54	148
Healthcare	102	143	171
Consumer staples	84	53	105
Industrials	83	79	124
Energy	74	77	115
Consumer discretionary	73	329	128
Telecommunication	66	13	81
Financials	61	264	89
Materials	34	47	41

SOURCE: The authors.

challenges, industry changes, and company acquisitions, the road will also be
lengthy; and (3) for all, recovering from large-scale disruption is not for the
faint hearted. We have seen from the evidence here that it can require one,
two, or even three years just to bring a company's value back to where it was
before the disruption. It took UnitedHealth's stock more than three years to
recover after the New York attorney general announced his investigation.

The long path to recovery can also be seen in the experience of British
Petroleum after the fatal explosion on its Deepwater Horizon platform
in the Gulf of Mexico in 2010. The resulting spill released more than four
million barrels of oil before a broken pipe was finally capped nearly three
months later. BP's stock price at first had only slowly declined, even after
emergency measures to stop the release had not succeeded. On the day of
the accident, April 20, 2010, its stock had been trading at $60 per share,
and ten days later it had only dropped to $49, the 18 percent decline less
than what might have then been expected, perhaps because it was still
seen as a short-term problem with a near-term fix. Institutional investors evidently remained cautiously optimistic that the well would soon be
capped.

As it became clear over the weeks that encapsulation of the wellhead
would take far longer than initially anticipated, and as the environmental

Table 11.3. STOCK PRICE RECOVERY TIME OF FIRMS FOLLOWING A 20%+
DECLINE RELATIVE TO INDUSTRY PEERS OVER 10 TRADING DAYS, BY RISK
FACTOR, RANKED BY RECOVERY TIME

Risk Factor	Mean Recovery Time in Weeks	Number of Events	Standard Deviation in Weeks
Competition	162	62	210
Industry	137	105	204
Acquisition	121	135	181
Investments	117	29	141
Operations	102	162	167
Macro	99	97	160
Legal	94	110	156
Earnings	93	546	147
Labor	90	62	162
Accounting	90	13	113
Marketing/Reputation	80	164	144
Credit Risk	79	55	108
Capital Expenditure	78	49	128
Key Personnel	72	92	141
Distribution	66	9	79
Government	61	74	133
Capital Structure	61	84	107
Catastrophes	58	19	77
Suppliers	55	13	42
Customer Concentrations	54	4	61
International	46	34	106
Intellectual Property	22	10	22

SOURCE: The authors.

and economic impacts were becoming more evident, BP's stock went into
free fall, reaching $29 per share by the end of June 2010, a more than 50 per-
cent decline since the start of the oil spill. As of September 2017, the share
price had rebounded to only $37, still far below the price of seven years ear-
lier. In other words, BP had yet to recover from its Gulf Coast disaster some
360 weeks later. Other elements affected its stock price, of course, including
an oil glut that depressed the earnings of all energy companies, but it may
always be that way: a wounded company becomes more fragile. In addition

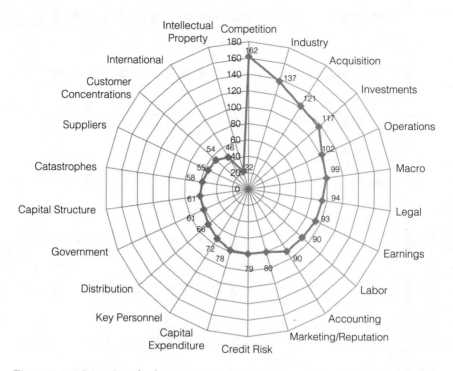

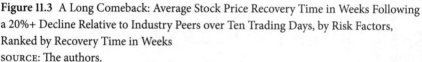

Figure 11.3 A Long Comeback: Average Stock Price Recovery Time in Weeks Following a 20%+ Decline Relative to Industry Peers over Ten Trading Days, by Risk Factors, Ranked by Recovery Time in Weeks
SOURCE: The authors.

to a prolonged loss of shareholder value—close to $100 billion came out of investor portfolios—BP removed its chief executive and disposed of $38 billion in noncore assets within the next three years to fund the massive liabilities occasioned by the oil spill.

Although other drivers are no doubt also significant, including a company's financial condition, executive quality, and board leadership, we have found that a firm's market and the nature of its risks are important determinants of its revival path. A company's sector and its specific hazards are reasonably good predictors of its time to recovery. Table 11.4 displays a more detailed characterization of the average time for stock prices to recover from a severe setback as a function of varied risk factors.

Many companies of course not only want to bounce back but also to spring ahead of where they were, implicitly building on the adage that with crisis comes opportunity. In the hands of deliberative directors and

Table 11.4. Average Stock Price Recovery Time in Weeks of Firms after a 20%+ Decline Relative to Industry Peers over 10 Trading Days, by Company Industry and Risk Factor

Industry / Risk Factor	Consumer Discretionary	Financials	Telecommuni-cations	Information Technology	Consumer Staples	Energy	Healthcare	Materials	Utilities	Industrials	Average
Accounting	28	–	–	6	–	–	–	169	178	16	90
Acquisition	56	81	–	182	27	46	165	47	75	230	121
Catastrophes	8	109	–	75	51	20	–	–	109	110	58
Capital Expenditure	48	41	–	145	–	18	100	–	66	126	78
Capital Structure	31	45	–	144	77	60	76	2	154	31	61
Competition	154	178	67	203	88	–	126	71	14	–	162
Credit Risk	48	77	–	5	–	6	4	20	188	18	79
Customer Concentration	23	–	–	12	–	–	–	–	159	–	54
Distribution	5	2	–	96	41	–	–	–	215	–	66
Earnings	61	52	121	132	105	84	122	39	67	85	93
Government	23	31	23	172	–	22	25	31	51	13	61
Industry	56	47	114	217	7	21	99	5	303	16	137
Intellectual Property	8	–	–	30	–	–	15	–	–	–	22
International	49	17	–	58	28	–	82	14	87	34	46
Investments	255	99	–	10	5	74	84	–	329	–	117
Key Personnel	85	64	–	73	88	178	15	33	–	8	72
Labor	50	17	2	177	185	20	36	9	59	19	90
Legal	89	60	10	103	28	89	104	9	291	47	94
Macro	60	67	120	190	88	45	–	32	219	31	99
Marketing/Reputation	82	65	73	93	56	–	59	56	–	45	80
Operations	74	38	4	141	55	123	88	20	219	57	102
Suppliers	30	–	–	3	88	71	–	39	–	–	55
Average	73	61	66	132	84	74	102	34	131	83	

SOURCE: The authors.

executives, with the usual resistance to change weakened by a calamity, a firm can jump forward, transforming a setback into recovery plus.

UnitedHealth did just that. Its stock traded for less than $20 in late 2008, and reached nearly $210 by November 2017, generating more than 10 times the market value—now $205 billion—than the company had created for investors just nine years earlier.

As company directors, executives, and risk managers become stronger in their risk oversight management, they should also become better at forecasting their financial performance. By creating fewer surprises for institutional investors, this in turn should reduce the magnitude and frequency of those rapid 20 percent downdrafts in company share prices compared to competitors. Supportive evidence comes from two university researchers who tracked eighty-five publicly traded US companies in 2011–2014. They found that firms with more sophisticated ways of taking risks into account in their planning proved more accurate when they publicly forecast their financial performance. And since professional investors dislike downward surprises in earnings, especially large ones, they look askance on executives who suggest future results that they fail to achieve. Better risk management can thus yield less stock volatility and more executive longevity.[16]

SAFEGUARDING VALUE

1. Institutional investors and individual shareholders seek to appreciate the risks in their portfolio, and companies now more extensively warn them of those business risks.
2. Deliberative thinking and risk practices have become more widespread among large companies, and institutional investors are less forgiving when directors, executives, and managers still fail to embrace them.
3. Shareholder reactions to unexpected downdrafts extend not only to stock selloffs, diminishing the market value of the firm, but also to dismissal or resignation of executives.
4. Firms can require a year or longer to fully restore the market value that had been destroyed by risk-induced losses in reputation, operations, and acquisitions. When the firm is shown to be at fault, market valuation can drop abruptly and take years to recover, if ever.

A Checklist for Action

In *The Power of Noticing,* Harvard's Max Bazerman cautioned against predictable pitfalls in making decisions, those suboptimal tendencies that are too often evident among organizational leaders—and that can lead to disaster if unchecked. When attention is preoccupied by immediate concerns and pressing issues, executives and managers tend to ignore small warning signs of impending disaster—sometimes even those staring them in the face—that can morph unattended into genuine threats. They sometimes also focus too narrowly, solving today's problems while leaving looming dangers for a later day. We have all witnessed a moment just before the end of a fiscal year or tax deadline when we or others dropped everything to finalize a closing or a submission by the cutoff.[1]

Understanding how and why these limiting factors can undermine the decisions of even the best-intentioned business leaders is a vital first step for company preparedness. Here we are well advised by the writings of Nobel Laureate Daniel Kahneman and best-selling author Michael Lewis. Kahneman's *Thinking, Fast and Slow,* and Lewis' *The Undoing Project* on the life of Kahneman and his university collaborator Amos Tversky illuminate the many biases and heuristics that can predictably cloud the decisions of business leaders when they really count—as in a catastrophic disaster.[2]

Cognitive limitations can be especially prevalent during extreme events. That said, those responsible for running some of the S&P 500 companies that we have studied here are better at managing disruptions when their colleagues help them think more deliberatively about how to deal with unexpected disruptions. Yet that cooperation can also come with a downside during a crisis when timeliness is essential: executive teams resolve and decide more slowly than would their members individually. "Organizations are better than individuals when it comes to avoiding errors," Kahneman cautioned, but "they naturally think more slowly."[3]

As discussed earlier in these pages, intensified global interdependencies, greater concentrations of people and assets at risk, and more complex regulations and markets, and other DISRUPT drivers, have impelled business leaders to become more aware of having all players at all levels pull together in a more disciplined manner to deal with the intensified risks that now threaten their enterprises. And fortunately, many companies have come to better anticipate disruptions that can cause long-term setbacks, and to put in place stronger risk-management capabilities to prevent them.

As a result, many business leaders have acquired a clearer line of sight into the hazards they face and have adopted a steadier hand for preventing and responding to them. Still, the path for dealing with adverse events remains tortuous, and many firms still have a way to go in dealing with them. In this final chapter, we extract the most evident factors that still thwart effective risk management, and we itemize a number of steps that companies have devised to surmount them. We conclude with a checklist for action.

EIGHT PITFALLS IN DEALING WITH EXTREME EVENTS

Drawing on our interviews, case studies, and prior research, here are eight reasons that some company directors, executives, and managers still do not deliberatively act on the likelihood and consequences of extreme events until it is too late. They serve as instructive warnings of how well-intended risk-management strategies can still go wrong.

Reason 1: Not Preparing for Low-Probability Events

Without specifying their willingness to accept some risks and avoid others, company leaders are less able to identify the hazards that require attention. An executive with one financial institution reported, for instance, that her firm had done no contingency planning for an event like 9/11 because she and her colleagues had never imagined—like the rest of us—that such a terrorist attack could ever happen. With no backup facilities, the firm was forced in the wake of the attack to move its workforce into subpar temporary quarters for nearly a year. Similarly, a chemical company had never considered that it could be hit by a hurricane of Katrina's force, and it consequently had no backup when a plant that had been the sole producer of an essential ingredient was taken offline.

Reason 2: Underappreciation of Global Connections

A flattened world has facilitated international trade but also proliferated risks, given companies' increased reliance on dispersed networks of suppliers and distributors. Manufacturers depending on a single supply source, for instance, can face disruptions from disasters on the opposite side of the globe, as the auto industry experienced in the wake of Japan's 9.0-magnitude earthquake in 2011.

Reason 3: Thinking "It Will Not Happen to Us"

Company leaders may perceive the likelihood of a disastrous event as so low that it simply "will not happen to us." Directors, executives, and managers should not believe that threats or incidents at other firms are unique to them, devoid of implications or warnings for others. This "not-invented-here" syndrome, a well-known impediment to product innovation, can also lead company officials to ignore what other companies have put in place to guard against disaster.

Reason 4: Fighting the Last War

When company leaders believe that the next disruptive event will somehow be similar to the last one, they are likely to be ill-prepared for the coming one. Learning from after-action reviews is essential, but so too is recognizing that the next disaster is unlikely to resemble the most recent setback. In the case of the Germanwings air crash, the suicidal copilot locked out the pilot with a door bolt that was intended to prevent a recurrence of the terrorist seizure of four aircraft on 9/11.

Reason 5: Risk Denial

When large-scale risks threaten a firm, one understandable response has been denial. Even if grudgingly accepting that possibility in private, directors, executives, and managers may also want to avoid a public reputation for pessimism or issuing Cassandra-like forecasts. Many financial institutions, for example, ignored early warning signs of the 2008–2009 collapse that would take many of them down, denying that mortgage-backed securities might massively implode.

Reason 6: Near Miss as No Problem

Business leaders are likely to congratulate themselves on avoiding a disruptive event, rather than asking why they were fortunate *not* to have been hit this time. A counterfactual question for surmounting this shortcoming would be: "Can we gain insights from a near miss if it had actually turned into a hit instead?"

Reason 7: Avoiding High Upfront Costs Due to Myopia

Many firms are reluctant to engage in protective measures because of their high upfront costs, downplaying the long-term benefits of otherwise sensible investments. A principal driver may be a measure's costly impact on the year-end balance sheet, which seemingly gives business leaders little to crow about if a disaster does not happen. But, akin to insurance, the best result is when there is no payoff. Despite the upfront costs, the firm should celebrate *not* having experienced a disruptive event for which it had prepared.

Reason 8: Fear of Becoming Noncompetitive

Firms may be reluctant to undertake protective measures for fear that doing so would make the firm less competitive. California-based banks, for example, do not require earthquake insurance as a precondition for a home mortgage. Some executives we interviewed mentioned that requiring such coverage might lead cost-conscious customers to choose another bank that does not require it. The result has been a grievous underinsuring of the home mortgage market in California, with less than 10 percent of homeowners having earthquake coverage. This presents no financial problem for either the banks or homeowners—until the "Big One" hits.

FIFTEEN STEPS TOWARD MASTERING CATASTROPHIC RISK

Drawing on this research and related studies, we propose a set of fifteen management practices for company leaders to overcome systematic biases and reduce the likelihood and the impacts of large-scale disruptions. Some of these steps utilize concepts associated with choice architecture introduced by Richard Thaler and Cass Sunstein in *Nudge* and a behavioral risk audit proposed by Robert Meyer and Howard Kunreuther in *The Ostrich Paradox: Why We Underprepare for Disasters*. The behavioral risk audit is a matrix of six behavioral biases together with tactics to overcome them. On the premise that we can all become better at catastrophic risk management if we learn from one another, we encourage readers to share experiences, tactics, and nudges at cat-risk@wharton.upenn.edu.[4]

Step 1: View Risk Management as a Value-Creating Strategy

Risk management should be viewed as a long-term investment in staying competitive by creating sustainable value and protecting the firm and its reputation rather than a short-run burden on management's time and the company's budget.

Step 2: Prioritize Risks

Given everyone's limited time for reflection and action, it can be useful to focus attention on the risks of greatest consequence and mark others for future study. Prioritizing facilitates the development of a nuanced and data-rich catastrophic risk-management regimen.

Step 3: Stretch Time Horizons

Taken individually, extreme events are relatively rare. If the likelihood of a specific disaster or adverse event this year is one in a hundred, that seemingly remote probability may understandably result in our failing to pay much attention. On the other hand, if we redo the math to report the probability over the next thirty years, we learn that it is one in four, and that may be more than enough to lead companies to take protective measures now rather than viewing the event as below their threshold level of concern.

Step 4: Anticipate the Worst

Scenario planning across a range of severe events is always wise, but remember to include worst cases even if the firm has never seen one. It is also critical to have a clear understanding of the underlying assumptions on which scenario planning is based. Given the great uncertainties associated with extreme events, firms can wisely run their algorithms with a range of outcomes, likelihoods, and timeframes. These kinds of sensitivity analyses and stress testing enable firms to determine where the benefits of preventive measures exceed their costs for a wide variety of consequences. Less quantitative outcome metrics can be equally important, such as brand and reputation, as Walmart appreciated in the wake of Hurricane Katrina and Lawson Inc. learned after the Fukushima meltdown.

Step 5: Know Your Risk Appetite and Risk Tolerance

Some firms, notably financial institutions, have developed ways to quantify their risk appetite and their tolerance for taking on risks. By specifying these two metrics, companies can better determine the risks they are willing to take and the protective measures required as a result.

Step 6: Disclose Your Risks

Reporting your company's risks is essential for keeping investors informed of what they should know about the firm's potential downdrafts. Public reporting also imposes discipline within the organization and may benefit the industry as firms learn from one another what is most worrisome.

Step 7: Link Compensation to Share Price

Large drops in share prices and market value are potent reminders of the tangible costs of disruptive events not only to investors but also to business leaders whose compensation is now largely contingent on company share price. Tying more pay to multiyear performance-based incentives like stock options can remind those most responsible for company performance of the need for long-term risk antidotes.

Step 8: Set the Tone

Directors set the tone for the C-suite and subordinates. Executives and managers will likely pay much more attention to the firm's disrupters if the board takes risk management seriously. If directors display little concern with how the firm deals with extreme risks, executives and managers are likely to follow suit.

Step 9: Conduct After-Action Reviews

Disciplined learning from both near misses and direct hits can be invaluable. A common form of intuitive thinking that can distort disaster planning, availability bias, may be turned on its head to special advantage here. Given that a close call or real disruption just occurred, a company's leadership is more open to doing something now than before the adverse event to prevent a recurrence.

Step 10: Learn from Competitor Misfortunes

Some might have a tendency to gloat over competitor calamities, but the latter's setbacks actually present a unique learning opportunity for others wishing to avoid the same. Trade and professional associations can play a vital role in disseminating experienced-based lessons and creating spaces where directors and executives can learn from counterparts in other organizations.

Step 11: Act Fast, Even with Imperfect Information

Company calamities are by definition fast-moving and widely impacting, which often limits the information available to those responsible for surmounting the adversities. Complete data for making management decisions are never available, and even less so in the midst of a crisis, but that is precisely when fast and informed decisions are needed. As we have seen in the escalating crisis at Deutsche Bank in the wake of the Fukushima meltdown, and at Lufthansa after the pilot-induced crash, risk managers and company executives made quicker decisions with less certainty than they would have under normal circumstances.

Step 12: Diversify Suppliers

The best time to appreciate if a firm has sufficiently diverse sources of supply is before one is taken offline. We have seen earthquakes and floods disrupt global supply chains, and many companies are taking steps to diversify their suppliers. It would have been even better if they had done so beforehand.

Step 13: Insure Against Adverse Events

By transferring financial exposure to a third party through insurance, firms are able to increase their risk appetite and risk tolerance, knowing they have protection against large losses. When a firm cannot secure insurance against a given risk at an attractive price, however, it may opt to self-insure, though the high price of insurance could be viewed as a market signal that the risk is not worth taking.

Step 14: Everybody Is Responsible

Enterprise risk management can best be viewed as the responsibility of all, from front-line managers to the risk-analysis team to the internal audit group to top executives. Directors can also provide invaluable guidance on risks and their mitigation, if they serve not just as a watchdog for investors but also a partner with executives.

Step 15: Be Unsurprised by Surprise

In a DISRUPT environment, catastrophic situations rarely provide sufficient warning in advance of their occurrence. Preparedness for shocks has become an essential company capacity according to most of the firms in our

study. The unexpected is to be expected, as is a readiness to think deliberatively and to act with alacrity.

We conclude *Mastering Catastrophic Risk* with a checklist for company
action. The rationale and utility of such a list has been well argued by sur-
geon and writer Atul Gawande in his *Checklist Manifesto*. For transforming
deliberative thinking into deliberative action, he has forcefully made the
case for a short list of mission-critical guidelines. Each is essential and all
are required, whether for conducting surgery, piloting an aircraft, or leading
a company in a more risky era. For managing corporate disruptions, here is
our mission-critical checklist.[5]

THE MISSION-CRITICAL CHECKLIST

1. *Catastrophes are on the rise, and your firm may be next in line to suffer
   one.* Don't pretend it can't happen to you, and instead imagine five
   potential disruptions that could hit this year or next if one of your
   current assumptions turns out to be wrong.
2. *Involve personnel at all levels in designing risk-management and
   crisis-response strategies.* Involve company directors, top executives,
   managers, and front-line employees in taking steps now to prepare
   for the unexpected. Tapping outside expertise can help you put the
   different parts of the puzzle together and save you time.
3. *Recognize behavioral biases and simplified rules that misdirect
   company decisions.* Engage in deliberative thinking and systematic
   analysis by recognizing that intuitive ideas can lead business leaders
   to misestimate their low-probability risks and then mismanage
   recovery efforts when they materialize.
4. *Identify and appraise the risks you face.* Prioritize the enterprise risks
   that demand attention now by building on what directors, executives,
   and managers separately see, and recognize the hazards that can
   threaten the firm as a whole.
5. *Define your firm's risk appetite and risk tolerance.* Identify and balance
   risk appetite and tolerance in mapping your company's overall
   strategy.
6. *Take steps now to invest in protective measures.* Invest in measures
   where the long-term expected benefits justify the upfront costs.

7. *Learn from your own adverse events and those of others.* Identify a dozen management practices from disruptions you've experienced and those of other firms to design an architecture and culture of preparedness and resilience.

8. *Strategize for recovery.* Incorporate enterprise risk management into your business strategy. Put practices in place that will guide and sustain the firm for what may be an extended period following an adverse event.

9. *Protect against extremes through risk transfer.* When available, use insurance and other measures to buffer against low-probability, high-consequence risks that may gravely disrupt the firm.

10. *Attract and prepare the next generation of company leaders.* Prepare directors, executives, and managers to become more agile in avoiding systematic biases, engage them in deliberative thinking, and build strategic risk-management practices with clear accountability. Capitalize on your firm's setbacks and those of others, when the readiness to learn is greatest. Make the mastery of catastrophic risk a source of competitive advantage.

Epilogue

On a Rainy Day

Urgent. Need to talk, now!
—CHIEF OF STAFF TO CHIEF EXECUTIVE OFFICER

It had been another long week. More like a marathon, in fact. Since George Taylor had been appointed six weeks ago as the new chief executive of Great Ventures Co., his plate has been full, with endless meetings in three countries during the past five days, and it had been raining heavily the entire time. Despite his hectic schedule, George felt good and was excited about the opportunity to drive profitable growth and increase the value of his new enterprise. Next Tuesday would be a big day, his first meeting with the governing board since he had assumed the position of CEO.

George had a successful career, most recently as executive vice president of another large firm in the same industry. He was highly regarded by his colleagues who saw him as a business leader who liked to get the job done through teamwork. The company he left had built its reputation on strong risk-management practices and a balance between short-term return and long-term value. But sometimes it lacked the appetite for risk-taking that George had come to savor.

The more enterprising culture that had drawn him to Great Ventures had evidently been paying off, as both customers and investors had found the company an attractive "buy." Since the firm was added to the S&P 500 seven years ago, it had doubled in size, mostly through acquisitions. Its success had been reported in the business media, customers had been flock-ing, and the big financial institutions had become bullish.

George liked to go for a jog in the evening to exercise—and to clear his thoughts. But now the rain was coming down in buckets, so no jogging tonight. He instead turned on the TV in his hotel room to check the sports news, a well-deserved respite after the nonstop week.

Then it came. Not an email message, just a text. George was surprised to receive one from his chief of staff who was three thousand miles away on another continent. It must be in the middle of the night for her, he thought.

"Urgent. Need to talk, now! —Jen."

Then another text message:

"Two government investigations announced. US and Asia."

He quickly confirmed on his smartphone that the federal government would announce on Monday a detailed investigation of Great Ventures' practices. News travels fast. Another inquiry might be launched by one of the governments in Asia where the firm also had large operations. "Nothing more is known at this point," Jen told George in a brief call.

Tuesday's governing board meeting where he was planning to unveil his three-year vision and strategy for Great Ventures would now be very differ-ent. The lack of any real information about why one, and maybe even two governments wanted to investigate the company made his situation even more challenging.

George had done his share of due diligence before accepting the CEO position. The financial results of the company had been stellar.

His head buzzed with a slew of questions, and he knew that his direc-tors would be wondering much the same: Could the speed at which Great Ventures had grown have triggered inappropriate or even illicit actions? Who was involved? Were some of our products at issue? What about our flagship offering? What was the extent of the damage? How will investors react?

While George knew he would not be personally implicated since he had just joined the firm, he of course felt fully responsible for the enterprise and its 24,000 employees. As the top executive of a corporation with numer-ous operating divisions and products at home and abroad, he had antici-pated that he might one day have to face a daunting disruption. But he never imagined that it would come so soon.

Some companies prepare for such crises by making risk management a core component of their business strategy and heavily investing in it. Could he count on the knowledge and support of his own executive team and from the governing board to deal with the impending investigation? George considered lessons learned from other companies that could serve as role models. Their experience might steady his hand, suggesting the pitfalls to avoid and steps to take.

It was now 3 a.m. As he looked out the window, he saw that the rain had finally stopped. But he appreciated that a storm of another kind was coming, and he hoped his directors and managers were ready to cope with it.

ACKNOWLEDGMENTS

Along with the two of us, our former colleague Erwann Michel-Kerjan was part of the leadership team of this study over the period 2011 to 2016, when he was Executive Director of the Wharton Risk Management and Decision Processes Center.

Mastering Catastrophic Risk has truly been a collaborative effort. It could not have been completed without the active participation of the following individuals, who assisted us in arranging and transcribing the interviews with company directors, executives, and managers; analyzing the interviews and the firms' 10-K reports; detailing stock price movements among the S&P 500 firms; and editing the book. (Their titles and affiliations were those held during the project period.)

Luis Ballesteros, Research Associate, Wharton School, University of Pennsylvania (and now Assistant Professor, George Washington University)

Preston Cline, Director, Wharton Leadership Ventures, McNulty Leadership Program, Wharton School

Carol Heller, Senior Communications Manager, Center for Risk Management and Decision Processes, Wharton School

Rebecca R. Henderson, Research Associate, Wharton School

Matthew J. Hill, Project Manager, Center for Risk Management and Decision Processes, Wharton School

Richard Jungwoo Hong, Research Associate, Wharton School

Jeffrey Klein, Executive Director, McNulty Leadership Program, Wharton School

Nicole Kwok, Research Assistant, Wharton School

Ann Miller, Administrative Assistant, Wharton School

We also thank friends and colleagues for their invaluable guidance, support, and insights during the completion of this project.

Beth Alioto, Senior Contract Administrator, University of Pennsylvania

Peter Andres, Vice President, Deutsche Lufthansa AG

Scott C. Belden, Senior Vice President of Reinsurance, Travelers Companies, Inc.

Sourav Bose, Research Assistant, Wharton School

Laura Boudreau, Research Assistant, Wharton School

Karen Campbell, Senior Research Fellow, Center for Risk Management and Decision Processes, Wharton School

Cary Coglianese, Professor of Law, and Director, Penn Program on Regulation, University of Pennsylvania

Jeffrey Czajkowski, Senior Research Fellow, Center for Risk Management and Decision Processes, Wharton School

Elaine Dezenski, Senior Director and Head of Partnering Against Corruption Initiative, World Economic Forum

Steve Dreyer, Managing Director, Investor Communications, S&P Global Ratings

Chioma Fitzgerald, Business Administrator, Center for Risk Management and Decision Processes, Wharton School

Erin Haberman, Program Officer, Travelers Foundation

Laurence Hazell, Director, Governance Specialist, Standard & Poor's Ratings Services

W. Lee Howell, Managing Director, Centre for Global Events and Risk Response Network, World Economic Forum

Danbi Hwang, Research Assistant, Wharton School

Marlene Ibsen, Chief Executive Officer, Travelers Foundation

Bruce R. Jones, Executive Vice President, Enterprise Risk Management, Chief Risk Officer, Travelers Companies

Daniel Kahneman, Professor of Psychology Emeritus, Princeton University

Larry Knafo, Crisis Management Global Head, Deutsche Bank AG

Linda Kronfeld, Senior Philanthropic Advisor, Principal Gifts, University of Pennsylvania

Sara Labrum, Research Associate, Wharton School

Shaun Lee, Research Assistant, Wharton School

Wing Li, Research Assistant, Wharton School

Samuel Lundquist, Vice Dean, External Affairs, Wharton School

Mani Mahesh, Research Associate, Wharton School

Alison Matejczyk, Senior Executive Director, Development, Wharton School

Joy McKenzie, Research Assistant, Wharton School

Robert Meyer, Professor of Marketing, Co-Director, Center for Risk Management and Decision Processes, Wharton School

Victor Meyer, Corporate Security and Business Continuity, Deutsche Bank AG

Eric Nelson, Senior Vice President, Catastrophe Underwriting, Risk, Travelers Companies

Gregory Nini, Assistant Professor, Business Economics and Public Policy, Wharton School

Sean Niznik, Research Assistant, Wharton School

Scott Parris, Executive Editor, Economics and Finance, Oxford University Press

Nyzinga Patterson, Business Administrator, Center for Risk Management and Decision Processes, Wharton School

Burkhard Pedell, Professor and Chair, Management Accounting and Control, Institute for Business Administration, University of Stuttgart, Germany

David Pervin, Acquisitions Editor, Economics, Business and Management, and Politics, Oxford University Press

Edward P. Pieters, Associate Director, Office Research Services, University of Pennsylvania

Gilbert Probst, Managing Director and Dean, Leadership Office and Academic Affairs, World Economic Forum

Lucy Provost, Associate Director, Office of Corporate and Foundation Relations, Wharton School

Maria Puciata, Administrative Assistant, Center for Risk Management and Decision Processes, Wharton School

Coy Purcell, Associate Director, Corporate Contracts, Office of Research Services, University of Pennsylvania

Alan D. Schnitzer, Chief Executive Officer, Travelers Companies, Inc.

Klaus Schwab, Founder and Executive Chairman, World Economic Forum

Karishma Tank, Research Associate, Wharton School

Gautham Venkatesan, Research Associate, Wharton School

Joan K. Woodward, Executive Vice President, Public Policy, and President, The Travelers Institute, Travelers Companies, Inc.

Richard Zeckhauser, Frank P. Ramsey Professor of Political Economy, Kennedy School of Government, Harvard University

Finally, we thank the company directors, executives and managers in the US and Europe who have collaborated with us.

S&P 500 Directors, Executives, and Managers Interviewed

This book had its genesis in 2010 when we at the Wharton Risk Management and Decision Processes Center and the Wharton Leadership Center discussed our mutual interests in better understanding how some of the largest companies were dealing with adverse events that had a disruptive effect not only on their own operations but also a wider impact. Our primary research agenda has been to conduct personal interviews with key decision makers to identify the steps they had taken to prepare their companies for potentially disruptive events, and how they had learned from their experiences and those of others.

A generous grant to our two research centers from the Travelers Foundation enabled us to conduct interviews with directors, executives, and managers at 102 of the companies among the Standard and Poor's 500 largest publicly traded companies, ranked by market value, listed on the New York Stock Exchange and Nasdaq. The value of firms in the S&P 500 in 2017 stood at more than $20 trillion, constituting some three-quarters of the market capitalization of all publicly traded companies in the United States. To be included in the index, a company required a value of at least $6.1 billion in 2017.[1]

In approaching the leaders of those firms across industry sectors for interviews, we reported that our two research centers were conducting a study on the role of directors, executives, and managers in dealing with catastrophic risks broadly defined, and that the study's results should be of practical interest to them.

An external advisory board provided project guidance in the design and conduct of the study. They are not responsible for the research findings or views expressed in this book. Its members (with their position listed at the time of their involvement) were:

Chair: Jay S. Fishman, Chair and Chief Executive Officer, Travelers
  Companies
Paul C. Curnin, Partner, Simpson Thacher & Bartlett LLP
Luis Custodio, Vice President, Chief Risk Officer and Pension
  Management, IBM
William Egan, Global Head of Financial Institutions, Bank of America
Peter Kellogg, Chief Financial Officer, Merck & Co.
Joe Morton, Vice President of Corporate Security, IBM
Pierre Ozendo, Chair and Chief Executive Officer, Swiss Re Americas
Stephen Propper, Assistant Treasurer, Merck & Co.
Thomas Ridge, US Secretary of Homeland Security, 2003–2005
J. Eric Smith, Chief Executive Officer and President, Swiss Re Americas
Research Advisor: Paul Slovic, President, Decision Research

We also received guidance and assistance from a range of university students, faculty colleagues, academic researchers, and business leaders, including a number who attended a working conference at the Wharton School. The research team recorded and transcribed the interviews—more than 350,000 words in total—and used a qualitative data analysis software package, NVivo, to identify the major themes running through the interviews. We assured those interviewed of confidentiality for both themselves and their companies, and have included no identifying references in the text. Our interviews were guided by the questions below, and we followed up with requests for data, documentation, and elaboration of points that emerged during the course of our dialog with the company directors, executives, and managers:

Adverse Events

What are one or two of the most adverse events that you have faced as a
  firm?
What steps did you take in the moment to respond to those events?
In hindsight, what would you have done differently?

Distribution of Responsibility

Taking the last adverse event, what roles did people play?
How is risk management structured in your organization? Who
  does what?

Risk Identification, Assessment, and Mitigation

What are the risks that really keep you up at night?

What formal or informal processes do you use to identify and assess those risks?

How do you mitigate or moderate those risks?

Balancing Risks and Rewards

How do you manage the tension between growing your business and minimizing risk?

What are the trade-offs?

Advice and Conclusion

Based on your own personal experience, what advice for managing catastrophic risk would you give to the leaders of other companies?

Is there anything we haven't asked you that we should have asked?

Analysis of 10-K Risk Factors Reported by Companies

As noted in chapter 9, the research team analyzed trends gleaned from risk factors that companies disclosed in section 1A of their annual 10-K reports. The task for the research team was to accurately assign the thousands of 10-K risks from hundreds of reports into the twenty-one categories selected for analysis. In order to convert the 10-Ks into useful data, we undertook a coding process:

1. *Determine risk factor categories.* Previous work by Wharton colleagues consolidated 116 distinct risks generated from a random sampling of the 10-K risk disclosures of 122 firms into twenty-nine categories. We further streamlined the twenty-nine risk categories to twenty-one, combining closely related risks. For example, we grouped "regulation" and "taxation" under "government."[1]
2. *Assign risks to categories.* To facilitate standardization in coding, we created a set of definitions, examples, and keywords for each of the risk factors, as summarized in Table A2.1, below. Members of our research team began with a 10 percent sample of the risks disclosed in the 10-K reports. We compared coding by research team members to ensure consistency and then proceeded to code the risks into their appropriate categories.
3. *Conduct analysis.* To analyze variation in the risk factors over time and among industry sectors, we organized the 10-K data using a data analysis software package, NVivo. The program is widely used in the research community to organize and analyze qualitative data, including that from interviews and reports. We calculated the sample-wide variation in reference to each of the risk factors, recognizing that some industries are more prone to certain risks than others.

Table A2.1. RISK FACTORS, EXAMPLES, AND KEYWORDS

Risk Factor	Definition	Example	Keywords (illustrative)
Accounting	Change in accounting regulations that can affect the financial standing of the company.	"We must comply with generally accepted accounting principles established by the Financial Accounting Standards Board."	Accounting, accounting practices, books, auditor, audit, accounting irregularities, financial statements
Acquisition	Risk associated with all phases of acquisition (pre, during, post) that may result in business value loss (e.g., unmet synergy, operational disruption, changes in management).	"The integration of firm A and other acquired businesses may present significant challenges to us."	Acquisitions, acquire, divest, sell unit, sale, merger, merger agreement, joint venture, synergies, spin off, split, buyout, alliance, offer, bid, restructuring, hostile takeover
Capital Expenditure	Investment in a company's business requiring substantial funds for items such as facilities, equipment, fixed assets, R&D, or new product development.	"We are developing new products that complement our traditional memory products or leverage their underlying design or process technology."	Plant expenditures, plant expansion, capital investment, plant closing costs, capital spending expenses
Capital Structure	The way a firm finances its overall operations and growth by using different sources of funds. (The debt-to-equity ratio is a financial metric used to assess a company's capital structure.)	"We are subject to the risks associated with debt financing, including the risk that our cash flow will be insufficient to meet required payments of principal and interest."	Debt, cash position, credit rating, covenants, highly leveraged, refinancing, interest rates, commercial paper, lines of credit, credit line, junk status, equity, financing, equity offering, stock price, dividends, share dilution, lenders, buyback, raise capital, bonds, loan

Competition	Potential disadvantage in the market as a direct result of the competitors' activity or a business's strategic mishap.	"Increased competition could result in fewer submissions, lower premium rates, and less favorable policy terms and conditions, which could reduce our margins."	Competition, competitor, competing product, decreased market share, increased market share, strategic advantage
Credit Risk	Risks related to not receiving payment for delivered goods or services; the risk of companies defaulting on payments.	"EME's operations are exposed to the risk that counterparties will not perform their obligations."	Credit risk
Customer Concentration	Growth in specific customer segments (by geography, industry, large players) that creates an overreliance on a small group of clients, posing business risks.	"Since we depend on a few brokers for a large portion of our revenues, loss of business provided by any one of them could adversely affect us."	Reliance on a small number of suppliers/ contractors/clients
Disasters	Environmental conditions / terrorist activities / acts of wars / pandemics. Cyber risk is also coded in this category.	"Extreme weather conditions in the areas in which the Company's stores are located could adversely affect the Company's business."	Pandemics, epidemics, oil spill, terrorism, September 11, act of terrorism, hurricane, weather, war, disaster, catastrophe, storms, tornado, tsunami, tropical storm, cyberattack

(continued)

Table A2.1. CONTINUED

Risk Factor	Definition	Example	Keywords (illustrative)
Distribution	Changes or unforeseen events during the passing of goods from a business to its external B2B or B2C customers.	"In the event that commercial transportation is curtailed or substantially delayed, our business may be adversely impacted, as we may have difficulty shipping merchandise to our distribution centers and stores."	Distribution, distribution channels
Government	Governmental acts and regulations that affect the way a company conducts its business.	"We are subject to extensive government regulation and supervision, including regulation and supervision in non-US jurisdictions, which may limit our ability to pay dividends or make other capital distributions and violations of which could have a material adverse effect on our business, financial condition and results of operations."	Government, Congress, taxes, regulation, SEC, Securities and Exchange Commission, president, Obamacare, healthcare plan, government contract, economic stimulus, bailout, troubled asset relief program, US Treasury, Volcker, Basel II and III, Dodd-Frank, oversight
Industry	Industry risks that not only affect the company, but also other players in the industry.	"The payments industry is highly competitive and includes, in addition to credit card networks, evolving alternative payment mechanisms and systems."	Industry risks

Intellectual Property	Risk associated with security of or changes to the sustained advantage from the business's intellectual property. Any threats to IP.	"With respect to patents and patent applications we have licensed in, there can be no assurance that additional patents will be issued to any of the third parties from whom we have licensed patent rights."	Patents, licenses
International	Currency fluctuations in a company's international business operations. Any risks associated with operations abroad (government/legal).	"The enactment of provincial legislation or regulations in Canada to lower pharmaceutical product pricing and service fees may adversely affect our pharmaceutical distribution business in Canada, including the profitability of that business."	International expansion, international economies/markets, emerging markets, non-US subsidiaries, foreign currencies, foreign currency changes, exchange rate, currency translations, strong/weak US dollar
Investments	Pension/retirement benefits and any capital put into other firms.	"Our pension plans are underfunded, and may require significant future contributions, which could have an adverse impact on our business."	Pension liability, pension liabilities, investment
Key Personnel	The loss of potential key executives in the company that may result in adverse effects. Reliance of a company's success on key executives.	"There is substantial competition for qualified personnel in the real estate industry, and the loss of several of our key personnel could adversely affect the company."	Resigned, fired, CEO, COO, CFO, board member, deaths, injured

(continued)

Table A2.1. CONTINUED

Risk Factor	Definition	Example	Keywords (illustrative)
Labor	Recruiting and retaining employees, errors that employees may incur.	"Our businesses require the retention and recruitment of a skilled workforce, and the loss of employees could result in the failure to implement our business plans."	Talents, recruitment, new expertise, retirement
Legal	The possibility that legal action will be taken because of a corporation's actions, inactions, products, services, or other events. Potential/ongoing lawsuits that will affect the company adversely.	"We are involved in numerous legal proceedings arising out of the conduct of our business, including litigation with customers, employment-related lawsuits, class actions, purported class actions, and actions brought by governmental authorities."	Lawsuit, legal proceedings, legal challenges, court, sued, suing, damages, litigation, contract disputes, ruling, judge, penalties, hearing, appeal, evidence, legal costs, liability, allegations, defendant, plaintiff, lawyers, trial, federal panel, jurisdiction
Macro	Activities happening in the aggregate economy that affect the operations of the company; demand for its products/services.		Demand contraction, low economic growth

Marketing/ Reputation Risks	Any risks related to the firm's brand, reputation, image, product pricing, and market share.	"The success of our branded products relies in large part on the favorable image they enjoy with consumers."	Marketing, reputation, market share, market expansion, customer focus, segmenting, brand, image, product mix, pricing
Operations	Risk associated with mismanaged or unforeseen activities in the internal operation of a business, e.g., production, manufacturing, etc.	"The size and complexity of our computer systems make them potentially vulnerable to breakdown, malicious intrusion, and random attack."	Quality control, product quality, product launch
Suppliers	Variations in the supply delivery processes that pose business risks, and changes in the bargaining power of suppliers driven by supply availability.	"In order to sustain and grow its business, the company must successfully replace the crude oil and natural gas it produces with additional reserves."	Suppliers, supplies, input costs, raw material costs, high oil prices, high fuel costs, fuel expenses, smaller margin

SOURCE: Authors.

PROLOGUE
1. Walmart, 2017.
2. Andrews, 2010.
3. Ochs, 2016. Cowley, 2017a, 2017b.
4. Brodeur et al., 2010.
5. The advisory board is identified in Appendix 1.
6. Additional information on the interviews appears in Appendix. 1.

CHAPTER 1
1. Kalavar and Mysore, 2017; Luis Ballesteros provided data from Factiva, drawing on newspapers, trade publications, magazines, newswires, press releases, television and radio transcripts, digital video and audio clips, corporate websites and reports, institutional websites and reports, and government websites and reports.
2. Author estimates from the programs of the annual meeting of the World Economic Forum, 1997–2014.
3. Standard and Poor's, 2013.
4. Goldin and Mariathasan, 2014
5. Kunreuther and Heal, 2002.
6. Dawson and Takahashi, 2011.
7. Heal et al., 2006; Kearns, 2005.
8. Auserwald et al., 2006; Feinstein, 2006.
9. Eckerman, 2005; Warren, 1999.
10. Morgenson, 2008; Hurtado, 2016.
11. Thomson, 2013.
12. Gallup, 2016.
13. Population Reference Bureau, 2017.
14. National Oceanic and Atmospheric Administration, 2016.
15. Pielke Jr. et al., 2008.
16. Kunreuther and Michel-Kerjan, 2011.
17. Houser et al., 2014.
18. Kalavar and Mysore, 2017.
19. Cheong, 2015; Dieterich, 2015; Gandel, 2015; Shell, 2017.
20. Korolov, 2015.
21. *Economist*, 2014.

22. Bernile, Bhatwat, and Rau, 2017
23. Bernile, Bhatwat, and Rau, 2017; Malmendier, Tate, and Yan, 2011.

CHAPTER 2
1. Muller and Kräussl, 2011.
2. Schwabe, Cory, and Newcomb, 2009; Kaufmann, 2011; Kilian and Murphy, 2014.
3. Useem and Leonard, 2012.
4. Boehm, Flaaen, and Pandalai-Nayar, 2015.
5. World Economic Forum, 2012.

CHAPTER 3
1. March and Simon, 1958; Cyert and March, 1963.
2. Cyert and March, 1963.
3. Kahneman, 2011.
4. Slovic, 2000.
5. Russo and Schoemaker, 1989.
6. Tversky and Kahneman, 1973.
7. Fischhoff, 2003.
8. Rerup, 2009.
9. Lampel et al., 2009; Zollo, 2009.
10. Kunreuther, Pauly, and McMorrow 2013.
11. Baker et al., 2007; Garicano and Rayo, 2016.
12. Yoshida and Fukada, 2011.
13. Samuelson and Zeckhauser, 1988; Tversky and Kahneman, 1991; Levinthal and March, 1993; Arkes and Blumer, 1985; Garicano and Rayo, 2016.
14. Garicano and Rayo, 2016; Levinthal and March, 1993; Samuelson and Zeckhauser, 1988; Tversky and Kahneman, 1991.
15. Cohen, March, and Olsen, 1972.
16. Kunreuther and Bowman, 1997.

CHAPTER 4
1. Risk and Insurance Management Society, 2012.
2. Aon Risk Solutions, 2017.
3. Risk and Insurance Management Society, 2012.
4. Hughes and Currie, 2010.
5. Rerup, 2009.
6. Vaughan, 1997a, 1997b; Boyd, 2011; National Aeronautics and Space Administration, 2003; McDonald and Robinson, 2010; Pate-Cornell and Fischbeck, 1994.

CHAPTER 5
1. March, Sproull, and Tamuz, 1991.
2. Baum and Dahlin, 2007; Madsen, 2009.
3. DiMaggio and Powell, 1983; Levitt and March, 1988.

CHAPTER 6
1. Low, 2016.

2. Information on the air crash and its crisis management was obtained from an interview with Peter Andres, Lufthansa vice president, on October 5 and December 1, 2016, and a host of sources, including Bureau d'Enquêtes et d'Analyses, 2016; DePietro, 2015; *Economist*, 2015.
3. Kottasova and Thompson, 2015.
4. Bureau d'Enquêtes et d'Analyses, 2016.
5. Neilan, 2015.
6. Baum, 2016.
7. Juma and Hassan, 2014.
8. Clark and Bilefsky, 2016.
9. World Bank Group, 2012.
10. Palca, 2011.
11. Lawrence, 2011.
12. Deutsche Bank, 2012.
13. Pedell, 2014; Burkhard Pedell is chair of Management Accounting and Control in the Institute of Business Administration at the University of Stuttgart, Stuttgart, Germany.

CHAPTER 7

1. Lipton, 2015; see also National Association of Corporate Directors, 2014.
2. Fraser, 2016; Charan, Carey, and Useem, 2014.
3. Charan, Carey, and Useem, 2014.
4. PricewaterhouseCoopers, 2016b.
5. PricewaterhouseCoopers, 2016b.
6. This section draws on Useem, 2010.
7. Useem, 2010.
8. Kiel, 2008.
9. Kahneman, 2011.
10. De la Merced and Sorkin, 2015.
11. This section draws on Useem, 2006, and Charan, Carey, and Useem, 2014.
12. Spencer Stuart, 2015, 2016; also see Conference Board, 2007; Beaumier and DeLoach, 2012.
13. Ernst & Young, 2014.
14. Ittner and Keusch, 2017.
15. Useem and Zelleke, 2006.
16. Ponemon Institute, 2015; Beasley, Branson, and Hancock, 2015; Pricewaterhouse Coopers, 2016b.
17. Spencer Stuart, 2015; also see Zukis, 2016.
18. Adapted from Useem, 2006.
19. Boeing, 2017; Airbus, 2017. It should be noted that the price of a Boeing 787 is about $250 million, compared to about $433 million for the Airbus A380.
20. Schwartz, 2016.
21. Schwartz, 2016; Nottingham, 2016.
22. Ailworth, 2017.
23. Brodeur et al., 2010.

24. Business Roundtable, 2016.
25. Ingley and van der Walt, 2008; Ittner and Keusch, 2017; Committee of Sponsoring Organizations of the Treadway Commission, 2009.

CHAPTER 8

1. De Alessi, 1975; Douty 1972; Ballesteros and Useem 2015; Ballesteros 2015. Luis Ballesteros is Assistant Professor at George Washington University. His research interests include competitive strategy and international business, and he is particularly focused on the business drivers behind the provision of collective goods, such as disaster relief, by commercial firms and the impact of their giving on social welfare and economic redistribution. Luis has worked for JP Morgan Chase, the World Bank, and the United Nations Development Program, and he holds degrees from the Massachusetts Institute of Technology and the Mexican Autonomous Institute of Technology, and a doctoral degree from the Wharton School, University of Pennsylvania.
2. Ballesteros, 2013, 2015; UN Office for the Coordination of Humanitarian Affairs, 2015; White and Lang, 2012; Ballesteros, Useem, and Wry, 2017; Silverblatt, 2016; Ballesteros and Useem, 2015.
3. United Nations High-Level Panel, 2016.
4. UN Office for the Coordination of Humanitarian Affairs, 2015; major natural disasters are those that meet at least one of the following criteria: ten or more people killed, a hundred or more people affected, a declaration of a state of emergency, or a call for international assistance. The analysis focuses on disasters whose deaths were above the mean; Becerra et al., 2014.
5. Bevere et al., 2015; Cummins and Mahul, 2009; Munich Re, 2013; Staib and Puttaiah, 2015; Kunreuther and Michel-Kerjan, 2011; New York City, 2013; CNN, 2017.
6. Ballesteros, 2013, 2015; Ballesteros, Useem, and Wry, 2017.
7. This section draws on Ballesteros, Useem, and Wry, 2017
8. Manager, International Public Affairs, Coca-Cola Company, in interview with one of the authors.
9. See De Alessi, 1975; Gao, 2011; White and Lang, 2012; Cavallo and Daude, 2011; Khan and Kumar, 1997; Camerer and Fehr, 2002; Douty, 1972; Hirshleifer, 1963; Kunreuther, 1996.
10. Porter and Kramer, 2002; Saiia et al., 2003; Wokutch et al., 2013; De Alessi, 1975; Hirshleifer, 1963.
11. Ballesteros, Useem, and Wry, 2017.
12. Ballesteros, Useem, and Wry, 2017.
13. United Nations Development Program, 2017.
14. Ballesteros, Useem, and Wry, 2017.
15. Useem, Kunreuther, and Michel-Kerjan, 2015.
16. Ballesteros, Useem, and Wry, 2017.
17. Ballesteros, Useem, and Wry, 2017.
18. Dacy and Kunreuther, 1968; Cavallo, Cavallo, and Rigobon, 2014.
19. Useem, Kunreuther, and Michel-Kerjan, 2015.
20. *Nation*, 2011.
21. Henry Schein, 2014; World Economic Forum, 2015; Ebola Private Sector Mobilization Group, 2015.
22. Ballesteros, Useem, and Wry, 2017.

CHAPTER 9

1. Riley et al., 2014.
2. Mulligan, 2014.
3. Tobias, 2014.
4. https://www.sec.gov/Archives/edgar/data/27419/000002741917000008/tgt-20170128x10k.htm
5. Weiss and Miller, 2015.
6. Consumer Financial Protection Bureau, 2017.
7. Bao and Datta, 2014; Campbell et al., 2014.
8. The disclosure was even more specific: "The nature of our business involves the receipt and storage of personal information about our guests and team members. We have a program in place to detect and respond to data security incidents. To date, all incidents we have experienced have been insignificant. If we experience a significant data security breach or fail to detect and appropriately respond to a significant data security breach, we could be exposed to government enforcement actions and private litigation. In addition, our guests could lose confidence in our ability to protect their personal information, which could cause them to discontinue usage of RED cards, decline to use our pharmacy services, or stop shopping with us altogether. The loss of confidence from a significant data security breach involving team members could hurt our reputation, cause team member recruiting and retention challenges, increase our labor costs and affect how we operate our business." Target's 2012 10-K report.
9. Target, 2014
10. Of those firms, five were not listed in the index in 2007, and we excluded them from our analysis for 2014.
11. Jiao, 2011. According to the author, "These rankings represent assessments of the completeness, clarity, and timeliness of firms' disclosures by leading financial analysts, and encompass both the qualitative and quantitative aspects of corporate disclosures. They span the period from 1979 to 1996 and cover hundreds of firms in more than forty industries each year. In sum, they are the most extensive measure of disclosure quality and accounting transparency available."
12. Campbell et al., 2014.
13. This subsection is based on public documents from S&P that describe their methodology. We thank Steven Dreyer and Laurence Hazell for their willingness to share the information and for dialogue on risk management and ratings of firms.
14. Institutional Shareholder Services, 2017; Glass Lewis, 2017.

CHAPTER 10

1. Guess Inc., 2015.
2. Chhaochharia and Grinstein, 2007; Jain and Rezaee, 2006; Wintoki, 2007; Zhang, 2005.
3. Davis Polk & Wardell LLP, 2016; https://www.sec.gov/Archives/edgar/data/1390777/000119312512085349/d260593d10k.htm
4. PricewaterhouseCoopers, 2016a, 2016b.
5. Coglianese, 2012.
6. *The Economist*, 2005.
7. Kunreuther and Michel-Kerjan, 2004; Michel-Kerjan and Kunreuther, 2017.
8. Heal and Kunreuther, 2010.

CHAPTER 11

1. Richard Jungwoo Hong provided research assistance on this chapter.
2. New York's Attorney General Office, 2008; Abelson, 2008.
3. Associated Press, 2008.
4. Brought by the Litigation Center of the American Medical Association and State Medical Societies, the Medical Society of the State of New York, and the Missouri State Medical Association. The class action also focused on the same issue but had been languishing for years until the New York attorney general started his own investigation.
5. Creswell and Maheshwari, 2017.
6. This section draws on Cremer and Schwartz, 2015; Gates et al., 2017; Reuters, 2016; Petcu, 2017.
7. Chu, 2015, 2017.
8. Ruddick, 2015.
9. Ewing and Tabuchi, 2016.
10. Ewing, 2017a, 2017b.
11. Ewing, 2017b.
12. Rao, 2017.
13. Spencer Stuart, 2016.
14. If an event was less than three days away from another event of interest, then these were considered as one single event.
15. NewsMaker, 2012.
16. Ittner and Michels, 2017; Ittner and Keusch, 2017.

CHAPTER 12

1. Bazerman, 2014.
2. Kahneman, 2011; Lewis, 2016.
3. Kahneman, 2011, p. 418.
4. Thaler and Sunstein, 2008; Meyer and Kunreuther, 2017.
5. Gawande, 2011.

APPENDIX 1

1. http://www.businessinsider.com/sp-500-market-cap-crosses-20-trillion-for-the-first-time-2017-2; https://data.worldbank.org/indicator/CM.MKT.LCAP.CD?locations=US.

   Financial analyst Henry Poor developed an annual listing of publicly held railroad companies in the nineteenth century, and merged it with the "Standard" Statistics Bureau in 1941 to constitute Standard and Poor's, which established the S&P 500 index in 1957; S&P 500, 2017.

APPENDIX 2

1. Our methodology follows a type of dictionary and supervised learning approach, modeled after Campbell et al., 2014; Huang and Li, 2011; and Mirakhur, Nini, and Asher, 2011. We believe the set of risks that large corporations are discussing in their 10-K is fairly well known. More recently, researchers have proposed ways to estimate rather than predefine a set of risk-factor categories and simultaneously assigned part of the 10-K to these categories (Bao and Datta, 2014). Several of the "new" risks that the authors generate through this method were already listed in Mirakhur, Nini, and Asher, 2011.

REFERENCES

Abelson, Reed. "Inquiry Set on Health Care Billing." *New York Times*, February 14, 2008.

Ailworth, Erin. "Occidental Holders Back Climate Review." *Wall Street Journal*, May 13–14, 2017.

Airbus, "Orders and Deliveries," 2017, http://www.aircraft.airbus.com/market/orders-deliveries.

Aldrich, Daniel P. "How Social Ties Make Us Resilient to Trauma." *The Conversation*, May 23, 2017, https://theconversation.com/how-social-ties-make-us-resilient-to-trauma-78223.

Andrews, Suzanna. "Larry Fink's $12 Trillion Shadow." *Vanity Fair*, April 2010.

Aon Risk Solutions. *Global Risk Management Survey*. Aon, 2017, http://www.aon.com/2017-global-risk-management-survey/index.html.

Arkes, Hal, and Catherine Blumer. "The Psychology of Sunk Cost." *Organizational Behavior and Human Decision Process* 35(1) (1985): 124–140.

Associated Press. "Cuomo Expands Health Insurer Investigation." March 6, 2008, http://www.crainsnewyork.com/article/20080306/FREE/360210861/.

Auserwald, Phillip. E., Lewis M. Branscomb, Todd M. La Porte, and Erwann O. Michel-Kerjan. "Leadership: Who Will Act? Integrating Public and Private Interests to Make a Safer World," in *Seeds of Disaster, Roots of Response: How Private Action Can Reduce Public Vulnerability*, edited by Phillip E. Auserwald, 483–505. New York: Cambridge University Press, 2006.

Baker, James A., III, Frank L. "Skip" Bowman, Glenn Erwin, Slade Gorton, Dennis Hendershot, Nancy Leveson, Sharon Priest, Isadore "Irv" Rosenthal, Paul V. Tebo, Douglas A. Wiegmann, and L. Duane Wilson. The Report of the BP U.S. Refineries Independent Safety Review Panel. 2007, http://www.csb.gov/assets/1/19/Baker_panel_report1.pdf.

Ballesteros, Luis. "The Drivers of Corporate Philanthropic Catastrophe Response: The Community-Event-Firm Triad." Philadelphia: Wharton School Research Paper, University of Pennsylvania, 2013.

Ballesteros, Luis. "Markets as Clubs: A Study of the Role of Economic Reliance in Corporate Provision of Collective Goods." Philadelphia: Wharton School Research Service, 2015, http://proceedings.aom.org/content/2015/1/19077.abstract.

Ballesteros, Luis, and Michael Useem. "Black Swans and the Social Value of Corporate Disaster Giving." *Wharton School Research Paper* (84). 2015.

Ballesteros, Luis, Michael Useem, and Tyler Wry. "Masters of Disasters? An Empirical Analysis of How Societies Benefit from Corporate Disaster Aid." *Academy of Management Journal*, 60(5)(2017): 1682–1708.

Bao, Yang, and Anindya Datta. "Simultaneously Discovering and Quantifying Risk Types from Textual Risk Disclosures." *Management Science* 60(6) (2014): 1371–1391.

Baum, Joel A. C., and Kristina B. Dahlin. "Aspiration Performance and Railroads' Patterns of Learning from Train Wrecks and Crashes." *Organization Science* 18(3) (2007): 368–385.

Baum, Philip. *Violence in the Skies: A History of Aircraft Hijacking and Bombing*. Chichester: Summersdale Publishers, 2016.

Bazerman, Max. *The Power of Noticing*. New York: Simon and Schuster, 2014.

Bazerman, Max, and Don A. Moore. *Judgment in Managerial Decision Making*. Hoboken, NJ: Wiley, 2008.

Beasley, Mark, Bruce Banson, and Bonnie Hancock. *2015 Report on the Current State of Enterprise Risk Oversight*. Raleigh: North Carolina State University Poole College of Management, 2015, https://erm.ncsu.edu/az/erm/i/chan/library/AICPA_ERM_Research_Study_2015.pdf.

Beaumier, Carol, and Jim DeLoach. *Risk Oversight: Should Your Board Have a Separate Risk Committee?* Conference Board, 2012, www.conference-board.org/retrievefile.cfm?filename=TCB-DN-V4N1-12.pdf&type=subsite.

Becerra, Oscar, Eduardo Cavallo, and Ilan Noy. "Foreign Aid in the Aftermath of Large Natural Disasters." *Review of Development Economics* 18(3) (2014): 445–460.

Bernile, Gennaro, Vineet Bhagwat, and P. Raghavendra Rau. "What Doesn't Kill You Will Only Make You More Risk-Loving: Early-Life Disasters and CEO Behavior." *Journal of Finance* 72(1) (2017): 167–206.

Bevere, Lucia, Kirsten Orwig, and Rajeev Sharan. "Natural Catastrophes and Man-Made Disasters in 2014: Convective and Winter Storms Generate Most Losses." Technical report, Zurich, Switzerland: Swiss Re. 2015, http://www.actuarialpost.co.uk/downloads/cat_1/sigma2_2015_en.pdf.

Boehm, Christoph, Aaron Flaaen, and Nitya Pandalai-Nayar. "Input Linkages and the Transmission of Shocks: Firm-Level Evidence from the 2011 Tōhoku Earthquake." US Census Bureau Center for Economic Studies Paper No. CES-WP-15-28. 2015.

Boeing Company, "Boeing 787: Orders and Deliveries," 2017, http://active.boeing.com/commercial/orders/displaystandardreport.cfm?cboCurrentModel=787&optReportType=AllModels&cboAllModel=787&ViewReportF=View+Report

Bowman, Edward, and Howard Kunreuther. "Post-Bhopal Behaviour at a Chemical Company." *Journal of Management Studies* 25(4) (1988): 387–402.

Boyd, Roddy. *Fatal Risk: A Cautionary Tale of AIG's Corporate Suicide*. Hoboken, NJ: Wiley, 2011.

Brodeur, André, Kevin Buehler, Michael Patsalos-Fox, and Martin Pergler. *A Board Perspective on Enterprise Risk Management*. McKinsey and Company, 2010.

Bureau d'Enquêtes et d'Analyses. Final Report, Accident on 24 March 2015, 2016, https://www.bea.aero/uploads/tx_elydbrapports/BEA2015-0125.en-LR.pdf.

Business Roundtable. Principles of Corporate Governance, 2016, https:// businessround-table.org/sites/default/files/Principles-of-Corporate-Governance-2016.pdf.

Camerer, Colin F., and Ernst Fehr. "Measuring Social Norms and Preferences Using Experimental Games: A Guide for Social Scientists." 2002, http://people.hss.caltech.edu/~camerer/Camerer-Fehrjan30.pdf.

Campbell, John L., Hsinchun Chen, Dan S. Dhaliwal, Hsin-min Lu, and Logan B. Steele. "The Information Content of Mandatory Risk Factor Disclosures in Corporate Filings." *Review of Accounting Studies* 19(1) (2014): 396–455.

Cavallo, Eduardo, Alberto Cavallo, and Roberto Rigobon. "Prices and Supply Disruptions during Natural Disasters." *Review of Income and Wealth* 60(S2) (2014): S449–S471.

Cavallo, Eduardo, and Christian Daude. "Public Investment in Developing Countries: A Blessing or a Curse?" *Journal of Comparative Economics* 39(1) (2011): 65–81.

Charan, Ram, Dennis Carey, and Michael Useem. *Boards That Lead*. Cambridge, MA: Harvard Business Review Press, 2014.

Cheong, Cintia. "Cyber Crime Costs Global Economy $445bn a Year." *The Actuary*, September 24, 2015, http://www.theactuary.com/news/2015/09/cyber-crime-costs-global-economy-445bn-a-year/.

Chhaochhariam, Vidhi, and Yaniv Grinstein. "Corporate Governance and Firm Value: The Impact of the 2002 Governance Rules." *Journal of Finance* 62(4) (2007): 1789–1825.

Chu, Jennifer. "Volkswagen's Emissions Cheat to Cause 60 Premature Deaths in U.S." *MIT News*, October 28, 2015, http://news.mit.edu/2015/volkswagen-emissions-cheat-cause-60-premature-deaths-1029.

Chu, Jennifer. "Volkswagen's Excess Emissions Will Lead to 1,200 Premature Deaths in Europe." *MIT News*, March 3, 2017, http://news.mit.edu/2017/volkswagen-emissions-premature-deaths-europe-0303.

Clark, Nicola, and Dan Bilefsky. "Germanwings Pilot Was Locked Out of Cockpit before Crash in France." *New York Times*, March 25, 2016.

CNN. "Hurricane Katrina Statistics Fast Facts." http://www.cnn.com/2013/08/23/us/hurricane-katrina-statistics-fast-facts/index.html.

Coglianese, Cary. "Measuring Regulatory Performance: Evaluating the Impact of Regulation and Regulatory Policy." Organisation for Economic Cooperation and Development, 2012, https://www.oecd.org/gov/regulatory-policy/1_coglianese%20web.pdf.

Cohen, Michael D., James G. March, and Johan P. Olsen. "A Garbage Can Model of Organizational Choice." *Administrative Science Quarterly* (March 1972): 1–25.

Committee of Sponsoring Organizations of the Treadway Commission. "Effective Enterprise Risk Oversight: The Role of the Board of Directors." 2009, www.coso.org/documents/COSOBoardsERM4pager-FINALRELEASEVERSION82409_001.pdf.

Conference Board. *Emerging Governance Practices in Enterprise Risk Management*. 2007, https://www.conference-board.org/publications/publicationdetail.cfm?publicationid=1271&centerId=5.

Consumer Financial Protection Bureau. *Monthly Complaint Report*, April 2017, http:// files.consumerfinance.gov/f/documents/201704_cfpb_Monthly-Complaint-Report .pdf.

Cowley, Stacy, "Wells Fargo Vice Chairwoman to Succeed Departing Chairman," *New York Times*, August 15, 2017a.

Cowley, Stacy, "Wells Fargo Review Finds 1.4 Million More Suspect Accounts," *New York Times*, August 31, 2017b.

Cox, Jeff. "Wells Fargo Getting Smacked by Wall Street Analysts." CNBC, October 5, 2016, http://www.cnbc.com/2016/10/05/wells-fargo-getting-smacked-by-wall-street-analysts-fitch-raymond-james-and-goldman-sachs.html.

Cremer, Andreas, and Jan Schwartz. "VW Looks to Cutbacks and Electric Cars to Overcome Scandal." *New York Times*, October 13, 2015.

Creswell, Julie, and Sapna Maheshwari. "United Grapples with PR Crisis over Videos of Man Being Dragged Off Plane." *New York Times*, April 11, 2017.

Cummins, J. David, and Olivier Mahul. *Catastrophe Risk Financing in Developing Countries: Principles for Public Intervention*. World Bank, 2009, http://siteresources .worldbank.org/FINANCIALSECTOR/Resources/CATRISKbook.pdf.

Cyert, Richard M., and James Geoffrey March. *A Behavioral Theory of the Firm*. Englewood Cliffs, NJ: Prentice-Hall, Inc., 1963.

Dacy, Douglas, and Howard Kunreuther. *The Economics of Natural Disasters*. New York: Free Press, 1968.

Davis Polk and Wardell, LLP. Dodd–Frank Progress Report, 2016, https://www .davispolk.com/Dodd–Frank-Rulemaking-Progress-Report.

Dawson, Chester and Yoshio Takahashi. "Thai Floods Force Toyota to Suspend U.S. Production." *Wall Street Journal*, October 28, 2011.

Dawson, Chester, and Yoshio Takahashi. "Toyota Makes New Push to Avoid Recalls." *Wall Street Journal*, February 24, 2011.

De Alessi, Louis. "Toward an Analysis of Postdisaster Cooperation." *American Economic Review*, 65(1) (1975): 127–138.

De la Merced, Michael J., and Andrew Ross Sorkin. "G.E. to Retreat from Finance in Post-Crisis Reorganization." *New York Times*, April 12, 2015.

Deloitte. *Risk Intelligent Governance: Lessons from State-of-the-Art Board Practices*, 2014, https://www2.deloitte.com/us/en/pages/risk/articles/risk-intelligent-governance-lessons-from-state-of-the-art-board-practices.html.

Deutsche Bank AG. "Deutsche Bank Careers: Operational Risk/Business Continuity Management Framework Specialist (m/f) Frankfurt am Main." January 5, 2012.

Dieterich, Chris. "Americans Worry About Falling Victim to Cyberattacks More Than Any Other Type of Crime.'" *Barron's*, September 8, 2015, http://www.barrons.com/ articles/americans-worry-about-falling-victim-to-cyberattacks-more-than-any-other-type-of-crime-1441740930.

DePietro, Ben. "Lufthansa's Response to Germanwings Crash." *Wall Street Journal*, April 6, 2015, https://blogs.wsj.com/riskandcompliance/2015/04/06/crisis-of-the-week-lufthansas-response-to-germanwings-crash/.

DiMaggio, Paul J., and Walter W. Powell. "The Iron Cage Revisited: Institutional Isomorphism and Collective Rationality in Organizational Fields." *American Sociological Review* 48(2) (1983): 147–160.

Douty, Christopher M. "Disasters and Charity: Some Aspects of Cooperative Economic Behavior." *American Economic Review* 62(4) (1972): 580–590.

Ebola Private Sector Mobilisation Group. 2015, https://www.epsmg.com/

Eckerman, Ingrid. *The Bhopal Saga—Causes and Consequences of the World's Largest Industrial Disaster*. Hyderabad: Universities Press, 2005.

Economist. "A Human Response to a Human Tragedy." March 30, 2015, www.economist .com/blogs/gulliver/2015/03/germanwings-flight-9525.

Ernst & Young. *Let's Talk: Governance*. EY Center for Board Matters, 2014, http://www .ey.com/Publication/vwLUAssets/EY_-_Lets_talk:_fovernance/$FILE/EY-lets-talk-governance.pdf.

Ewing, Jack. "Matthias Müller, VW Chief, Is Suspected of Market Manipulation." *New York Times*, May 17, 2017a.

Ewing, Jack. "VW Engineers Wanted O.K. from the Top for Emissions Fraud, Documents Show." *New York Times*, May 17, 2017b.

Ewing, Jack, and Hiroko Tabuchi. "Volkswagen Scandal Reaches All the Way to the Top, Lawsuits Say." *New York Times*, July 19, 2016.

Feinstein, Jack. "Managing Reliability in Electric Power Companies," in *Seeds of Disaster, Roots of Response: How Private Action Can Reduce Public Vulnerability*, edited by P. Auerswald, L. Branscomb, T. LaPorte, and E. Michel-Kerjan, 164–193. New York: Cambridge University Press, 2006.

Fischhoff, Baruch. "Hindsight ≠ Foresight: The Effect of Outcome Knowledge on Judgment under Uncertainty." *Quality & Safety in Health Care* 12(4) (2013): 304–312.

Fraser, John R. S. "The Role of the Board in Risk Management Oversight," in *The Handbook of Board Governance*, edited by Richard LeBlanc, 283–304. Hoboken, NJ: Wiley, 2016.

Gallup. "Partisan Divide on Government Regulations Remains Wide." September 28, 2016, http://www.gallup.com/poll/195893/partisan-divide-government-regulations-remains-wide.aspx.

Gandel, Stephen. "Lloyd's CEO: Cyber Attacks Cost Companies $400 Billion Every Year." *Fortune*, January 23, 2015, http://fortune.com/2015/01/23/cyber-attack-insurance-lloyds/.

Gao, Yongqiang. "Philanthropic Disaster Relief Giving as a Response to Institutional Pressure: Evidence from China." *Journal of Business Research* 64(12) (2011): 1377–1382.

Garicano, Luis, and Luis Rayo. "Why Organizations Fail: Models and Cases." *Journal of Economic Perspectives* 54(1) (2016): 137–192.

Gates, Guilbert, Jack Ewing, Karl Russell, and Derek Watkins. "How Volkswagen's 'Defeat Devices' Worked." *New York Times*, March 16, 2017.

Gawande, Atul. *The Checklist Manifesto: How to Get Things Right*. New York: Picador, 2011.

Glass Lewis. "An Overview of the Glass Lewis Approach to Proxy Advice," 2017, http:// www.glasslewis.com/wp-content/uploads/2016/11/2017_Guideline_US.pdf.

Goldin, Ian, and Mike Mariathasan. *The Butterfly Defect: How Globalization Creates Systemic Risks, and What to Do About It.* Princeton, NJ: Princeton University Press, 2014.

Guess Inc. 10-K, 2015, http://investors.guess.com/mobile.view?c=92506&v=202&d =3&id=aHR0cDovL2FwaS50ZW5rd2l6YXJkLmNvbvS9maWxpbmcuYXNweD9pcD2lw YWdlPTEwMTc1MzM4JkRTRVE9MSSZTRVE9MjEmU1FERVNDPVNFQ1RJT 05fUEFHRSZleHA9JnNiYnpD01Nw%3D%3D.

Heal, Geoff and Howard Kunreuther. "Environment and Energy: Catastrophic Liabilities from Nuclear Power Plants." In: *Measuring and Managing Federal Financial Risk.* Deborah Lucas, editor. University of Chicago Press, 2010.

Heal, Geoffrey, Michael Kearns, Paul Kleindorfer, and Howard Kunreuther. "Interdependent Security in Interconnected Networks," in *Seeds of Disaster, Roots of Response,* edited by L. Auerswald, L. Branscomb, T. La Porte, and Erwann Michel-Kerjan, 258–278. New York: Cambridge University Press, 2006.

Henry Schein. Corporate Social Responsibility Review. 2014, https://www.henryschein .com/us-en/Images/Corporate/2014HenryScheinCSR.pdf.

Hirshleifer, Jack. *Disaster and Recovery: A Historical Survey.* Defense Technical Information Center Document. Santa Monica, CA: Rand Corp., 1963.

Houser, Trevor, Solomon Hsiang, Robert Kopp, and Kate Larsen. *American Climate Prospectus: Economic Risks in the United States.* New York: Rhodium Group LLC, 2014.

Hughes, Christopher, and Antony Currie. "A Slip Too Many for BP's Chief." *New York Times,* June 8, 2010.

Huang, Ke-Wei, and Zhuolun Li. "A Multilabel Text Classification Algorithm for Labeling Risk Factors in SEC Form 10-K." *ACM Transactions on Management Information Systems* 2(3) (2011): 18.1–18.19.

Hurtado, Patricia. "The London Whale." *Bloomberg,* February 23, 2016, https://www .bloomberg.com/quicktake/the-london-whale.

Ingley, Coral, and Nick van der Walt. "Risk Management and Board Effectiveness." *International Studies of Management and Organization* 38(3) (2008): 43–70.

Institutional Shareholder Services, *Quality Score Overview and Updates,* February 2017, https://www.issgovernance.com/file/products/iss-qualityscore-techdoc-feb-1-2017 .pdf?elqTrackId=8cadbcc86ae9444ab3ec5ec3e2e55837&elq=1b262cefl14f4e3882bf41 7f3d661257&elqaid=479&elqat=1&elqCampaignId.

Ittner, Christopher D., and Thomas Keusch. "The Influence of Board of Directors' Risk Oversight on Risk Management Maturity and Firm Risk-Taking." Unpublished paper, 2017.

Ittner, Christopher D., and Thomas Keusch. "Incorporating Risk Considerations into Planning and Control Systems," in *The Routledge Companion to Accounting and Risk,* edited by Philip Linsley and Margaret Woods, 150–171. New York: Routledge, 2016.

Ittner, Christopher D., and Jeremy Michels. "Risk-Based Forecasting and Planning and Management Earnings Forecast." Unpublished paper, 2017.

Jain, Pankaj K., and Zabihollah Rezaee. "The Sarbanes-Oxley Act of 2002 and Capital-Market Behavior: Early Evidence." *Contemporary Accounting Research* 23(3) (2006): 629–654.

Jiao, Yawen. "Corporate Disclosure, Market Valuation, and Firm Performance." *Financial Management* 40(3) (2011): 647–676.

Juma, Muhamed, and Amro Hassan. "Islamist Militias Seize Main Libya Airport as Conflict Deepens." *Los Angeles Times,* August 24, 2014.

Kahneman, Daniel. *Thinking, Fast and Slow.* New York: Macmillan, 2011.

Kalavar, Sanjay, and Mihir Mysore. "Are You Prepared for a Corporate Crisis?" *McKinsey Quarterly,* April 2017.

Kaufmann, Robert K. "The Role of Market Fundamentals and Speculation in Recent Price Changes for Crude Oil." *Energy Policy* 39(1) (2011): 105–115.

Kearns, Michael. "Economics, Computer Science, and Policy." *Issues in Science and Technology* 21(2) (2005): 37–47.

Khan, Mohsin S., and Manmohan S. Kumar. "Public and Private Investment and the Growth Process in Developing Countries." *Oxford Bulletin of Economics and Statistics* 59(1) (1997): 69–88.

Kiel, Paul. "AIG's Spiral Downward: A Timeline." *ProPublica,* November 14, 2008, http://www.propublica.org/article/article-aigs-downward-spiral-1114.

Kilian, Lutz, and Daniel P. Murphy. "The Role of Inventories and Speculative Trading in the Global Market for Crude Oil." *Journal of Applied Econometrics* 29(3) (2014): 454–478.

Korolov, Maria. "Data Breach Costs Now Average $154 Per Record." CSO, May 27, 2015, http://www.csoonline.com/article/2926727/data-protection/ponemon-data-breach-costs-now-average-154-per-record.html.

Kottasova, Ivana, and Mark Thompson. "'Deliberate Crash' a Huge Blow to Lufthansa." *Money CNN,* March 26, 2015, http://money.cnn.com/2015/03/26/news/companies/lufthansa-germanwings-crash.

Kunreuther, Howard. "Mitigating Disaster Losses through Insurance." *Journal of Risk and Uncertainty* 12(2) (1996): 171–187.

Kunreuther, Howard, and Edward H. Bowman. "A Dynamic Model of Organizational Decision Making: Chemco Revisited Six Years after Bhopal." *Organization Science* 8(4) (1997): 404–413.

Kunreuther, Howard, and Geoffrey Heal. "A Firm Can Only Go Bankrupt Once." Philadelphia: Wharton Risk Management and Decision Processes Center, University of Pennsylvania, Working Paper, 2002.

Kunreuther, Howard, and Erwann Michel-Kerjan. "Challenges for Terrorism Insurance in the United States." *Journal of Economic Perspectives* 18(4) (2004): 201–214.

Kunreuther, Howard, and Erwann Michel-Kerjan. *At War with the Weather: Managing Large-Scale Risks in a New Era of Catastrophes.* New York: MIT Press, 2011.

Kunreuther, Howard, Mark V. Pauly, and S. McMorrow. *Insurance and Behavioral Economics: Improving Decisions in the Most Misunderstood Industry.* New York: Cambridge University Press, 2013.

Lampel, Joseph, Jamal Shamsie, and Zur Shapira. "Experiencing the Improbable: Rare Events and Organizational Learning." *Organization Science* 20(5) (2009): 835–845.

Lawrence, Chris. "Pentagon Clears Exit of Some Military Family Members from Japan." Cable News Network, March 17, 2011.

Levitt, Barbara, and James G. March. "Organizational Learning." *Annual Review of Sociology* 14 (1988): 319–338.

Levinthal, Daniel A., and J. G. March. "The Myopia of Learning." *Strategic Management Journal* 14 (1993): 95–112.

Lewis, Michael. *The Undoing Project: A Friendship That Changed Our Minds.* New York: Norton, 2016.

Lipton, Martin. "Is Activism Moving In-House?" International Business Council, World Economic Forum, Geneva, Switzerland, August 27–28, 2015.

Low, Harry. "Germanwings Crash: Have Cockpit Doors Changed?" *BBC News*, March 24, 2016, http://www.bbc.com/news/magazine-35802645.

Lufthansa Group. Annual Report. 2012, https://investor-relations.lufthansagroup.com/fileadmin/downloads/en/financial-reports/annual-reports/LH-AR-2012-e.pdf.

Madsen, Peter M. "These Lives Will Not Be Lost in Vain: Organizational Learning from Disaster in U.S. Coal Mining." *Organization Science* 20(5) (2009): 861–875.

Malmendier, Ulrike, Geoffrey Tate, and Jon Yan. "Overconfidence and Early-Life Experiences: The Effect of Managerial Traits on Corporate Financial Policies." *Journal of Finance* 66 (2011): 1687–1733.

March, James G., and Herbert A. Simon. *Organizations.* New York: Free Press, 1958.

March, James G., Lee S. Sproull, and Michal Tamuz. "Learning from Samples of One or Fewer." *Organization Science* 2(1) (1991): 1–13.

McDonald, Lawrence G., and Patrick Robinson. *A Colossal Failure of Common Sense: The Inside Story of the Collapse of Lehman Brothers.* New York: Crown Business, 2010.

Meyer, Robert and Howard Kunreuther. *The Ostrich Paradox: Why We Underprepare for Disasters.* Wharton Digital Press, 2017.

Michel-Kerjan, Erwann, and Howard Kunreuther. "Redesigning Flood Insurance." *Science* 333 (6041) (2011): 408–409.

Michel-Kerjan, Erwann, and Howard Kunreuther. "A Successful (Yet Somewhat Untested) Case of Disaster Financing: Terrorism Insurance under TRIA, 2002–2020." Philadelphia: Wharton Risk Management and Decision Processes Center, University of Pennsylvania, 2017.

Mirakhur, Yatin, Gregory Nini, and Martin Asher. "Risk Disclosure in SEC Corporate Filings." Working paper. Philadelphia: Wharton School, University of Pennsylvania, 2011, 2011. http://repository.upenn.edu/cgi/viewcontent.cgi?article=1088&context=wharton_research_scholars.

Morgenson, Gretchen. "Behind Insurer's Crisis, Blind Eye to a Web of Risk." *New York Times*, September 28, 2008.

Muller, Alan, and Roman Kräussl. "Doing Good Deeds in Times of Need: A Strategic Perspective on Disaster Donation." *Strategic Management Journal* 32(9) (2011): 911–929.

Mulligan, John. *Protecting Personal Consumer Information from Cyber Attacks.* Senate Committee on Commerce, Science and Transportation, March 26, 2014, https://corporate.target.com/_media/TargetCorp/global/PDF/Target-SJC-032614.pdf.

Munich Re. *Loss Events Worldwide 1980–2014.* 2015, http://www.munichre.com/site/corporate/get/documents_E-1260878433/mr/assetpool.shared/Documents/5_

Touch/_NatCatService/Significant-Natural-Catastrophes/2014/10-deadliest-events-worldwide.pdf.

Nation. "Siam Cement CEO as Businessman of the Year." December 30, 2011, http://www.nationmultimedia.com/business/Siam-Cement-CEO-as-Businessman-of-the-Year-30172913.html.

National Aeronautics and Space Administration. *Report of Columbia Accident Investigation.* Washington, DC. 2003, https://www.nasa.gov/columbia/home/CAIB_Vol1.html.

National Association of Corporate Directors. "Board Oversight of Reputation Risk." Washington, DC. 2014.

National Oceanic and Atmospheric Administration. *National Coastal Population Report: Population Trends from 1970 to 2020.* Washington, DC. 2016, https://coast.noaa.gov/digitalcoast/training/population-report.html.

Neilan, Catherine. "Airline Share Prices Have Been Hit after Officials Reveal Co-Pilot of Germanwings 4U9525 Intended to 'Destroy the Plane.'" *CityA.M.*, March 26, 2015, http://www.cityam.com/212550/airline-share-prices-are-tanking-after-officials-reveal-co-pilot-germanwings-4u9525-intended.

New York's Attorney General Office. "Cuomo Announces Industry-Wide Investigation into Health Insurers; Fraudulent Reimbursement Scheme." February 13, 2008.

New York City. PlaNYC: A Stronger More Resilient NYC. New York City, Mayor's Office of Long Term Planning and Sustainability. 2013. http://www.nyc.gov/html/sirr/html/report/report.shtml.

NewsMaker. "DealBook: U.S. Markets Closed on Tuesday." *First Business News*, October 30, 2012, https://firstbusinessnews.net/dealbook-u-s-markets-closed-on-tuesday.

Nottingham, Lucy. "Unlock Growth by Integrating Sustainability: How to Overcome the Barriers." New York: Marsh & McLennan Companies, 2016.

Ochs, Susan M. "The Leadership Blind Spots at Wells Fargo." *Harvard Business Review*, October 2016, https://hbr.org/2016/10/the-leadership-blind-spots-at-wells-fargo.

Palca, Joe. "Explainer: What Are Spent Fuel Rods?" National Public Radio, March 15, 2011.

Pate-Cornell, E., and P. Fischbeck. "Risk Management for the Tiles of the Space Shuttle." *Interfaces* 24(1) (1994): 74–86.

Petcu, Sorin. "VW Presents Its Long-Term Plan Aimed to Overcome the Diesel Scandal." *InAutoNews*, June 16, 2017, http://www.inautonews.com/vw-presents-its-long-term-plan-aimed-to-overcome-the-diesel-scandal.

Pedell, Burkhard. "Leadership in Dealing with Serious Risks: Strategies for Improving Resilience of Companies." University of Stuttgart, working paper, 2014.

Pielke, Roger A., Jr., Joel Gratz, Christopher W. Landsea, Douglas Collins, Mark A. Saunders, and Rade Musulin. "Normalized Hurricane Damage in the United States: 1900–2005." *Natural Hazards Review* 9(1) (2008): 29–42.

Ponemon Institute. "Defining the Gap: The Cybersecurity Governance Study." 2015.

Population Reference Bureau. *Human Population: Urbanization, 2017.* http://www.prb.org/Publications/Lesson-Plans/HumanPopulation/Urbanization.aspx.

Porter, Michael E., and Mark R. Kramer. "The Competitive Advantage of Corporate Philanthropy." *Harvard Business Review* 80(12) (2002): 56–68.

PricewaterhouseCoopers. *PwC State of Compliance Study 2016: Laying a Strategic Foundation for Strong Compliance Risk Management.* 2016a, www.pwc.com/us/stateofcompliance.

PricewaterhouseCoopers. *19th Annual Global CEO Survey.* 2016b, https://www.pwc.com/gx/en/ceo-survey/2016/landing-page/pwc-19th-annual-global-ceo-survey.pdf.

Rao, Prashant S. "VW Executive, Hired to Help Overhaul Carmaker's Culture, Is to Leave." *New York Times,* January 26, 2017.

Rerup, Claus. "Attentional Triangulation: Learning from Unexpected Rare Crises." *Organization Science* 20(5) (2009): 876–893.

Reuters. "VW Will Offer U.S. Diesel Scandal Customers Generous Compensation, Paper Says." *Automotive News Europe,* February 7, 2016, http://europe.autonews.com/article/20160207/ANE/160209871/vw-will-offer-u.s.-diesel-scandal-customers-generous-compensation.

Riley, Michael, Ben Elgin, Dune Lawrence, and Carol Matlack. "Missed Alarms and 40 Million Stolen Credit Card Numbers: How Target Blew It." *Bloomberg,* March 13, 2014.

Risk and Insurance Management Society. "Exploring Risk Appetite and Risk Tolerance." 2012, https://www.rims.org/resources/ERM/Documents/RIMS_Exploring_Risk_Appetite_Risk_Tolerance_0412.pdf.

Ruddick, Graham. "Volkswagen Scandal: US Chief Says Carmaker 'Totally Screwed Up.'" *The Guardian,* September 22, 2015, https://www.theguardian.com/business/2015/sep/22/volkswagen-scandal-us-chief-carmaker-totally-screwed-up-michael-horn.

Russo, Edward J., and Paul Schoemaker. *Decision Traps.* New York: Doubleday, 1989.

Saiia, David H., Archie B. Carroll, and Ann K. Buchholt. "Philanthropy as Strategy: When Corporate Charity 'Begins at Home.'" *Business & Society* 42(2) (2003): 169–201.

Samuelson, Willaim, and Richard Zeckhauser. "Status Quo Bias in Decision Making." *Journal of Risk and Uncertainty* 1(1) (1988): 7–59.

Schwabe, Paul, Karlynn Cory, and James Newcomb. *Renewable Energy Project Financing: Impacts of the Financial Crisis and Federal Legislation.* National Renewable Energy Lab, Golden, Colorado, 2009.

Schwartz, John. "Climate Change Activists: Either Prod Exxon Mobil or Dump It." *New York Times,* May 26, 2016.

Shell, Adam. "Equifax Data Breach: Number of Victims May Never Be Known." *USA Today.* September 17, 2017, https://www.usatoday.com/story/money/2017/09/17/equifax-data-breach-number-victims-may-never-known/670618001/

Silverblatt, Howard. "S&P500 2015: Global Sales," *S&P Dow Jones Indices,* 2016, http://us.spindices.com/documents/research/research-sp-500-2015-global-sales.pdf.

Slovic, Paul, ed. *The Perception of Risk.* Virginia: Earthscan, 2000.

Spencer Stuart. Spencer Stuart Board Index. Chicago, IL, 2014.

Spencer Stuart. Spencer Stuart Board Index. Chicago, IL, 2015.

Spencer Stuart. Spencer Stuart Board Index. Chicago, IL, 2016.

Staib, Daniel, and Mahesh Puttaiah, "World Insurance in 2014: Back to Life," 2014, Swiss R, Sigma, 4, 2015, http://www.swissre.com/reinsurance/insurers/sigma_42015_world_insurance_in_2014_back_to_life.html

Standard and Poor's. *Evaluating Insurers' Enterprise Risk Management Practice.* New York. 2013.

Standard and Poor's. S&P500. *S&P Dow Jones Indices*, 2017, http://us.spindices.com/indices/equity/sp-500.

Statistics Bureau of Japan. Population Census, Preliminary Counts of the 2010 Population Census of Japan, May 11, 2011.

Target Corporation. 2012 Form 10-K. https://corporate.target.com/annual-reports/2012/10-k/10-K-Part-I/Item-1A-Risk-Factors.

Target Corporation. 2014 Form 10-K. https://corporate.target.com/_media/TargetCorp/annualreports/2014/pdf/10K-Target-2014-Annual-Report-5.pdf.

Thaler, Richard and Cass Sunstein. *Nudge: The Gentle Power of Choice Architecture.* New Haven, CT: Yale University Pres, 2008.

Thomson, Derek. "How Airline Ticket Prices Fell 50% in 30 Years (and Why Nobody Noticed)." *The Atlantic*, February 28, 2013.

Tobias, Sharone. "The Year in Cyberattacks." *Newsweek*, December 31, 2014.

Tversky, Amos, and Daniel Kahneman. "Availability: A Heuristic for Judging Frequency and Probability." *Cognitive Psychology* 5(2) (1973): 207–232.

Tversky, Amos, and Daniel Kahneman. "Loss Aversion in Riskless Choice: A Reference-Dependent Model." *Quarterly Journal of Economics* 106 (1991): 1039–1061.

UN Development Program. Human Development Reports. 2017, http://hdr.undp.org/en/content/human-development-index-hdi.

UN High-Level Panel on Humanitarian Financing Report to the Secretary-General. "Too Important to Fail—Addressing the Humanitarian Financing Gap." 2016, http://www.un.org/news/WEB-1521765-E-OCHA-Report-on-Humanitarian-Financing.pdf.

UN Office for the Coordination of Humanitarian Affairs. Financial Tracking Service, 2015.

Useem, Michael. "How Well-Run Boards Make Decisions." *Harvard Business Review* (November 2006): 130–138.

Useem, Michael. "Developing Leadership to Avert and Mitigate Disasters," in *Learning from Catastrophes: Strategies for Reaction and Response*, edited by Howard Kunreuther and Michael Useem, 249–306. Saddle River, NJ: Pearson, 2010.

Useem, Michael, Howard Kunreuther, and Erwann Michel-Kerjan. *Leadership Dispatches: Chile's Extraordinary Comeback from Disaster.* Redwood City, CA: Stanford University Press, 2015.

Useem, Michael, and Herman B. Leonard Jr. "Catastrophic Risk Management at Deutsche Bank." Philadelphia: Wharton School, University of Pennsylvania, 2012.

Useem, Michael, and Andy Zelleke. "Oversight and Delegation in Corporate Governance: Deciding What the Board Should Decide." *Corporate Governance: An International Review* 14(1) (2006): 2–12.

US Securities and Exchange Commission. *How to Read a Read a 10-K*. April 14, 2016, https://www.sec.gov/answers/reada10k.htm.

Vaughan, Diane. *The Challenger Launch Decision: Risky Technology, Culture, and Deviance at NASA*. Chicago: University of Chicago Press, 1997a.

Vaughan, Diane. "The Trickle Down Effect: Policy Decisions, Risky Work, and the Challenger Tragedy." *California Management Review* 39(2) (1997b): 80–102.

Walmart News. "Walmart Announces a New Customer Campaign to Assist with 2017 U.S. Hurricane Relief." September 10, 2017. https://news.walmart.com/2017/09/10/walmart-announces-a-new-customer-campaign-to-assist-with-2017-us-hurricane-relief.

Warren, Susan. "Dow Chemical to Acquire Union Carbide." *Wall Street Journal*, August 5, 1999.

Weiss, Eric, and Rena Miller. "The Target and Other Financial Data Breaches: Frequently Asked Questions." Washington, DC: Congressional Research Service, 2015.

White, Stacey, and Hardin Lang. "Corporate Engagement in Natural Disaster Response." Center for Strategic and International Studies. http://csis.org/files/publication/120117_White_CorporateEngagement_Web.pdf, 2012.

Willsher, Kim. "Germanwings Crash: Victims' Relatives Say Lufthansa Should Have Stopped Pilot Flying." *The Guardian*, March 13, 2016, https://www.the-guardian.com/world/2016/mar/13/germanwings-pilot-psychiatrists-two-weeks-before-crash-final-report.

Wintoki, M. Babajide. "Corporate Boards and Regulation: The Effect of The Sarbanes-Oxley Act and the Exchange Listing Requirements on Firm Value." *Journal of Corporate Finance* 13(2) (2007): 229–250.

Wokutch, Richard E., Manisha Singal, Yaniv Poria, and Michelle Hong. "Crisis Situations and Role of Strategic CSR in Decision-Making." *Academy of Management Proceedings* (1) (2013): 16136.

World Economic Forum. Global Risks Report. Geneva: 2012.

World Economic Forum. Global Risks Report. Geneva: 2015.

World Bank Group. World Development Indicators. 2012. https://data.worldbank.org/data-catalog/world-development-indicators

Yoshida, Reiji, and Takahiro Fukada. "Fukushima Plant Site Originally Was a Hill Safe from Tsunami." *Japan Times*, July 13, 2011, http://www.japantimes.co.jp/news/2011/07/13/national/fukushima-plant-site-originally-was-a-hill-safe-from-tsunami/#.WRyyYOvys-V.

Zhang, Ivy Xiying. "Economic Consequences of the Sarbanes–Oxley Act of 2002." *Journal of Accounting and Economics* 44(1) (2005): 74–115.

Zollo, Maurizio. "Superstitious Learning with Rare Strategic Decisions: Theory and Evidence from Corporate Acquisitions." *Organization Science* 20 (2009): 894–908.

Zukis, Bob. "Information Technology and Cybersecurity Governance in a Digital World," in *The Handbook of Board Governance*, edited by Richard LeBlanc, 557–573. Hoboken, NJ: Wiley, 2016.

ABOUT THE AUTHORS

Howard Kunreuther is James G. Dinan Professor of Decision Sciences and Public Policy, and Codirector, Center for Risk Management and Decision Processes, Wharton School, University of Pennsylvania (https://riskcenter.wharton.upenn.edu/). He has a long-standing interest in ways that society can better manage low-probability, high-consequence events related to technological and natural hazards. He is a fellow of the American Association for the Advancement of Science, and distinguished fellow of the Society for Risk Analysis. His recent books include *The Ostrich Paradox: Why We Underprepare for Disasters* with Robert Meyer (Wharton Digital Press), *Insurance and Behavioral Economics* with Mark Pauly and Stacey McMorrow (Cambridge University Press) and *Leadership Dispatches: Chile's Extraordinary Comeback from Disaster* with Erwann Michel-Kerjan and Michael Useem (Stanford University Press).

Michael Useem is William and Jaclyn Egan Professor of Management and Director of the Center for Leadership and Change Management (https://leadershipcenter.wharton .upenn.edu/) and faculty director of the McNulty Leadership Program at the Wharton School of the University of Pennsylvania. His university teaching includes MBA and executive-MBA courses on leadership and change, and he offers programs on leadership, governance, and decision-making for managers in the United States, Asia, Europe, and Latin America. He also works on leadership development and governance with many organizations in the private, public, and nonprofit sectors. He is the author of *The Leadership Moment, Investor Capitalism,* and *The Leader's Checklist;* coauthor and coeditor with Howard Kunreuther of *Learning from Catastrophes;* and coauthor of *The India Way, Boards That Lead, Leadership Dispatches,* and *The Strategic Leader's Roadmap.*